Transcendent Teacher Learner Relationships

Transcendent Teacher Learner Relationships

The Way of the Shamanic Teacher (Second Edition)

By

Hunter O'Hara

BRILL
SENSE

LEIDEN | BOSTON

Cover illustration: Alphonse Osbert (1857–1939), *Le Mystère de la nuit*, 1897, oil on canvas, 36 × 56 cm, private collection © Thomas Hennocque

All chapters in this book have undergone peer review.

The Library of Congress Cataloging-in-Publication Data is available online at http://catalog.loc.gov

Typeface for the Latin, Greek, and Cyrillic scripts: "Brill". See and download: brill.com/brill-typeface.

ISBN 978-90-04-44530-7 (paperback)
ISBN 978-90-04-44531-4 (hardback)
ISBN 978-90-04-44532-1 (e-book)

Copyright 2021 by Hunter O'Hara, except where stated otherwise. Published by Koninklijke Brill NV, Leiden, The Netherlands.
Koninklijke Brill NV incorporates the imprints Brill, Brill Hes & De Graaf, Brill Nijhoff, Brill Rodopi, Brill Sense, Hotei Publishing, mentis Verlag, Verlag Ferdinand Schöningh and Wilhelm Fink Verlag.
Koninklijke Brill NV reserves the right to protect this publication against unauthorized use. Requests for re-use and/or translations must be addressed to Koninklijke Brill NV via brill.com or copyright.com.

This book is printed on acid-free paper and produced in a sustainable manner.

Advance Praise for
Transcendent Teacher Learner Relationships

Second Edition

"Captivating, scholarly and invaluable, Hunter O'Hara's work beautifully illuminates the profound importance of developing and nurturing transcendent relationships within the teaching-learning community. Readers will be heartened by remarkable stories of transcendence that are built on the foundations of openness, trust, care, risk-taking, and love. A vital and timely work, Dr. O'Hara's phenomenal book will certainly benefit all teacher education programs, enlightening and empowering current and pre-service teachers, giving them strength, hope, and courage."
– **Joan Ports, D.Ed., Assistant Professor of Early Childhood Education, Towson University**

"With this second edition, Dr. O'Hara represents the embodiment of transcendence in teacher learner relationships. Captivating stories of learners and teachers, told in their own words, are intertwined with a deep examination of transcendent philosophy.

Thought provoking discussion aligns with illustrative narratives of the real lives of learners and teachers, in their roles as Transcendent Relators and Transcendent Shamanic Teachers. Ultimately, Dr. O'Hara leads us to an understanding of the Shamanic Teacher who creates change and healing, and 'shapes events and divines the hidden' to provide healing and relief from past traumas. Readers of this book will be struck by the relevant synthesis and the application to their own lives. Integrating the work of a broad range of notable thinkers and writers, this work is well grounded in the literature and based on thorough research methods.

In the four years after the publication of the first edition of *Transcendent Teacher Learner Relationships*, Dr. O'Hara's teaching has guided the development of more than 500 learners. Along with his learners, he himself has continued to develop his own growing practice of transcendence. With a relationship based on a sense of openness and mutual respect, his learners, and those who have become teachers, were not hesitant to offer their critiques and suggestions for this edition. Seeking input from these learners, past and present, and truly hearing them is characteristic of the sense of security and mutuality in a transcendent environment.

This book invites the reader to be part of Dr. O'Hara's personal life journey to transcendence. We are also privileged to meet a diverse group of individuals who are made real by Dr. O'Hara as they show us their various lives as transcendent teachers and leaners. Readers will be able to find themselves in these stories.

The research has been conducted over time, using a systematic heuristic and planful approach to what can be learned from the collection of voices and stories. The study's compelling stories from learners and teachers who were co-researchers became part of the research findings.

The book provides valuable applications, perspectives, practices, and ways of seeing dichotomies of schools of transcendence in contrast to traditional schools. Among so much more that we can learn throughout this book, we may aspire to internalize the 'general dispositions of transcendence': Hope, Creativity, Awareness, Faithful Doubt, and Wonder, Awe and Reverence.

Perhaps, readers who find themselves currently in transcendent relationships will be validated and inspired to continue, as they themselves become models to their own learners. Others may find themselves hoping to follow this path. Deeply inspired, all will thoughtfully examine their own practices and their guiding philosophies. In sum, it is clear from this work that transcendence may set the stage for the future, becoming the expected and not the exception to the rule.

I look forward to more from Dr. O'Hara and to the change and growth experienced by all of us who have been touched by his work. He provides hope for transcendence among teachers, learners, and schools. Learning to live the way of transcendence is a goal."

– **Edyth James Wheeler, Ph.D., Professor Emerita, Towson University**

First Edition

"Hunter O'Hara crafts a rare work of significance that encapsulates the art of great teaching. The focus of the book on the transcendent teacher learner relationship reveals the core of educational effectiveness. Wrapped up in the unique package of teacher as *shaman*, this book gifts the reader great insight and powerful examples. Revives teaching as joyous – a must read for all educators."

– **Patty O'Grady, Associate Professor, The University of Tampa**

"I like much of what Dr. O'Hara has to say, very much of what he has to say. Obviously written by a careful scholar and person of integrity and rather beautiful

ideas. There is something lovely and authentic and very personal about his work. I feel the rarity of what he talks about."
– **Maxine Greene, Ph.D., Teachers College, Columbia University**

"I entered into Hunter O'Hara's work and experienced many moments that moved me deeply, at times with great joy but also with feelings of sadness in the awareness that transcendent relationships are rare and that many children and adults go through an entire lifetime without knowing one of life's treasures – the mystery, beauty, and wonder of a loving relationship. His writing is vivid and alive and with passion and depth portrays the nature and essence of the constituents of a transcendent relationship."
– **Clark Moustakas, Ed.D., Ph.D., founder of the Center for Humanistic Studies (now the Michigan School of Professional Psychology)**

Theoni and Veronica   *Hunter and Jerry*

Helen and Anne
Photo credit: Thaxter P. Spencer, 1888, R. Stanton Avery Special
Collections, New England Geneological Society.
Color: Patty Allison, at *Imbued with Hues,* Facebook

Contents

Acknowledgements XVII

1 **The Nature of the Transcendent Relationship** 1
   1 Dash and the Electrician: A Parable of a Transcendent Relationship 4
   2 Analysis 4
   3 Teacher and Learner 6
   4 The King's Speech 6
   5 The Transcendent Teacher 7
   6 The Transcendent Teacher Learner Relationship 9
   7 The Author's Background with Teaching and Learning Encounters 13
   8 The Good, the Bad and the Ugly 14
   9 The Mother as Teacher 15
   10 Life at School 15
   11 How People Acted at School 16
   12 Life at Home 17
   13 What I Needed at School 18
   14 Teacher Realness 19
   15 Mrs. Peggy Pridemore, Transcendent Teacher 20
   16 Down the Road 20
   17 A Reflection before a Storm, then Sunshine 21
   18 Teacher Power and Relationships 22
   19 Questions for Thought 24

2 **The Nature of the Transcendent Shamanic Teacher** 26
   1 Anne and Helen 26
   2 Transcendent Shamanic Teaching 28
   3 The Transcendent Shamanic Teacher Merges with the Learner 30
   4 Transcendent Shamanic Teaching as a Glamorous Act 30
   5 Transcendent Shamanic Teaching Uplifts, Heals and Mobilizes the Learner 32
   6 A Note Regarding the Unencumbered Learner and the Transcendent Shamanic Teacher 33
   7 The Origins of Transcendent Shamans 34
   8 Portrait of Veronica and Theoni 36
   9 Veronica Risks 40
   10 Final Thoughts from Theoni 45

    11   Transcendent Shamanism in the Everyday Context   47
    12   Questions for Thought   49

3   Portrait of Transcendent Shamanic Teacher: Peggy (Mrs. Pridemore)   51
    1   Peggy the Learner and Her Transcendent Teacher Mr. Santon   51
    2   Peggy the Teacher   54
    3   Charley   56
    4   Peggy and Hunter   57
    5   A Moment of Peggy's Teaching: An Act of Glamour and Power   58
    6   Questions for Thought   60

4   An Ethic of Care, Tact and Tone   62
    1   An Ethic of Care   62
    2   Obstacles to Caring for the Learner   67
    3   Tact   69
    4   Tone   73
    5   Questions for Thought   74

5   Portrait of Transcendent Relator: Jean   76
    1   At Home   76
    2   Frances   77
    3   Ms. Nettie   77
    4   The Pedagogy of Manners   78
    5   Being Open   78
    6   The Art of Conversation   79
    7   Freedom and Affection   81
    8   Questions for Thought   81

6   Trust, Freedom and Mother Love   83
    1   The Facilitator   84
    2   Three Essential Attitudes of the Facilitator   85
    3   A Bit on Trust from Rogers   89
    4   The Move toward Freedom   90
    5   Mother Love   91
    6   Questions for Thought   96

7   Portraits of Transcendent Relators: Lauren and Kathy   98
    1   Portrait of Lauren   98
    2   Lauren's School Experiences   99
    3   Lauren's Connection with Her Teacher   100

CONTENTS   XIII

      4   Portrait of Kathy   102
      5   Kathy in High School   103
      6   Kathy at College   106
      7   Questions for Thought   107

8   **Risk, Authority and Trust**   108
      1   Authority and Corresponding Risk   108
      2   The Dilemma of Building a New Authority Dynamic   111
      3   Trust   113
      4   An Atmosphere of Security   115
      5   The Revelation of the Teacher's Innermost Self   117
      6   Morning Spirit   119
      7   Questions for Thought   120

9   **Portraits of Transcendent Relators: Jerry and Transcendent Shamanic Teacher Leslie**   122
      1   Jerry   122
      2   A Cold Teacher (Ms. Gilzenskolds [A Pseudonym])   122
      3   Leslie, a Caring Teacher   122
      4   Jerry at Saint Albans High School   123
      5   A Little Thing   124
      6   Affirming the Learner's Individuality   125
      7   Portrait of Transcendent Shamanic Teacher: Leslie (Jerry's Professor)   126
      8   Spiritual Professor   128
      9   Direct Professor   128
     10   Beloved Professor   129
     11   Challenging Professor   129
     12   Pushing Professor   129
     13   Graceful Professor   130
     14   Leslie the Teacher   130
     15   Putting Oneself in the Place of the Learner   131
     16   Jerry (Prior Portrait) and Leslie   131
     17   Risk   132
     18   Questions for Thought   133

10   **Balance, Transcendence and Dispositions**   135
      1   Maxine Greene, Freedom and Negotiation   135
      2   Freedom and Discipline   139
      3   The Transcendence Space   141
      4   Hospitality   142

    5   Teacher Reflection   144
    6   Transcendence   145
    7   Hope   146
    8   Creativity   146
    9   Awareness   148
    10 Faithful Doubt   149
    11 Wonder, Awe and Reverence   150
    12 Questions for Thought   153

11 **Portraits of Transcendent Relators: Kellen and Dr. Ball**   154
    1   Kellen   154
    2   Kellen's Life   155
    3   Jan   155
    4   Dr. Noy   156
    5   Dr. Ball   158
    6   Portrait of Dr. Ball (Kellen's Professor)   160
    7   The Service   160
    8   More Background   161
    9   Dr. Ball, the Teacher   162
    10 The Teacher as Empowerer, Not as Helper   162
    11 Humor and Answers   164
    12 Questions for Thought   165

12 **Reconciliation, Banking Education, Problem Posing Education, the I-It and I-Thou Relationships, and the Teacher as Midwife**   166
    1   Reconciliation between Teacher and Student   167
    2   Banking Education   167
    3   Problem Posing Education   168
    4   The I-It Relationship   172
    5   The I-Thou Relationship   173
    6   Becoming Mutual   174
    7   Dialogue and Inclusion   176
    8   The Teacher as Midwife   177
    9   Communion   179
    10 Questions for Thought   183

13 **Portrait of Transcendent Shamanic Teacher: Laura**   184
    1   Laura   184
    2   First Transcendence   185
    3   The Confrontation   186
    4   The Transformation   187

CONTENTS

- 5 A Mutual Relationship 187
- 6 Laura the Teacher 187
- 7 Equality and Freedom 188
- 8 Humor 189
- 9 The Mutual Exchange 189
- 10 Reciprocal Relationships 190
- 11 Questions for Thought 191

14 **Power, Rhythm, the Turning Point, Limits, Limitations and Labeling** 192
- 1 Compelling Powers and Rhythm 192
- 2 Establishing a Bond with the Learner 194
- 3 The Turning Point 196
- 4 Limits and Limitations 198
- 5 The Damaging Impact of Labels 199
- 6 Precocious Learners and Labeling 200
- 7 Questions for Thought 201

15 **Portrait of Transcendent Shamanic Teacher: Beth** 203
- 1 Beth 203
- 2 Beth's Classroom 203
- 3 Beth the Teacher 206
- 4 Alexander 208
- 5 Removing Barriers 210
- 6 Questions for Thought 210

16 **The Transcendent Teacher-Learner Relationship: A Class Investigation** 212
- 1 Introduction/Perspectives of the Research 213
- 2 Methods/Data Source 214
- 3 Composite Narratives 215
- 4 Summary and Implications 222
- 5 Implications for Early Childhood Teacher Educators 223
- 6 Questions for Thought 224

17 **Miracles Can Happen: The School of Transcendence** 225
- 1 Perspectives on Education 225
- 2 Methods/Data Source 227
- 3 Findings 228
- 4 Philosophical Orientation and Approach to Creating Learning Encounters 228

    5   Curricula   229
    6   Planning and Scheduling   230
    7   Assessment and Evaluation   230
    8   Physical Space   231
    9   School Community Interpersonal Relationships   232
    10   Traditional Schools as Places of Violence   232
    11   Governance of the School of Transcendence   233
    12   Transcendence-Oriented Approaches Implemented in Reggio Emilia Schools   234
    13   Metaphors for the School of Transcendence   235
    14   Conclusion   238
    15   Questions for Thought   239

18   Putting It All Together   240
    1   A Synthesis of the Research on Transcendent Teacher Learner Relationships   241
    2   Transcendent Impact   244
    3   Community   245
    4   The Transformative Impact of the Transcendent Teacher Learner Relationship   245
    5   Questions for Thought   246

Appendix A: Heuristic Research Methodology and Procedures   249
Appendix B: Transcendent Teacher Inventory   254
Appendix C: Role Play Scenarios   260

References   261

Acknowledgements

This book is the result of the tremendous help, inspiration, and encouragement that I received from many people including my teachers, my learners and my colleagues. First of all, I would like to thank Greg Zechman who has been with this project since the original conception of the research thirty years ago, continuing in that role with this new edition. He has pondered, edited and advised me well. He has worked selflessly and tirelessly to help ensure that teachers and learners can benefit from the publication of this book. Without Mr. Zechman's contributions, neither edition of this book would exist.

I am also deeply indebted to my undergraduate and graduate students at The University of Tampa and Towson University whose help has been invaluable in offering suggestions, asking challenging questions and especially bringing their voices to the text. I owe thanks to my colleagues at The University of Tampa, Department of Education and Towson University Department of Early Childhood Education, who have continually supported, encouraged and critiqued my writing.

I am particularly grateful to Tom Morgan, my high school English teacher, without whom I would not have had the courage to emerge as a writer. Kudos to Jerry Crank and Kathy Bagley Blust who have inspired me and have also been deeply committed to the publication of this work, having also advised me well. Ryan Neal asked me about the role of transcendent shamanic teachers in the lives of learners who have experienced minimal trauma in their lives. Thus, in this edition and, thanks to him, I have included that content. I credit M. Lynne Squires has been a writing co-dreamer for several decades. She played a pivotal role in securing the art for the front cover of this book and I extend my thanks to her. I am grateful to Cheryl Eary, the architect for the promotion of this book.

Maxine Greene of Teacher's College provided a great source of inspiration for this work in addition to serving on my doctoral committee and being my friend and mentor until her death in 2014.

Jeanne Gerlach deftly served as chair of my doctoral committee that included David Bess, Scott Bower, Samuel Stack, and Jody Wolfe. Each of them provided superb guidance. Jody Wolfe, in particular, was a source of great encouragement and reassurance to me throughout the process.

Theoni Soublis has inspired me and acted as my muse in the completion of this work. Her teaching first provoked me to conceive the phenomenon of shamanic teaching.

I am grateful to John Bennett at Brill | Sense for agreeing to publish a second edition of this book. I was fortunate to work with Jolanda Karada, also at

Brill | Sense, throughout the process of publishing both editions of this book. Like Mr. Zechman, she is thorough, supportive, timely and a magnificently effective production editor. I hope one day to cross the Atlantic and meet her face to face.

Patty O'Grady spent considerable time coaching, problem solving and helping me shape this work in the boldest manner possible. She also carefully tutored me in the process of finding an appropriate home for this work.

Finally, I am grateful to my family and friends who have offered their continuous encouragement, especially my husband, Larry, who in his role as listener, helper and Encourager-in-Chief, provided me with patience for my interminable time spent before the computer.

I thank Jean O'Hara, Ann Mullins, Mary Ann O'Hara, James Skeen, Peggy Pridemore, Norma Matassini, Barbara Hruska, Beth Wilson, Leslie Pettys, and Laura Van Vorhis. Each one has been an enormous source of wisdom, inspiration and affirmation.

CHAPTER 1

The Nature of the Transcendent Relationship

> Some say that my teaching is nonsense. Others call it lofty but impractical. But to those who have looked inside themselves, This nonsense makes perfect sense. And to those who put it into practice, The loftiness has roots that go deep.
>
> LAO TZU (1999, number 67)

∴

The first edition of *Transcendent Teacher Learner Relationships: The Way of the Shamanic Teacher* was published in 2015. Since then, I have taught nearly five hundred students using that edition as a professor at The University of Tampa. Over that period of time my students have not been bashful in terms of making recommendations for the second edition of my book, now in your hands. As always, the feedback that I receive from my learners is invaluable. Indeed they help me be a better teacher, a better professor, a better person and, in this example, a better author. My learners tell me, on a regular basis, that not only will they apply the transcendence philosophy contained in this book with their learners but also in their relationships with family, friends, significant others, co-workers, and anyone with whom they may cross paths. Their recommendations, as well as my own evaluation of the first edition put me on a path toward including ever more clarity of concept articulation, the addition of comparison and contrast charts, an inventory for evaluating teachers for transcendence dispositions, as well as the addition of vast numbers of examples of how those myriad concepts and phenomena, contained herein, are conceived, implemented and maintained. I have repeated several quotes from portrait chapters in this book because those quotes effectively demonstrate multiple transcendence concepts.

I have been a teacher for more than four decades. I believe that teaching is one of the most powerful professions one can pursue. The profession endows teachers with the power to inform others, to strengthen them, and power to enable and liberate them intellectually, socially, spiritually and aesthetically. And as I work to accomplish this with others I accomplish it for myself.

Teaching others has given me an abundance of creative opportunity and more satisfaction than virtually any other facet of my life. My learners, as I shall call them, are my family and friends. I never forget that they continue to inspire me when I need it most. As a teacher, I am also a learner and I learn from them every day.

When I was in doctoral school, I needed a research topic that would sustain my interest for a year or more. I was keenly aware of how important my teaching and learning relationships were to me. And so began my careful observation and study of such relationships, a research focus that is ongoing (O'Hara, 1992, 1994a, 1994b, 1995, 2005, 2011, 2015, 2020, see heuristic research methodology in Appendix A).

Forces continue to converge on the teaching profession, learning environments and learners that have the potential to upset all that I and so many other teachers and learners value. Such forces include relentless testing and test-driven curricula, the standardization of classroom schedules, scripted teacher language, and language that usurps the teacher's professional judgment, timing and expertise. Teachers are forced to categorize learners in terms of perceived ability thereby creating a kind of pedagogical caste system. Even as the enormously expensive standards-based approach fails to produce promised results, the very power of the teachers to act and transform others as well as themselves is threatened. Despite the barriers placed before them by individuals, entities and institutions who do not seem to have a learner's best interest at heart, I continue to see evidence of teachers and learners overcoming these obstacles and transcending these barriers. I am inspired anew.

In the pilot study for my dissertation (O'Hara, 1994a, 1994b), I spoke with teachers in Denmark who had taught behind the "iron curtain" of the former Soviet Union. Those teachers, like so many teachers in the United States today, worked in intensely prohibitive schools where their professional judgment was not valued. Their teaching language, content and interaction with learners was highly restricted or imposed from without. And yet those obstacles failed to inhibit these teachers' commitment to their learners. Even when their actions and devotion to learners could have landed them in jail, they closed their classroom doors and did what they knew was best for their learners. Indeed, this is an awe-inspiring historical context for any situation where teacher learner relationships are studied closely. The former Soviet Union teachers interviewed held true to Albert Einstein's admonitions, "Only a life lived for others is worthwhile" (Schlipp, 1991, p. 650) and "Never do anything against conscience even when the state demands it" (Schlipp, 1991, p. 653).

And thus, this work is about the incredible power of human relationships to transcend barriers, to transform the old and to create something wonderful and new. All of this is contained in the stories that follow, factual portraits as I shall call them, of hope and wonderment, those of teachers and learners relating in marvelous ways, ways that enabled them to reshape their existence. These teachers and learners have experienced relationships that extend beyond or transcend the limits of ordinary experience, limits that would otherwise have circumscribed the nature of their interaction and accomplishments. Their transcendent relationships are characterized by mutual trust, mutual care and mutual respect. As a result of the process of going beyond the ordinary, not only have their experiences with teaching and learning become more deeply meaningful, but participant perceptions of their world and lives have expanded positively as well. The transcendence process inspired them to find new direction and to change their life paths for the better. While the portraits are those of teachers and learners, the dynamics of their human relationships are universal.

The perspectives of multiple education philosophers, psychologists, theorists and practitioners who have written about the various hallmarks of transcendent relationships are presented herein. Throughout this book, the intent is to construct a vision, a philosophy that provides a set of principles that guide teachers as they facilitate a particular type of human relationship that not only remedies learner non-engagement in the learning process but also transcends the barriers that have led to impersonal interaction or even estrangement between teachers and learners.

Readers who have encountered transcendent relationships will note how familiar these stories may seem. Those who have not encountered them may feel cheated. Either way, I encourage you to consider where such transcendent relationships could lead if they were to become commonplace, and imagine the implications if transcendence were the standard to which all teacher-learner relators aspired.

Transcendent relationships should not be confused with mentorship or perceptions of mentorship in which the relationship is designed for only the teacher to meet the various receptive needs of the student. Transcendent relationships are mutually beneficial. Teacher and learner go beyond their traditionally imposed roles so that both individuals experience positive, life altering phenomena. Transcendent relationships are characterized by *the mutuality that leads to joint pilgrimages and transformation for both relators.* Transcendent relationships are appropriate relationships, that is, they are proper, well-suited and lawful relationships. The parable that follows is intended to offer some clarity about how transcendence occurs in everyday life, beyond the classroom. The parable shows how momentous and profound common life encounters become when relators transcend the limits of ordinary experience.

1 Dash and the Electrician: A Parable of a Transcendent Relationship

The wiring in Dash's Victorian era house was old and dangerous. Dash was concerned that an electrical fire might occur so he called an electrician to do the job of rewiring the house. It was a hot June day when the electrician arrived and the shy-seeming electrician quietly introduced himself as Orlando Constantine. Orlando went to work.

A couple of hours later, Dash offered Orlando a glass of iced tea. Orlando accepted and Dash invited Orlando to sit with him as they drank. Dash thanked Orlando for his highly competent electrical work. Dash's sincere manner took Orlando off guard. Dash's warm, social personality put the otherwise reserved Orlando at ease. Orlando paused for a bit, then began to talk. He mentioned that his adoptive father was also an electrician. When Dash told Orlando he was adopted as well, Dash asked Orlando how old Orlando was when he was adopted. Orlando answered "eighteen months."

Intrigued, they continued to discuss how old they were when they learned that they were adopted and their attempts to find their biological family. Orlando had not been able to locate his biological family but Dash had managed to locate his family. Both had had tremendously positive experiences with their adoptive families. As the conversation continued, the two also discovered that they were both runners. More conversation ensued. After that day and long after the rewiring was completed, Orlando and Dash were close friends. They ran together each weekend and at one point Orlando saved Dash's life when a drunk driver swerved into their running lane and nearly collided with Dash. Trust between the two continued to grow and ultimately it was Dash who helped Orlando through the most trying times of his life, including his mother's death and his back surgery.

The two continued to remain friends for the rest of their lives. All of this was the result of Dash's call for an electrician to come to his house to carry out a professional task. Dash's offer of iced tea led to more than two hours of interaction that day. The outcome is that Dash and Orlando transcended traditional professional/client roles and a rich relationship followed.

2 Analysis

Occurrences such as the one experienced by Orlando and Dash may not be rare, but the genesis of the relationship is somewhat serendipitous. A fortunate discovery of friendship occurred in an unexpected, perhaps providential, manner. The emergence of an authentic relationship, one that is not defined by professional roles, could not have occurred, had Dash not created an atmosphere in which an otherwise wary individual, Orlando, could relax and open up over a glass of iced tea. Dash could not have known where his action as an inviting and open host to his electrician would lead. Dash's simple, gracious and welcoming act facilitated Orlando's comfort and safety levels thereby ushering in their deeply valued ongoing friendship.

Typically clients do not interact with professionals who are performing a service for them in such a personable way or make the professional feel like a guest in their home. Dash risked that Orlando would reject his offer to sit with him. But because Dash did offer, Orlando was enabled to feel safe enough to open up to a stranger in a way that he would not have done otherwise.

When individuals step outside traditional interactive roles such as the one described, marvelous events may occur. Indeed, relationships that transcend traditional roles in ways that are authentic, as in the example of Dash and Orlando, can become mutually respectful, trusting, caring and mutually transformative. Such relationships are unexpected joys that are available *only* if one reaches out to the other in an unexpected way.

Teachers and learners do not have much opportunity to sit and talk over a glass of iced tea, as did Dash and Orlando. The reader will recall that Dash and Orlando were able to begin a friendship, an authentic relationship, in a couple of hours.

Teachers and learners may interact each day during class, as learners are gathering, as the teacher circulates throughout the classroom, when they are having lunch or as learners are exiting the classroom. Over a semester, a year, or multiple years, teachers and learners have many hours of opportunity to come to see each other as more than persons in their traditional roles. At the same time, teachers can invite transcendence with all learners in the classroom by creating a warm, social, nurturing, loving atmosphere as described below.

In a warm atmosphere, learners feel safe to take risks that they would not ordinarily take, as in Orlando's example. Learners feel safe to reach out to the transcendent host teacher who stays *with* the learner, struggles with the learner and never abandons him or her throughout their connection. The transcendent teacher cares for the learner in a *steadfast* manner and so the learner is enabled to trust the teacher in ways that would not be possible without the transcending host teacher's strong commitment to the learner. Teacher and learner begin a promenade down a path of mutual awakening as they both begin to learn from each other.

3 Teacher and Learner

A mutual awakening process, such as the one described above, exceeds usual limits for teacher learner interaction. Indeed, such phenomena lie outside ordinary experience. As in the examples of Dash and Orlando, when teacher and learner connect in profound ways, the result can be a mutually transformative, transcendent encounter for *both*. The concern in a transcendent teacher learner relationship is not whether the teacher is trustworthy, a liar, or whether the teacher can be trusted to be fair with grades. One expects that of non-transcendent teachers. The concern is whether the learner can trust the transcendent teacher to create and maintain a warm, safe, social, loving and nurturing environment. Many traditionally oriented teachers have high expectations for learners but the atmosphere they create may not be warm, safe, social, nurturing or loving. The reader will note that the transcendent relationship characteristics and qualities described throughout this book are both unique and sophisticated. Likewise the depiction that follows of *The King's Speech* (Canning, Sherman, & Unwin, 2010) conveys the unique and sophisticated nature of transcendent teacher learner relationships.

4 The King's Speech

As portrayed in the film, King George VI of England had developed a strong stammer. The King was compelled to overcome his stammer so he could deliver speeches and represent the United Kingdom effectively throughout and beyond WWII. The King was called upon by his teacher, Lionel Logue, to relax protocol and to approach his speech therapist teacher and commoner as an equal. The teacher even insisted on calling the King by his nickname "Bertie," a name used only by his family and never by commoners. The King resisted at first, but mutuality between the two came about when the teacher, Lionel, modeled a manner of being that was supremely non-pretentious, one that exceeded class and station.

In the film, both the King and his teacher mutually submerged themselves in the process of enabling the King to speak without stammering. The process of overcoming the stammer took an enormous toll on the King and his teacher as they labored diligently throughout the process.

The teacher stayed close beside the King both in terms of proximity and emotional support, throughout the King's physical, emotional and spiritual struggle. Lionel, a fully devoted teacher called upon the King to trust his pedagogy without doubt or reservation. Again, the King resisted but ultimately complied. Lionel worked tirelessly to inspire the King to have confidence in himself; to believe in his own strength and capacity for success, despite the humiliation the King had suffered as a child from his father and nanny. Indeed, the King continued to suffer as an adult from the actions of his father, his brother David, and others. The teacher on the other hand, never abandoned the King, pedagogically, emotionally or spiritually.

Finally, the time for the King's speech arrived. The teacher and the King were alone together during the speech that was to be broadcast throughout the world. Both remained face to face as the teacher conducted the King through the speech. To everyone's joy, the King's speech was profoundly successful. All were elated. Following the speech, the King referred to his teacher as "friend," despite his teacher's professional role and status as a commoner. Afterward, the King elevated his teacher's status in British society and the two remained friends for the rest of their lives.

Throughout, the teacher and the King interacted in ways that went beyond tradition both socially and pedagogically. With the teacher's guidance, the King and the teacher imagined what did not yet exist and brought what was imagined into reality. They were able to go beyond, to transcend boundaries that might have prevented the King's success and ultimately the friendship that emerged between the King and his teacher.

The King and the teacher shared a transcendent teacher learner relationship. Just as the barriers implied by royalty and commoner status at first stood between the King and the teacher, the barriers of tradition have historically stood between teachers and learners. In other words, the barriers of class and profession have stood in the way of authentic mutual teacher learner relationships. As a result, trust, authentic interaction, care and transformation could not emerge. Teachers and learners that adhered to traditional interactive models were rendered unable to establish the kind of connection that can lead to the most powerful, most meaningful learning encounters one can imagine.

5 The Transcendent Teacher

The transcendent teacher creates a safe, warm nurturing environment that invites transcendence to occur, the teacher remaining fully devoted to the learner throughout their interaction. The transcendent teacher is focused on the learner's holistic development. The teacher's behavior consistently demonstrates a deep commitment to each learner's social, emotional, spiritual, physical as well as intellectual development. The teacher, as in the example of *The King's Speech,* never faltered in terms of his commitment to the King, a commitment that put Lionel's high expectations for the King's success center stage. Transcendent teachers, such as Lionel, do not waiver in terms of the demands and expectations they place on the learner. Teacher and learner stay face-to-face, if you will, throughout the learning encounter. The transcendent teacher creates a learning environment that is full of change, movement and conversation, an environment in which, again, the teacher learns from learners as well as the reverse.

Throughout this process, the transcendent teacher acts as a catalyst for the learner's development, remaining firm, demanding and compelling. There is nothing, in this sense, that is commonly referred to as "soft." The rigorous transcendence process requires grit and determination on the part of both learner and teacher. Transcendent teachers tend to be more demanding than traditional teachers. Transcending barriers and obstacles is not always fun, enjoyable or even amusing. However, the results of a transcendent learning encounter and relationship are always rewarding and liberating for both learner and teacher.

The transcendent teacher converses regularly with learners about *trans-curricular,* as well as curricular topics. I assert the term trans-curricular, instead of extra-curricular, to refer to exceeding or extending the intended curriculum in terms of content, importance, meaning and depth of learning. Thus, trans-curriculum includes content that is of equal importance, or more importance than the intended curriculum. During conversations, the transcendent teacher gathers valuable data that directly assists in creating the most transformative learning context possible to accommodate the learner's maximal development. The transcendent teacher shares appropriate, relevant, personal information that relates directly to what is being taught. The transcendent teacher shares what they value and is sacred to them, what helped them become the person they are, and who they want to be.

Within the context of a math lesson for example, the transcendent teacher may share their own personal struggles with math. They may share the process that helped them meet those challenges and who helped them, all the while extending variant help, as needed, to learners during the lesson at hand. Transcendent teachers reveal their own struggles with content and how they overcame those struggles to help learners understand that difficulty and struggle are natural, expected and valued dimensions of the learning process, a process that occurs even for highly regarded teachers who may otherwise appear to learners to be virtually omnipotent. In addition to frequent conversation, transcendent teachers appraise learner development carefully via intense and regular observation along with other interactions throughout the learning process.

Moreover, transcendent teachers are not concerned with, or reliant on *pre-determining* a learner's capacity or potential for development. Standardized test scores that are limiting, stigmatizing and purport to measure ability or potential for learning are only remotely or occasionally relevant for transcendent teachers who are devoted to maximizing learner achievement. Informal teacher's lounge conversations about learners have no place in the transcendent teacher's psyche. Instead, transcendent teachers act to remove limiting labels that impose developmental barriers on learners, which helps widen the learner's developmental scope to hitherto unknown and unexpected realms. That widening occurs even as the achievement gap narrows. The transcendent teacher, not confined by artificial or archaic ability estimations, moves forward *boldly* with high expectations for all learners. Thus, the learner's capacity for development is operationalized and maximized in the intended context, and the learner's development extends to and enriches other developmental realms and dimensions.

James Skeen describes profound trans-curricular learning that occurred with his transcendent teacher. James' learning included the realization of his gifts, what he has to offer the world as well as the intended curricular learning that occurred during his encounters with his transcendent teacher.

> What I actually learned from my transcendent teacher is that I am a force of nature. I learned that my boundless empathy is not a weakness but, in fact, a superpower. I was taught that my family's financial standing was no indication of my intelligence. I was taught that my quirks and eccentricity are what make me magnificent to behold. I learned confidence. I learned that I am worth fighting for. I learned that it is okay and healthy to stand out as an individual. But, to also bring my flame into the group so we can all benefit from one another's powers of acceptance, creativity, love, humor and understanding. I learned these things, of myself and of others, because my transcendent shaman understood teaching to be a deeply individual experience, not just books, lesson plans and regurgitated seminars of decades-old "get them ready for the workforce" educational philosophy.... Oh, and I actually learned to sing, read music and dance.

6   The Transcendent Teacher Learner Relationship

Transcendent teacher learner relationships are comprised of the components identified below.

6.1   *Transcendent Atmosphere*
Acting in good faith, the transcendent teacher, in a manner that is analogous to that of a host for the learner, deliberately creates a warm social atmosphere in

which all members of the teaching/learning community feel cared for, valued and valuable. The teacher facilitates the learner's feelings of self-valuing, both as a learner and as a human being. The learner's sense of self-valuing emerges as the teacher highlights the learner's unique combination of competencies, intelligences, modalities and capacities. In a non-competitive community where all learners are valued for their divergent gifts, learners are freed to feel comfortable to be themselves. They feel relaxed, safe and free to take positive risks that would not be possible in non-transcendent atmospheres. The transcendent atmosphere is socially, emotionally, spiritually, intellectually and physically safe. A transcendent atmosphere feels joyous and familiar to learners. The tone is bright and homey. In Chapter 7, Lauren describes the transcendent atmosphere. "People were laughing and carrying on, like back home with your father, mother and relatives just laughing and having a good time together ... but ... [the teacher] didn't allow any foolishness. [He] cut up and [he] joked, but it was [his] own way. [He] gave us enough room, but [he] had discipline."

6.2 *Transcendent Interaction*

As a safe, warm social atmosphere is created, learners begin to trust teachers to maintain the transcendent atmosphere and to know that the teacher is their supporter and co-investigator. The transcendent teacher invites transcendent interaction via their expressions of trust, respect and care for the learner. Thus, the interaction that emerges is *mutually loving, mutually respectful, mutually trusting* and *mutually developmental*. Teachers and learners interact authentically, free of the barriers that false roles impose.

In Chapter 3, Peggy shares how teacher/learner mutuality functions. "Teaching is like a light that shines back and forth from teacher to student, and then from student to teacher, and so on, depending on the situation. Rigidity prevents that shifting, a rigidity that comes when teachers assume an all-knowing, attitude." Moreover, for Jerry in Chapter 9, "There is a feeling that *we're in this together.* I like the equality I feel with her. It's not that ... I know as much as she does, or that my knowledge is equivalent to hers. It's not that kind of equality. It's not so much she treats me like an adult, but that she treats me as an equal" (emphasis added)."

In her novel, *Jane Eyre* (1847), Charlotte Bronte, herself a teacher, captures the perspective of the transcendent teacher regarding the mutuality that arises in such contexts. "I am not talking to you now through the medium of custom, conventionalities, nor even of mortal flesh: *It is my spirit that addresses your spirit ... equal – as we are!*" (p. 386, emphasis added). Thus, mutuality in transcendence is a soul-to-soul connection.

Aligning this mutuality and authenticity with the teacher's professional and traditional duties and responsibilities requires a sophisticated balancing effort on the part of the transcendent teacher. The teacher therefore, must establish high expectations and facilitate exceptional motivation for each member of the learning community, expectations that are uniquely designed for each learner. In the process of establishing and maintaining these expectations the transcendent teacher remains leader and supervisor. The transcendent teacher is firm, reliable, and fully committed to each learner's personal evolution and development. Lauren continues,

> When [he] said [he] would do something, I knew I could depend on [him] to do everything in [his] power to get it done. I did not have to keep asking [him] ... This is where the trust came into our relationship ... I knew that it was taken care of ...
>
> [He] energized us and we took an interest. [He] had such a sense of pride about it; [he] wanted us to be the best we could be, and that made us work harder. And then *we* had a sense of pride ... We were motivated and excited about what we were doing. I respected [him] because of [his] honesty, what [he] stood for. [He] never gave me any reason to question [his] judgment or put down anyone for any reason. [He] gave me encouragement, advice and feedback, and allowed me personal and mental growth. [He] helped me explore alternatives in my life, without being pushy. [His] insight was very important in my case.

6.3 *Transcendent Encounter*

When transcendent atmospheres and interaction are established and maintained, teachers and learners may experience a transformation that allows both of them to see their worlds differently. They are both nurtured and empowered as a result. Teacher and learner may now find themselves on a life path that has changed for the better. In Chapter 13, transcendent teacher Laura describes the mutually transformational nature of her encounter with Melinda:

> For a long time I thought I was the only one giving in that relationship, but looking back I realize ... she was giving to me all the while. As I watched her resolve family, social, and personal image issues, I finished resolving them in my own life. I wonder sometimes where I would be if she had not entered my life. A year passed before I really knew how much Melinda meant to me.

The transcendent relationship may continue long after the original teaching learning context has passed. Indeed, many transcendent relationships continue for a lifetime.

When a network or community of transcendent relationships develops in a classroom context, relators may undergo a group-wide, *community encounter*. That is, the entire group may share an encounter in which all relators, teachers as well as learners, are transformed, nurtured and empowered. Such a phenomenon occurs in two particular films, *Paperclips* (Fab et al., 2004), *Freedom Writers* (Devito, Shamberg, & Sher, 2007). In both films, within a context of transcendent community of learners and teachers, studies of the Holocaust lead to profound, transformative, life changing encounters for all involved. Community encounters also occur in several portraits contained herein, including that of Theoni and her learners in Chapter 2.

6.4 *The Transcendent Relationship Gestalt*

Transcendent teacher learner relationships occur because of a cluster of atmospheric and interactive features that converge in such a way that enables teacher and learner to transcend barriers and overcome obstacles. Barriers and obstacles transcended by participants in the heuristic studies that follow include those imposed by loneliness, poor self-esteem, repression, hopelessness, wheelchairs, shock treatments and even the contemplation of suicide. Visions of better realities take their place even as better realities emerge for transcendent relators. Despite the common atmospheric and interactive features of transcendent relationships, there can be no prescription, no recipe or list of behaviors that promise transcendence in relationships. Rather, relators bring their respective, enigmatic biographies to those relationships and each relator pair transcends uniquely because of the confluence of those biographies.

6.5 *Transcendent Relationships and Time*

Transcendent teacher learner relationships do not require extra time on the part of the teacher, but they do require extra effort. Roughly 95% of the time involved in facilitating transcendent relationships occurs during class instruction, transitions, before or after the bell rings, in the lunch room or in school hallways. Transcendent teacher relationships are not facilitated outside the traditional school classroom context even though they may continue after the original learning context has ended.

6.6 *Good Teachers and Transcendent Teachers: Contrast/Comparison*

All good teachers are to be valued and revered because they are critical to the foundation of an informed society. But the transcendent teacher emerges and acts on additional and deeper levels. For purposes of contrast/comparison, included below are contrasting descriptive phrases for the good teacher and the transcendent teacher.

6.6.1 The Good Teacher
- knows content well and teaches effectively to diverse populations;
- is committed to the facilitation of learner's academic growth and development;
- is approachable, kind and non-threatening, establishes and maintains a physically safe environment;
- is supportive of the learner and facilitates the learner's academic success; and
- is encouraging and may offer one-on-one support to learners.

6.6.2 The Transcendent Teacher
- is fully devoted to and facilitates the learner's social, emotional, physical, spiritual as well as intellectual growth and development;
- consistently creates a warm, social atmosphere wherein all learners feel valued and valuable;
- consistently establishes and sustains mutual respect, mutual trust and mutual care with learners;
- creates and maintains a community where learners also share mutual respect, mutual trust and mutual care with each other;
- acts as a co-investigator with learners, teaching them and learning alongside them;
- may experience a life changing event with learners that facilitates a life-long friendship;
- is firm, demanding and compelling even while creating an atmosphere where learners feel safe and encouraged to take positive risks; and
- is empathetic and genuine.

Note: The discourse herein focuses on a set of ideas or beliefs relating to the field of education, and is a critical analysis of fundamental assumptions or beliefs about how teaching and learning can occur. A transcendence philosophy of education is set forth in this book; philosophy in this sense refers to a set of principles that guide the practice of teaching and learning.

7 The Author's Background with Teaching and Learning Encounters

I have always been fascinated by teachers. I marvel at the sophisticated and elegant nature of the teaching process. Teaching is an immensely creative endeavor that demands well developed artistic and intellectual capacities as well as a finely honed understanding of human nature. The extraordinary teachers in my life created very powerful experiences that changed me in profound ways. I remember being so enamored with my first grade teacher. At six years of age I was horrified when I discovered the she was paid to do her work. I thought she was simply a kind, selfless woman who was motivated only to do good in the world. When I became a teacher and first walked into the classroom, I wanted to approximate that level of impact on my learners.

8   The Good, the Bad and the Ugly

When I completed eight years of public school teaching, I enrolled in a full time doctoral program. As part of my research, I thought about my learners, myself and the relationships I had with them. With mixed emotions I remembered my own teachers. As with all professions, some teachers are poor and others are superb. I evaluated each of my teachers – first grade through graduate school. There were over sixty. I ranked them in terms of their capacity to meet my developmental needs; academically, emotionally, socially, aesthetically and creatively. After decades in some cases, I found myself responding on an emotional level to those memories. Two teachers emerged in particular. At rock bottom of my teacher capability hierarchy was my fourth grade teacher, Ms. Bias – cold, unyielding and mean. I still see her looking down at me with her headache face, black glasses, crossed arms and hands with popping veins. Coupled with that image, I can still feel the razor sharp edge of her sarcasm. She took satisfaction from demeaning children. Ms. Bias frightened me and humiliated me. I atrophied in her class, and hid. I spent my time worrying about whether I was good enough to measure up to her unknowable expectations or whether I was going to be embarrassed soon.

By contrast, my senior high vocal music teacher, Peggy Pridemore, was at the top of my list. She was passionate, funny, dramatic and sometimes outrageous. She shared all of her emotions in class – joy, excitement, exuberance, anger and frustration. In that authentic environment I blossomed. She treated us with respect and she was genuine. She was an accessible, transcendent teacher, both in terms of her approach to teaching and her interpersonal interaction with her learners, as you will read later.

How could I not do well in her class? She told us, "for the next forty-five minutes, nothing, nothing else exists but you and me." Her actual name was Mrs. Pridemore and her impact on my life has been immeasurable. It is because of her that I became a teacher.

Of course, it is per chance that these teachers, worst to best, were named Bias and Pridemore respectively. Their very names imply two very different types of teachers, two very different ways of being human and responding to the high calling of being a teacher.

As I thought about my teachers, myself and my learners, I began to understand that significant, truly meaningful learning hinges on the quality of the relationship between teacher and learner. It was my relationships with teachers and learners that determined the quality of the learning experiences I had with them. I carefully pondered the qualities, dynamics and characteristics that created superb, deep and meaningful learning. Before I interviewed teachers and learners for my research, I first had to scrutinize my own encounters with teachers and learners.

9   The Mother as Teacher

I attribute my intermittently charmed early childhood to my mother Jean as my first teacher, my grandmothers Mary and Lottie, and my Aunt Ann. As my first teachers, each one was wise, strong and creative. Each innately understood child development. Even as a child, I admired them very much as they balanced my life experiences between freedom and clearly established limits. I never felt as if I needed to pursue their attention or approval. My mother was patient and available. Her emphasis, as my first teacher, was on my natural learning inclinations and because there was never pressure to hurry my development, my childhood memories with her are of an abundance of time, of fun, and of love.

10   Life at School

Before I entered school, I was completely ignorant of the notion of failure. My closest friends were in school before me and so I wanted to be in school also. One of my friends told me I would like elementary school. But when I finally went there I was discouraged and I experienced a distinct awareness that something important to me was ending. At school, for example, I did not have the kind of graceful learning and joy that I had learning with my mother and the others at home as my teachers. Before school, I was familiar only with nature's classroom of light, color, texture, and taste. The exhilaration of play, laughter and music were so much more engaging than what met me on the first day of school.

When my mother delivered me to the classroom door for my first day of school, I remember the teacher's distracted welcome. She promptly directed me to a hard chair with a cramping desktop. The room was a peculiar place with glaring fluorescent lights, where people sat in tight rows, hour after hour, with little activity. Uncomfortable learning experiences seemed to emerge like tumors on the flesh. You could speak only when given permission to do so, and you could act only in response to the teacher's direction. Both approaches inhibited my natural kinesthetically oriented inclinations and appetite to learn. They were so different from my mother's developmentally sound approach of encouraging free and tactile responses to the environment, with limits, and fluid conversation. Moreover, at school, there was no effort to connect what was to be learned with my life experience.

At the end of one school day, I laughed out loud when a friend joked in the cloakroom. The teacher came rushing in with fire in her eyes and shook me violently. I was mortified. I do not remember what she said; I only remember that she was angry with me because I had laughed. Like most, I have never responded well to violence, physical or emotional. In that moment of being shaken something shifted in me. I could no longer trust her. I could no longer trust school to be a safe place.

The ugliness and violence of that encounter stayed with me and it was hard to be comfortable with what would happen next. Some believe that violence toward children at home and at school is the primary cause of the violence of the culture we live in, the culture that so often horrifies us. I could never understand how people could expect to gain appropriate behavior from others by modeling and inflicting violence on them.

11   How People Acted at School

People at school seemed to distance themselves from each other and competed against each other, while the teacher seemed to encourage such behaviors. She seemed ill equipped to model more harmonious and natural ways of being, teaching and learning. In response to the arena that was created, students preened for the teacher, and vied for her attention. I wanted to resist that ritual, but to resist was like running the wrong direction on an escalator. I would have liked to have shared a conversation with the teacher; instead the tone of my interaction with her was flat. Rarely was it conversational or even personable.

To add to the mix, two years later I moved to a new neighborhood and another school. As a new child at that school, I was not well accepted by my peers. At my first school for example, on Valentine's Day I received a Valentine from each classmate. At this new school, people gave you Valentines only if they liked you. Most of them apparently did not like me because I did not receive many. I felt disconnected from my classmates and that was disorientating because the disconnection from them was so new to me. My experiences at the school grew more disappointing and painful.

Much of this school's focus was on competition between peers rather than the development of school community. I did not enjoy participating in competitive academic or sporting games and I did not have the athletic skills to do so if I had. I did not join in with enthusiasm and frequently I dropped the ball or messed up a play. It was my androgynous style that antagonized many of my peers, I think, more than my athletic ineptitude. They responded to my bumbling attempts at sports with taunting, harassment, and physical abuse. School was increasingly an emotionally and physically violent place for me. Most of this occurred under the teacher's supervision. I distinctly remember thinking, at the age of nine years, that my teacher was betraying me by not intervening on my behalf when I was abused by my peers.

My adult activist self now realizes that the all too common distortions of classroom justice such as these were manifestations of homophobia in my peers and teachers (O'Hara, 2014). My peers were not aware of the roots of their biases because I was a pre-sexual being. The outcome was that my peers, many of whom called me Helen instead of Hunter in front of teachers, felt justified in their behavior and that justification was given full support by the teacher's nonintervention. Could those teachers have believed that if they looked the other way, I would be shamed into being someone I was not intended to be? If not, what *were* they thinking? These injustices occurred at school, but what happened at home also predisposed me to need particular relationships with teachers.

12   Life at Home

Despite the marvelous events that occurred at our home and my mother's advanced developmental skills and awareness, all was not well there. My parents were alcoholics. Their alcoholism and particularly my father's violence permeated our home. We spent many school nights escaping that violence by attempting to sleep underneath our beds even as my father's loud music blared throughout the night. The suspense was heightened by the fact that my father kept a loaded rifle in the basement that he referred to during rants. Frequently on weekends we were forced by my father to flee our home, usually through narrow, elevated windows at the rear of the house only later to suddenly and surprisingly appear on the doorsteps of friends and family who were fortunately uniformly gracious in providing us refuge. When we returned home on Sunday evenings, by which time my father was finally sober and badly hung over, the house was usually wrecked and sometimes the floors were covered with glass that had been shattered by him in a drunken rage. On most Monday mornings, we pulled ourselves together and went to school.

13   What I Needed at School

With all of this at home, I felt that I needed for my teachers to recognize my worth and to believe that I could, and would, be successful. I wanted to be free of the violence that I associated with my father. I needed a warm, caring, nonthreatening classroom. Rewards, stars, badges, and praise were wholly inadequate. Much more than that, I needed to be respected and valued by my teachers and peers. I craved the briefest conversations with them, ones that transcended curricular concerns. I wanted to have a meaningful relationship, although I could not have described it in that way back then, I wanted my teacher to trust me and to always expect that I genuinely desired to do well in school.

My home encounters, such as those described above, colored my perceptions of the world. I began to understand that I lived in a different world from other people who did not know the chaos that the family disease of alcoholism causes. Because of these perceptions I secretly believed that my peers and teachers were hiding the realities of their home life from me and from others. I thought for example, surely "someone gets drunk in your family. Someone must get nasty, things must go haywire." When I saw little or no evidence of that in their behavior, or their words, I told myself that they were in denial of their life situations. Could it be that their world really was so secure and orderly? I searched for people to connect with who were real to *me*, who seemed to have genuine conflict and struggle in their lives and spoke about it.

As the years passed I also looked for teachers and peers who were *real*. Real people for me were not naïve, had not led overly sheltered lives, and they were open and honest about themselves as well as the injustices, the joys, and passion of life. When I was growing up people did not discuss alcoholism, abuse, neglect, bullying, codependence, homophobia or sexual orientation. From my perspective, this absence of realism left a vacuum in human interaction.

The silence contributed to my growing sense of alienation. I looked for dents in people's armor because those dents, and their exposed humanity, reassured me that I was not alone.

14   Teacher Realness

I remember that a few of my teachers were real, wonderful, warm, and caring people. Real teachers are open and genuine toward learners. One day I was honored when my third grade teacher, Mrs. Marsh, asked me to stay after school to help her with the bulletin boards. When we finished she offered to take me home, in *her* car. With bugging eyes I gave her directions to my house. How strange it seemed for me to direct her and I took that responsibility very seriously. When we arrived she said, "My goodness, I didn't know we lived this close to each other; we're neighbors." I distinctly recall the moment when she referred to me as "neighbor." That was the point when, for me, we became more real to each other. I remember dropping by her home to see her even when she was no longer my teacher. I began to understand and appreciate her more as a person and she became softer in her interaction with me. I began to visit her at home occasionally. She was no longer untouchable, and unable to reach out to me. Twenty years later she told me how important those visits were to her.

I am not sure what motivated me to visit Mrs. Marsh at her home. I know that her sophistication appealed to me. She loved to talk about the beauty of ballet noting the roundness and fluidity of the dancers' movements and how rich the experience is for the observer. She also talked about her own life, her struggles and delights as they emerged, moment by moment. And she was interested in other's life events as well.

I had a few good teachers when I went to junior high school and I enjoyed their quirky environments and the experiences they created very much. However, for whatever reason, I did not have conversations with those teachers about things *other* than classroom concerns. At the same time, their behaviors and respectful attitudes showed that those teachers cared for me and wanted to help me. They were good teachers. But what I really wanted from them I later desired from my learners: to share something of my life with them and they with me. My teachers were directing a large part of my existence; should I not know and understand them as human beings and as more than school employees? Should they not know me, more than just a name followed by numbers in a grade book? I did not know then that what I wanted was a transcendent teacher.

15   Mrs. Peggy Pridemore, Transcendent Teacher

As a sophomore, because of one teacher, I gained a sense of wonder and enthusiasm about my school experience. Mrs. Peggy Pridemore (also see Chapter 3) was unlike any person I had encountered at school. She was outrageous, enthusiastic and exciting. She lost her temper sometimes, but not in a mean way, and I felt like I understood, really understood why she did it. She had wonderful facial expressions and a compelling presence. I was attracted to her believability. With her genuine approach, she could create an intimate atmosphere with seventy people in the room. For me, her variant tone of voice and her facial expressions made learning experiences enthralling. I felt as if she were talking to me alone. She made the unfamiliar familiar, by telling personal stories and anecdotes to her students who were genuinely captivated by them and her.

Mrs. Pridemore explained very early on that our goal in her class would *not* be individual, independence-oriented learning pursuits. Rather, the goal would be what we could accomplish together through collaborative learning projects. I remember her talking about each of us being links in a chain, the chain itself worthless without the strength of each link. She held learners in high regard and I never felt that she took advantage of her position of authority in a negative way.

I remember the clothing she wore. She was glamorous, sophisticated and charismatic. Her humor and her persona were snappy, compelling, and engaging. She was powerful and at the same time she was not afraid to laugh or joke or to be irreverent. Never pretentious, she let you know that she had struggled in her life. We observed her in some of her difficult times and she became regal and strong, a model for standing by one's personal convictions. I was agog. I was home.

16   Down the Road

Our relationship deepened when I was teaching in Peggy's former position as a choral director at Saint Albans High School. Peggy encouraged me through a difficult first year that she found to be similar to her own first year experiences. During my first three years of teaching, I was dealing with a non-supportive administrator who did not value my work. My learners were not familiar with my approach to music teaching. Peggy derived a sense of fulfillment from helping me in a situation in which she herself had once felt horribly alone.

She was able to assure me that the negative situation I was experiencing would indeed pass.

She told me,

> I was really proud that you wanted my opinion, and I thought, "Gee, this guy thinks I'm worth something." It was so funny. You were saying, "Oh God, is this ever going to pass?" And I remembered how that felt. I was alone, but I was so glad that you weren't. And what you were going through was so similar to what I went through, and it was so easy to say, "Now look, this will pass. It will pass."

17 A Reflection before a Storm, then Sunshine

I realized there was an uncommon link between the two of us. As a teacher, I wanted to create the kind of ambiance with my learners that my mother and Peggy created with others and me. I wanted them to feel enabled as I had and for their encounters to be as graceful as mine had been.

I wanted to have conversations with my students, to provide an opportunity for them to release their unique creativity, to challenge and provoke them. I wanted them to know the same unconditional regard I had enjoyed. Certainly, developmental concerns were prominent in my mind and there seemed to me to be no reason why learners could not be treated with the same respect or regard that I would afford any other individual on the street. I would not be violent, either physically or interactionally. I would set a better standard than many of the teachers I was exposed to as a learner.

It was not easy at first to accomplish all of this. My senior high students and I had to develop a culture together which would not be easy. My predecessor, who came after Peggy, had allowed them a great amount of unbridled power and they had experienced a degree of success in a competition with that predecessor the year before I arrived.

I had a different new vision for them and I was determined that I would be successful. I was determined that they would be successful. I insisted on focus, compliance, and commitment from them. Many of them resisted me at every opportunity; the harder I struggled, the more they exerted opposition. I was only six years older than the senior students. I looked the same age as them, was tall, thin – and was gay. And they continued to resist and to defy me.

In the middle of all of this, a friend suggested, "Well you know, you *can* fail their asses." Her advice gave me a limited sense of relief, but ultimately I did not fail them. Still, their grades were not what they were accustomed to and they were astonished to see that I was, in fact, in charge. The day after the first report cards went home, you could have heard a pin drop in the rehearsal hall.

Nonetheless, my grading power play was an artificial measure and an artificial success. I learned I would need to compromise, to genuinely listen to their ideas and concerns, even if they were sometimes expressed in a hostile manner. More than this I realized that I would have to find a way to make my vision a part of the vision we created together. That was much easier said than done. Gradually, progress came and I developed very rewarding relationships with many of them. The groups successfully performed music. During my second year of teaching, the majority of my students returned to the groups and with familiarity came dramatic progress.

That year we still had to struggle and then collaborate to create a learning community that was full of trust, mutuality, care, and respect. Building a classroom culture is a complex, time-consuming process. My learners and I united in our pursuit of common goals, in this case, to create a powerful musical feeling while projecting it with intellect, sophistication and allure. The commitment and confidence gradually began, first with me and later with the enthusiasm of my learners.

At the beginning of my third year, I began to feel as if I had come home again, home to the richness of my childhood learning experiences and Mrs. Pridemore's music classes during my teen years. A special ambiance emerged as teacher and learners worked together collaboratively with mutual respect. I did not have to work hard to involve them. We fed power to each other. Once again I recognized that teaching and learning in transcendent ways feels good and it leads to superb results for everyone involved.

18   Teacher Power and Relationships

When I was five years old, a film titled *The Miracle Worker* (Coe, 1962) was released. As I listened to adults talk about it I was attracted to the words in the title. I did not really know what a miracle was or what a miracle worker could do but I intuitively recognized the power of those words. Dramatic images flooded my mind because the title sounded powerful, especially to my young ears. In my mind's eye I imagined a figure with a hand upraised in a divinely powerful way, light beaming down on the figure's shoulders. I could see people around the figure, their jaws dropped in astonishment. I imagined power surging around the room like an electrical current as someone or something was being transformed.

The Miracle Worker (Coe, 1962) became very important to me because the film is about a teacher who worked miracles with a blind and deaf child who ultimately became an international luminary. The movie inspires me even today because I am a teacher as well as a learner and I deeply admire what occurred in the relationship between Helen Keller and Anne Sullivan. I see such drama and excitement in that relationship as learner and teacher developed, resisted and then drew close, celebrated and changed together.

The film is a remarkable example of the marvelous power teachers have to create miraculous situations that transform the learner's life and their own lives as well. Sullivan and Keller were magnificently portrayed onstage and later on screen by actors Ann Bancroft and Patty Duke. Both won Oscars for their performance and Bancroft won a Tony award for her performance on stage.

In the early parts of the film, Anne Sullivan suffers abuse from Helen. Helen slaps Anne on occasion and otherwise makes Anne's life as Helen's teacher torturous. Anne wrestles Helen all over the dining room floor, for an interminable amount of time, ostensibly to teach Helen to fold her napkin and to use flatware when eating. Her real objective, of course, was to bring Helen back from the precipice of her dark, silent world. Describing Anne Sullivan as a miracle worker is not an exaggeration of her work as she transformed Helen over time, to the amazement and sometimes resistance of her parents, from an animal-like creature to one of the most remarkable women of the twentieth century. She did that with her innate understanding of development and with the beautifully tailored yet spontaneously created learning experiences she designed for Helen. Helen's transformation would not have been possible had Anne been unable to establish a powerful bond with Helen. In her autobiography Helen Keller (1988, pp. 29–30) describes her relationship with her teacher:

> It was my teacher's genius, her quick sympathy, her loving tact which made the first years of my education so beautiful. It was because she seized the right moment to impart knowledge that made it so pleasant and acceptable to me. She realized that a child's mind is like a shallow brook which ripples and dances merrily over the stony course of its education and reflects here a flower, there a bush, yonder a fleecy cloud …. My teacher is so near to me that I scarcely think of myself apart from her. How much of my delight in all beautiful things is innate, and how much is due to her influence, I can never tell. I feel that her being inseparable from my own, and that the footsteps of my life are in hers. All the best of mine belongs to her – there is not a talent, or an inspiration, or a joy in me that has not [been] awakened by her loving touch.

Helen's words are important because she describes the essence of a relationship that goes beyond what has occurred in traditional relationships between teachers and learners. The relationship between Helen and Anne was transcendent, just as mine was with Peggy. In both examples teacher as well as learner were transformed. Anne and Peggy grew as teachers and Helen and Hunter were transformed.

Questions for Thought

1. Citing particular terms and concepts identified in Chapter 1, how and why was Dash's and Orlando's relationship transcendent?

2. Define Hunter O'Hara's transcendent teacher. What is required to be a transcendent teacher?

3. What are the three fundamental components of O'Hara's transcendent teacher learner relationship?

4. Define O'Hara's transcendent atmosphere. How did Lionel Logue create such an atmosphere?

5. Define O'Hara's transcendent interaction. How is transcendent interaction created between teacher and learner? What makes interaction in relationships transcendent? How is O'Hara's transcendent interaction created between that teacher and learner?

6. Define O'Hara's encounter. How does it function? What is a community encounter and how does it function?

7. In your own words briefly describe O'Hara's transcendent teacher learner relationship.

8. How do teachers behave when they are "real?"

9. How were learning encounters at home and at school different for Hunter? As, in all examples, examine the narrative closely before you answer this question.

10. How is O'Hara's transcendent teacher distinguished from a person who is simply a good teacher?

11. Describe a learning situation that felt miraculous to you.

12. Citing particular terms and concepts identified in Chapter 1, describe a transcendent relationship you had with a teacher.

CHAPTER 2

The Nature of the Transcendent Shamanic Teacher

> I leaned in very close to Veronica and I said, "you can do this, you need to do this."
>
> THEONI

∴

Transcendent teachers may engage in what is described below as transcendent shamanic teaching. All shamanic teachers are also transcendent teachers by virtue of the transcendent atmosphere and interaction they create. Both transcendent and transcendent shamanic teachers deliberately act to remove barriers, overcome limitations for, and with, the learner. Both act to inspire, broaden and realize the learner's dreams. The transcendent shamanic teacher takes these processes a bit further and deeper.

I will provide a theoretical basis for transcendent shamanic teaching, describe the nature of a transcendent shamanic teacher and identify the processes of transcendent shamanic teaching. I also offer two teacher learner pair portraits to illustrate the power of transcendent shamanic teaching and to demonstrate how such teaching may impact learners and transcendent shamanic teachers in positive ways. I begin with Anne Sullivan's transcendent shamanic transformation of Helen Keller as portrayed in *The Miracle Worker* (Coe, 1962) and Keller's book, *The Story of My Life* (2015).

1   Anne and Helen

Soon after her arrival at the Keller home, Anne Sullivan ponders the enormity of her pending work with Helen Keller who cannot hear or see and is essentially wild. Anne grasps a pamphlet from the Perkins School for the Blind containing the following quote:

> Can nothing be done to disinter this human soul. The whole neighborhood would rush to save this woman if she were buried alive by a caving pit and labor with zeal until she was dug out. Now if there were one who

had as much patience and zeal, he might awaken her to a consciousness of her immortal nature. (Coe, 1962)

Anne has the requisite levels of patience and zeal for her transformational teaching task as she searches for inspiration in that pamphlet and begins to conceive a plan to transcend myriad barriers with Helen (Coe, 1962). Annie is the only person who detects the broad dimensions of Helen's intellect that, in Anne's words, "works like a mouse trap" albeit buried deep in Helen's dark, silent internal lair. Frustrated, Helen approaches her world aggressively as an animal. Thus she is allowed by her family and other caretakers to wander, to bite and to grunt and growl. Helen's one parent questions whether Helen should be left the way God means her to be, that is with minimal training to behave about as well as a dog. The other parent smothers Helen with an overprotective shroud.

Anne, alone and heretofore unaware of her uncanny teaching abilities, calibrates Helen's myriad capacities and designs a plan to operationalize those capacities. Anne uses her personal and ongoing struggles with her own eyesight, and even more her second sight, her intuition, to inform her strategy to facilitate the unfolding of her solitary vision for Helen's transcendence and transformation.

Anne acts to rescue Helen from the abyss; her intent is to heal Helen intellectually, emotionally, physically, socially and spiritually. As Helen begins to transform, Helen's family can only look on with astonishment. Anne's miraculous teaching unleashes the mind, body and spirit of an individual who will become one of the most prominent worldwide luminaries of the twentieth century. Helen, as Anne discerned, was to develop a powerful intellect as well as an evolving keen awareness of the world about her and its myriad social injustices. Helen was to become a highly literate author and speaker and in so doing revealed that she could see and hear more than many sighted, hearing persons (Hamilton, 2012).

Anne is referred to by Helen's parents and in the play and film as a *miracle worker*. Her achievement may be said to lie within the realm of the sacred, even as Anne's work defies traditional pedagogical thought and practice. There can be no prescription for Helen or Anne as Helen's dilemma and circumstances are so rare.

As Anne embarks on this remarkable journey, the bewildered Anne feels she needs a teacher herself. Anne must rely on what can now be viewed as her emerging shamanic clarity of vision to accomplish her mission. Anne draws on her inner *sharpsightedness*, her acute perception, intuition, discernment and understanding to reach Helen. She demonstrates a capacity to assess Helen's predicament and to draw sound conclusions, the outcomes of which were to benefit Helen day-by-day, frequently moment-by-moment for the rest of her life.

2   Transcendent Shamanic Teaching

As a transcendent shamanic teacher, Anne acts to uplift, heal and mobilize Helen, she draws from within for guidance. In *Shamanism and the Psychology of C. G. Jung: The Great Circle* (2002) Robert E. Ryan, J. D., Ph.D., describes the shaman as one who unleashes and revitalizes the health, illuminates the mind and spirit of the other. The shaman unearths "root matter" and reveals "deeper dimensions of the psyche" (p. 35). Like transcendent shamanic teacher Anne, Swiss psychoanalyst and psychiatrist Carl Jung, founder of analytical psychology, was guided by "a sort of predisposition, a dim foreknowledge emanating from the unconscious and guiding him in the direction of deeper understanding" (p. 36). In some sense, this process may be regarded as the simple, albeit broad-spectrum, use of intuition. Where intuition is interpreted as a process of contemplation that yields glimpses of greater knowledge, certainly that has occurred for Anne. Indeed many, including Albert Einstein, postulate that intuition is closely connected with the innovation involved in discovery.

Transcendent shamanic teaching, I argue, involves a more elaborate process than intuition. A *transcendent shamanic teacher* is defined as a transcendent teacher who also *shapes events and divines the hidden* for the purpose of healing others and alleviating traumas to the spiritual, social, intellectual and emotional selves of others. The transcendent shamanic teacher's compelling energy is powerful enough to overcome the learner's past conditioning. In Chapter 3, Peggy shares her transcendent shamanic teacher's compelling energy, "... he was constantly saying 'how lucky I am to be your teacher.' ... Well, he didn't need to hold my hand. He made it quite clear that I had to do this on my own." Peggy's transcendent shamanic teacher's compelling energy led to internal shifts inside Peggy:

> It was a shimmer, and at that moment, I couldn't do anything wrong. I really couldn't. And I didn't. It brought me dignity, grandeur. He made me feel like ... the most intelligent, and the most wonderful person in the world. Until then I felt that I could have just dropped in a hole somewhere and wouldn't have been missed. But he made me feel that I mattered, as if the world would have missed out if I weren't a part of it. This is the type

of human interaction that causes one to forget negative and sometimes even suicidal thoughts.

The transcendent shamanic teacher may penetrate the *pleroma*. Merriam Webster (2020) describes the pleroma as "the fullness of divine excellencies and powers." One may think of the pleroma as the ultimate database of divine wisdom, the totality of divine attributes, energies and virtues. The transcendent shamanic teacher accesses what is needed to uplift, to heal and to mobilize the learner. When the transcendent shaman penetrates the pleroma, they are able to grasp, to feel the learner's situation or dilemma *in its entirety* as well as to realize *the most elegant solution possible* to resolve a particular dilemma or to facilitate whatever growth may be called for within a given pedagogical context. The pleroma affords the shaman *wise insight and profound unravelment,* that is, via the pleroma the transcendent shaman is enabled to grasp, solve or explain the learner's dilemma in a way that heals the learner. A transfiguration, a complete change of their perception of life and life possibilities, emerges for the learner via their encounter with their transcendent shamanic teacher. Transcendent shamanic enlightenment may occur instantaneously or following deep contemplation over time. In fact, many believe that what is commonly referred to as genius actually has to do with one's capacity to access the pleroma while in pursuit of the answers to creative and profound questions that, when answered, lead to healing.

Shamanism is a part of many ancient and current religions. More recently, religious scholars have made cases that Jesus was a shamanic teacher (Keeney, 2006) and that Moses, Jesus Mary Magdalene as well as other prophets were all shamanic figures (Jones-Hunt, 2011; Bourgeault, 2010; Craffert, 2008).

Transcendent shamanic teachers such as Anne do not prepare themselves to penetrate the pleroma through traditional formal rituals such as drumming and chanting, although a kind of ritual does in fact unfold as Theoni and others will describe later. Such extraordinary teachers do not necessarily recognize that they respond in a transcendent shamanic capacity when they act to uplift, heal and mobilize the learner. I nonetheless argue that is precisely what they do. The transcendent shamanic teacher further acts as a muse for the learner, eliciting the learner's creative capacities and setting the learner on a path to positive action.

Note: The capacity for transcendent shamanism is innate. A person with transcendent shamanic capacities, who has never intentionally practiced transcendent shamanism, retains the transcendent shamanic capacity nonetheless.

3   The Transcendent Shamanic Teacher Merges with the Learner

In Harper Lee's magnificent book *To Kill a Mockingbird*, the character Scout recalls her father's words, "Atticus was right. One time he said you never really know a man until you stand in his shoes and walk around in them" (Lee, 1988, p. 279). In much the same way, a primary function of the shamanic teacher is the capacity to *merge* with the learner intellectually, emotionally and spiritually. The shamanic teacher masters the practice of *becoming as the learner* to facilitate that merger. The transcendent shamanic teacher merges with the learner to momentarily form one consciousness. Such a merger involves *compassion*, the etymological root of which means *to suffer with the other*.

In *The Religious Function of the Psyche* (2002), Jungian analyst at the C. G. Jung Institute in Chicago, Lionel Corbett explains that shamanism has to do with a capacity for "accurate active imagination" that is used to perceive the other's predicament or problem. The shaman merges her psyche with the other "by a process of extraordinary empathy" (p. 123). The shaman "hears the voice of the unconscious …" and then applies charisma along with the various capacities identified above to facilitate the connection with the learner (p. 123). The shaman diffuses normal boundaries so that a "soul-to-soul communication occurs" thereby facilitating shamanic healing (p. 124). What emerges is a "temporarily *shared self* that is the result of soul-to-soul contact" (p. 125). The shamanic teacher, like Corbett's psychotherapist, "hears what is not being said, or hears the voice of the unconscious as it rides 'piggy-back' on the [learner's] verbal productions" (p. 123). The transcendent shamanic teacher struggles with the learner, ponders and carefully analyzes the learner's predicament, or dilemma. The transcendent shamanic teacher may feel the learner's pain and joy, sometimes simultaneously. Thus, the transcendent shamanic teacher dons what could be conceived as a highly sophisticated empathic sensor web to accomplish such processes.

4   Transcendent Shamanic Teaching as a Glamorous Act

Transcendent shamanic teachers must *attract* the intellect and the imagination of the learner and thus I argue that shamanic teaching is by necessity a *glamorous act*. Today most people think of glamour as having to do with a luxurious or elegant appearance and manner of being as has been associated particularly with early Hollywood movie stars. Interestingly, glamour originally referred to casting a magic spell intended to make someone see something the spell caster wanted them to see, to cast the glamour (gramarye) in 1720 Scotland.

Indeed, there are parallels between extraordinary teaching and both current and original connotations of glamour. Both connotations have to do with the deployment of an attractive energy that generates appeal. Both suggest enchantment, adventure and fascination. Both refer to allurement, a compelling power one has over another. In *The Power of Glamour,* Annette Tapert (1998) further clarifies the historical context of glamour. Until the twentieth century "glamour was associated with the occult. Glamour denoted an attractiveness that was exciting, romantic, fascinating- attractiveness too powerful to be real. Such power had, therefore, to be aligned with sorcery" (p. 10). That is, glamour could then only be perceived as a supernatural power. It is of particular note in this context that glamour is cited in etymological dictionaries as an alteration of *grammar,* a term derived from the Latin *grammatica* that was often used in the Middle Ages to mean scholarship and learning.

For American playwright and essayist, Arthur Miller, "glamour, [is] that transhuman aura, the power to rearrange people's emotions which, in effect, is the power to control one's environment" (Willis, 2013, p. 3). Glamorous pedagogical charisma and power characterize transcendent shamanic teaching in foundational ways. Transcendent shamanic teaching engenders unusual activity in extraordinary learning environments as teachers create irresistible investigations of new ideas, new concepts for which learners become wide awake and enthralled. The teacher's glamorous, alluring energy also extends to, and permeates, the learning atmosphere, interpersonal interaction and the projects of the entire learning community. All members of such a community become energized. All are enchanted. In Chapter 3, Peggy describes the glamour of her teacher, Mr. Santon:

> And he spoke so quietly and with such command that you found yourself straining to hear him. He had ... [a] sophistication about him. He was very slick, full of culture, style and taste. So I felt very flattered that he even knew I was in the class ... and I thought, "oh, I want to know everything this man knows. My God, this person, this teacher, is just fantastic and he cares what happens to me!"

Such power, of course may be very difficult to generate and wield in environments where teaching is scripted, where curricula are test-driven or where measurement of finite outcomes is the preeminent goal. On the other hand as been indicated previously, teachers such as those in the former Soviet Union were able to transcend even daunting obstacles such as these.

As in the original connotation of glamour, the transcendent shamanic teacher leads the learner to see what that teacher intends for them to see. The learner must first be attracted before a spell can be cast. To attract Helen, Anne must first use guile and craftiness to contrive scenarios in which Anne stands between Helen and whatever Helen may want at a given moment. Once Helen is forced to confront Anne, Anne is able to cast her spell. Before long Anne and Helen are exploring nature together: trees, brooks, birds and hatching eggs. Helen is enchanted and fascinated. Helen explains,

> As my knowledge of things grew I felt more and more the delight of the world I was in. Long before I learned to do a sum in arithmetic or describe the shape of the earth, Miss Sullivan had taught me to find beauty in the fragrant woods, in every blade of grass, and in the curves and dimples of my baby sister's hand. (Keller, 2015, p. 13)

5 Transcendent Shamanic Teaching Uplifts, Heals and Mobilizes the Learner

The transcendent shamanic teacher *uplifts* the learner spiritually, socially, emotionally, as well as intellectually. The transcendent shamanic teacher's influence inspires hope in the learner. Again, prior to Anne's work with Helen, Helen was locked in a dark silent world and she was unable to connect with others in meaningful ways or to feel herself as a part of a much larger whole. She was viewed as not much more than an animal in need of training. Anne meant for her "to see" and in miraculous fashion Anne uplifted, inspired and liberated Helen to see past her optical darkness. Helen explains some of how Anne conveyed the nature of love to her at a very young age. "You cannot touch love … but you feel the sweetness that it pours into everything. Without love you would not be happy or want to play." Helen exclaims in response, "The beautiful truth burst upon my mind – I felt that there were invisible lines stretched between my spirit and the spirits of others" (Keller, 2015, p. 16). Thus uplifted and inspired, Helen was no longer isolated from others because of her physical limitations. Helen was rescued from social isolation and was thereby ultimately healed socially, intellectually and spiritually by Anne. Helen adds that she could not explain Anne's "peculiar sympathy" but that Anne made, "every subject so real that I could not help remembering what she taught" (p. 18). Anne's glamour, her "peculiar sympathy" as Helen calls it, enabled Anne to position herself between Helen and whatever Helen wanted, ultimately creating the bridge that Helen crossed, into Helen's healing.

The transcendent shamanic teacher enables the learner to reconcile that which has been formerly irreconcilable. The transcendent shamanic teacher *heals* the learner on multiple levels, some of which may be unimaginable for the learner, by enabling the learner to overcome the obstacles and barriers that have heretofore immobilized them. Again in this way, the learner is healed. Prior to Anne's work with Helen, Helen was locked in profound disconnect from those around her. Anne woke up Helen to the power of language to heal and to build upon that healing. Armed with language, Helen was able to reach out to her family and to the world around her, to be a powerful force in her own right.

6 A Note Regarding the Unencumbered Learner and the Transcendent Shamanic Teacher

Helen Keller and Veronica, later in this chapter, are perhaps more in need of healing than other learners. Helen and Veronica's healing encounters are broad-based, palpable and profound, however, the benefits of transcendent shamanic teaching extend to *all* learners. Many learners may not need help overcoming a major obstacle but will, nonetheless, derive benefits from, and enjoy, working in an uplifting, mobilizing and healing environment created by the transcendent shamanic teacher wherein atmospheric equilibrium is reliably established and maintained.

In Chapter 7, Kathy comes from a stable home life and has not been exposed to trauma or oppression at home or at school. And yet, she recalls how she gravitated to her transcendent shamanic teacher:

> ... we used to go to [my teacher's] office in the morning before school, we'd sit out and wait for [him] to get there and eat breakfast in the hall, and then go into [his] office. I don't know if we ever did anything constructive while we were there. It was more personal, more than just going down for classes. It was having a personal contact with the teacher. It helped to build the bond. I don't know exactly how to explain it. It reaffirmed, in my mind, that [he was] more of a personal type, that it wasn't just a strict role. ... I think I function better when I have a friend-friendship instead of a teacher-learner friendship or relationship. I think it goes back to respecting each other and having that loyalty and the honesty, and, at the heart of it all, it is a matter of being friends.

Beneath their enjoyment, learners may have emotional, social, intellectual and/or spiritual blocks of which they are not aware. They may experience transformation via working in the healing space and interaction created by the transcendent shamanic teacher, even in the absence of particular and/or known concerns.

Virtually all learners enjoy relative security, safety and confidence at the time of their encounters with a transcendent or transcendent shamanic teacher, even if they do not have major obstacles to overcome at that point of their lives. Later in life however, troubles may arise that take an enormous toll on that learner. Thus, such a person, now in difficult times, looks back on the healing environment created by their teacher in their past and draws strength from that. They may also reconnect with the healing teacher and/or their learner family for support and healing. In Chapter 3, Peggy describes such an encounter. Drawing strength from memories of her transcendent shamanic teacher Mr. Santon, she is able to transcend a traumatic period in her life and thus avoid suicide.

7 The Origins of Transcendent Shamans

Some say that a shaman is a person who has been to hell, escaped hell and then returns to hell to rescue others. Prior to her work with Helen Keller, Anne Sullivan, supreme example of a transcendent shamanic teacher, spent much of her childhood at the Tewksbury Almshouse for the poor. Anne was partially blind. At Tewksbury, the majority of the "inmates" were poor immigrants from Europe. Anne was regularly exposed to alcoholics in the throes of delirium tremens as well as others who were then labeled as "pauper insane." She witnessed Tewksbury's notorious cannibalism and sexual perversion. Undoubtedly, she was also on the receiving end of the outrageous cruelty to "inmates" meted out by the Tewksbury staff. An article that appeared in *The Lowell Weekly Sun* on April 24, 1883 reported the outcomes of an investigation of Tewkesbury. An excerpt follows:

> Frank Barker and his wife, who were at Tewksbury from 1876 to 1879, in charge of the insane ward, testified to cases of ill-treatment of patients, who were left for days without food, and unattended by a physician when sick; patients had holes eaten in their heads by vermin, which crawled about on the beds; Dr. Lathrop and the Marshes had their attention called to these matters at the time but showed cruel indifference; patients, about 70 in all, were bathed without any change being made in the water, though many of them had running sores. ("Tewksbury Almshouse investigation," 1883)

THE NATURE OF THE TRANSCENDENT SHAMANIC TEACHER 35

The investigation referred to above was launched in 1875. Transcendent shaman Anne escaped the hell of Tewksbury in 1877. She was delivered to the Perkins Institute for the Blind. She had nine operations on her eyes that were not fully successful. At Perkins, a school full of students from well-to-do families, Anne was subjected to economic bigotry on a regular basis. Anne nonetheless prevailed and thus, ultimately graduated valedictorian from the Perkins Institute. Anne shares how the terror of the early years at Tewksbury, the hell she escaped, never really left her:

> ... at times melancholy without reason grips me as in a vice [sic]. A word, an odd inflection, the way somebody crosses the street, brings all the past before me with such amazing clearness and completeness, my heart stops beating for a moment. Then everything around me seems as it was so many years ago. Even the ugly frame-buildings are revived. Again I see the unsightly folk who hobbled, cursed, fed and snored like animals. I shiver recalling how I looked upon scenes of vile exposure - the open heart of a derelict is not a pleasant thing. I doubt if life, or eternity for that matter, is long enough to erase the errors and ugly blots scored upon my brain by those dismal years. (Tewksbury Almshouse, n.d.)

A transcendent shamanic teacher such as Anne, having escaped hell, has a "calling" to help those in need, to ease other's suffering, and if possible, to heal them. Enduring and escaping a metaphoric hell is not required for one to become a transcendent shamanic teacher, however survival may provide a *very strong inclination* for one to act on improving the lives of others. The transcendent shamanic teacher may not always be aware of which learners experience healing or when that healing occurs. The transcendent shamanic teacher derives comfort and fulfillment from creating circumstances and processes that lead to the healing of others and, in that process of bringing about healing for others, heals themselves.

Transcendent shamanism is not a matter of a teacher mastering and applying a method or a strategy for healing. Instead, transcendent shamanism emerges from the teacher's deepest desire to actualize a motivation, to operationalize a philosophy in which the intent is to afford every learner, particularly those who are oppressed and/or have experienced trauma, the most advantageous development possible. The transcendent shamanic teacher remains by the learner's side throughout the learner's healing and transformation.

The transcendent shamanic teacher encourages, guides and directs thereby *mobilizing* or marshaling the learner to act in a concerted way to develop insight, to imagine a world as it might otherwise be and to become change agents in their worlds. The transcendent shamanic teacher significantly extends the learner's capacity to dream and to pursue dreams, to accomplish desired objectives, to develop critical awareness and to acquire a sense of her own capacity to create whatever an unleashed mind and heart may imagine. Anne was not content to see Helen evolve in less than remarkable ways. Anne's goals for Helen transcended how to behave well and the obeyence of family members. Rather, Anne wanted to put the world at Helen's fingertips. Moreover, Anne ultimately prepared Helen to meet the world as a fully accomplished, fully aware intellectual who, because of her awareness and insight was capable of, and succeeded in, transforming her world. In Chapter 15, Beth shares how the mobilization process worked for her:

> [She] recognized me as an individual. When I think about her I can remember the feeling of being close with her even clear across the room, the feeling she truly believed in me and who I was. She knew exactly what I was about and she still believed in me. I was valuable to her. Because of her, I made the conscious decision that I would be a teacher also. I want to make that kind of difference to someone.

Reversing the transcendent shamanic roles, I have experienced the phenomenon of being healed by my students. I once had blocks resulting from childhood trauma, blocks that prevented me from experiencing joy fully. In the process of working to create a joyful climate with my learners, I role-played the part of a joyous person with them. Delighted that my learners reflected genuine joy back to me, I found myself experiencing authentic joy. In other words, through working toward joy with me, my learners escorted me, their teacher, to joy.

> The Master allows things to happen. She shapes events as they come. She steps out of the way and lets the Tao speak for itself. (Lao Tzu, trans. 1999, p. 45)

8   Portrait of Veronica and Theoni

Veronica is a warm, gracious person. Overweight most of her life, she became the victim of the pain as well as the psychological, spiritual and emotional damage associated with relentless bullying. She explains,

> The bullying started from around first grade, and followed me until graduation. It was always name-calling and exclusion from groups and activities. The bullying almost always centered on my weight, but by the

time I got to high school – because I went to school with a lot of these individuals since elementary – it was basically "That is Veronica, and this is how we treat her." It was just understood that I was at the bottom of the social hierarchy. I failed ninth grade – skipping school and not doing my work because I did not want to be tormented and humiliated in my classes anymore – and by the end of tenth grade, my social anxiety disorder and depression really began to manifest.

Teachers and others looked the other way when Veronica was bullied and so she began to give up on life. She stopped grooming and hid herself as much as possible under a hood in public. Most onlookers were satisfied to ignore her. "I felt like I did not matter at all. I slept through most of my classes, or read other novels, and not a single one of my teachers ever asked me what was going on, or even reprimanded me for not being on task."

Veronica was somewhat awakened when during a mid term progress report one teacher, unlike *all* her other teachers, said to her, "I think you can do better than this." That teacher's comment became a first step in Veronica's path to healing:

> I respected Mr. Joeb, very much because he was an excellent teacher who connected well with his students through humor, but also through raising expectations for us. So, when I got my progress report and all my teachers just marked it with my failing grades, Mr. Joeb actually said something to me. He noticed me. This seems like such a small thing, but I remember that interaction fourteen years later. I really needed an adult in my life to look at me and say, "I see you. I know you exist, and you matter. And you're worthwhile." Mr. Joeb didn't even need to say all that; what he said was enough to keep me going.

Years later Veronica found herself in Theoni Soublis' class. Theoni is a veteran high school English teacher, now a teacher educator. In Theoni's class, Veronica and her colleagues were asked to read Chris Crutcher's enormously powerful *Staying Fat for Sarah Byrnes* (1993). The novel revolves around a small group of social misfits and their unwavering dedication to each other as they are collectively faced with family and peer abuse, school bullying trauma and other high school perils. These teens weave a life of friendship, trust, and survival.

Theoni explains,

> I use Crucher's *Staying Fat for Sarah Byrnes*; for its rich exploration of high school life; replete with its balance of unwavering friendship, bullying, child abuse, teen-pregnancy, religious dogmatism, powerful teachers,

sports and the personal relationships teammates build. Crutcher synthesizes a tremendous number of themes related to teen life in one novel that every single one of my students, over the past 14 years of teaching this novel, has been able to relate to some aspect of the book in a deep and meaningful way. If you went to high school, you will identify with this book.

Theoni describes how she crafted one example of a powerful learning experience in Veronica's class:

> The students are asked to utilize Louise Rosenblatt's (1938) Reader's Response Theory to complete the assignment. They must first read the book in it's entirety, and then respond to the text in a deep and meaningful way through writing. Rosenblatt affirms that when one brings a personal connection to the text, reading becomes a more significant and rich experience. The task of reading is no longer feared and arduous; instead it becomes an affirmation of life and an expressive opportunity. And that is one of my goals. I advise students that they will share their writing with their peers on the day the assignment is due. I caution them that they may want to think very deeply about their writing selection as they will be required to share the whole piece.
>
> There are many provocative themes in the book and they must be prepared to share the experience publicly. Most look at me with question and doubt, but once they read the novel they start to understand my caution and the emails begin: "Dr. Soublis, so I have to share the whole thing, it's very personal and I do not think I am ready. Dr. Soublis, I want to share an experience I had in high school, but I think my friends will laugh at me; do I have to share it? Dr. Soublis, can I write one piece for you and another to share in class?" The emails and office conferences continue and my response is always the same, *share what you are ready to share, but I promise you that if you are brave enough to share the truth your peers will surprise you.* Most take on the challenge. I believe deeply that students must share these personal experiences publicly in a small group setting with peers they are beginning to trust in order to empathize with the myriad of experiences students deal with in high school. My students are studying to become teachers; their high school experience is not the same as the experience of all other students. During high school, students choose to seek social relationships that fit their comfort zones; perhaps a sport, or drama club, or honor society, or debate team. Students migrate

THE NATURE OF THE TRANSCENDENT SHAMANIC TEACHER   39

> to organizations where they will feel welcome and included. But when those students turn into teachers, it is paramount to the teacher-student relationship that they support, encourage, and inspire students beyond what their own high school experience was.
>
> I want them to recognize, listen to, associate, understand, and commiserate with the social side of education to better prepare them to support their future students as they progress through similar experiences. The sharing of their connection to the novel is non-negotiable. As the teacher, I know something very profound will happen in that room when these stories of life are shared. The brave reader will be received with unbiased support and praise, and the listener will become more compassionate and giving than he/she may have ever thought possible. Such is the power of this assignment; I believe in Rosenblatt's theory to my core and I trust is will never fail to create the type of response of my students, one that is nurturing, supporting, and reaffirming. It never has.

Theoni describes a ritual process in which a customarily repeated act or series of acts that require careful attention to form and detail are operationalized. Such a ritual involves the observance of an established code of civility or politeness.

> To get the magic to happen, several ingredients must be used on behalf of the teacher: (1) the initial decision of what one would like to occur as a result of the lesson, the planning – select the appropriate materials to foster the desired effect, (2) atmosphere – one must pre-determine the setting. This means moving furniture, adjusting lighting, perhaps using props and (3) the ability to be silent. Teachers often feel the need to jump in, change the conversation, and rescue a drowning student. But we must trust in the well-constructed plan and be patient.

Theoni continues,

> When I have more than ten students, I divide the class into two groups. I know that the power of the sharing can occur when students are asked to listen to no more than seven or eight other experiences. If asked to listen to more, the energy diminishes. A student from each circle is sharing at the same time, so the noise level may get elevated. I weave around the two circles, listening to the personal reflections of my students. I stand close to a student who I know is struggling; I rest my hand on the

shoulder of a student who may begin to cry; I make eye-contact with a student after the story is over and mouth the words thank you; I kneel down next to a student and whisper, "that was the bravest thing I have ever heard." I am there to support, encourage, promote, and challenge. I know the magic that will reveal itself if the atmosphere is tended to appropriately. I intuitively make these connections with students; it may be experience, it may be my desire to make meaningful connections with these young adults, it may be my compassion for their situations that allows me to interact in such a way with my students. But because I take the risk to interact with them, they feel safe enough to continue and take the risk.

After we read the novel, the two small groups form a single circle. I sit with the students and we begin a discussion about the experience and we share our personal connections. First we talk about the novel – what we liked and didn't like, our expectations and revelations. Then we move into the reading experience, almost every year my non-readers in the class are thankful for introducing them to literature that they enjoy reading. Many of them become readers (some have actually become avid readers). I ask the class if another novel could have the effect *Staying Fat* does, the answer, every year, without fail is a resounding NO; thus I continue to use Crutcher's brilliant novel to facilitate the introspection of the teenage plight.

A summer passes before I have this cohort in class again, and when they return for their senior year I recognize the growth of the group. A chemical bond is created months prior that sustains the group. Some years, the bond is stronger than in other years. Sometimes the whole group works as a single unit, and other years segments of the group support one another. But the fact always remains that the individual students are more resilient because of the experience they shared together.

9 Veronica Risks

At first as Veronica began to respond in writing to her assignment was stumped as she tried to figure out what to say. She knew she connected very directly with Crucher's story but did she *dare* to share her story of abuse and abandonment? On one level she wanted to open up, but could she tolerate the pain required to write her story, the ripping open of so many old wounds?

At the same time she thought of the power that would emerge if she shared her bullying story with a roomful of future teachers. Could she write it for the sake of the welfare of all of the students who would be in her colleague's future classrooms?

> This definitely became what drove me to write my story, despite how painful it was. I knew that many people, many future teachers, have not experienced bullying. We learn about it in a clinical fashion in our "Classroom Management" courses, but I really wanted them to see and feel it. I wanted to say, "Look at me. I am thirty years old, and this still hurts me enough to put me in this state. Bullying is NOT a rite of passage; it is abuse."

Veronica took the risk in response to Theoni's challenge.

When she came to class, she was placed in a circle of half the class. Other learners began to read their stories and tears began to roll even as Veronica was aware that people were being kind to each other. Theoni's application of Rosenblatt's theory was coming to life. Veronica shares,

> This experience was definitely new to me. I had never been in a class where we were encouraged to deal with, and discuss, our feelings and personal experiences on such a level. I intentionally did not want to go first or last; I wanted to gauge how my group would react to other powerful stories. Once I saw that it was ok to tear up – others were – I knew it would be alright to tell my story. I also had a sort of false sense of courage, thinking I could probably make it through my story without crying. Although that wasn't the case, I still felt safe. It also helped that the group consisted of the half of the class with whom I felt most comfortable and shared good relationships.

Veronica's colleagues' stories were powerful and when it was time for Veronica to read her story there were no dry eyes. And so anticipatory silence fell upon Veronica.

> The first half of my paper was just the summary of the book, and I breezed through that with ease. As soon as I hit the first words of the first sentence on my personal connection, I broke down. My feelings about my experiences with bullying have always been very visceral – what I jokingly like to call "the ugly cry" always happens. I just shut down. I even tried to

hand my paper off to my friend sitting next to me, who reluctantly took it. I really did not want her to read it, and I knew it would be unnatural for her to do so, but I just needed to not be there in that moment. I felt really weak and upset with myself that I seemingly could not do this.

Veronica was paralyzed and had an overwhelming sense that it was impossible to rise to this supreme challenge. Theoni said,

> I saw Veronica hand her paper off to another student to read. I immediately made my way over to that group and stood behind Veronica. I wanted to take the paper out of the hand of her peer and give it back to Veronica, but I knew it needed to be Veronica's choice to continue.

Veronica's "ugly cry" came from the deepest regions of her being. When she handed the paper to a friend to read, Theoni guided from within by understanding and awareness, "I leaned in very close to Veronica and I said, 'you *can* do this, *you need* to do this.'"

Veronica describes her reaction in that moment,

> When Dr. Soublis said that, it felt like more of a reassurance than a demand. I felt like Dr. Soublis was telling me it's alright to be this upset, it's valid, and that it's alright if I'm crying and upset while I read. That was a part of the healing. That put power into it. Her telling me I had to read it myself made me feel stronger somehow. Dr. Soublis' tone was even and there was a soft strength to it, if that makes sense? She seemed sure in her words, and that transferred to me, making me feel sure. Most importantly, there was no negativity in her voice, no demand, just support.

Theoni, still standing behind her, put her hands on Veronica's shoulders and her chin on Veronica's head and quietly said, "It'll be okay." Theoni stayed close behind Veronica and Veronica continued to be soothed by Theoni's nearness and confidence in her.

> I felt stronger and stronger as I read it. I could hear the quiet feedback of my group as I read and whenever I occasionally looked up I could see there was sympathy, patience and interest. I think I was still tearful, but by the end of it, I felt empowered and I felt braver for having read it. I felt more composed once I was done reading. I was also relieved when my group had questions about my experience and I could answer them. There is nothing worse than crying in front of people and they just look

at you in awkward silence. Again, part of it was the support I felt coming from not just Dr. Soublis, but also my peers listening. Nobody seemed ambivalent towards me or my story. I gathered strength from that, knowing that my pain was not in vain. I felt like a great weight was lifted off me; it was *very* cathartic.

Part of Veronica's story read,

> When I was younger, I would have never thought to put how negatively I felt about those people on paper like she [Sarah Byrnes] did, but I could spread rumors, too, and I did. I despised the people who bullied me and I wanted them to have the greatest misfortunes for hurting me. I am older now, and a lot of that hatred is gone, but the pain still lingers. I sometimes consider finding some of those people on *Facebook* and writing them a private message telling them I hope their children never have to go through what they put me through, and how I waited six years before going to college because the idea of sitting in classrooms with people my age – possibly some of the same people I went to high school with – all over again felt like the worst form of hell. So yes, I understand Sarah Byrnes' dark side and I know why she was such a hard-ass – because she needed to protect herself.
>
> When I think of Sarah Byrnes, I think of her scars. Not the physical ones that everyone can see, but the ones inside her that she tries to cover up by being tough and belligerent. Every person has his or her own cross to bear, but I think those of us who wear our flaws on the outside have it the hardest because we cannot hide them – we just have to become stronger in spite of it.

As Theoni listened to Veronica's story,

> images of a lonely scared and helpless young girl crowded my head. Her descriptive prose made her personal plight come alive to her listeners. The entire group was riveted; the story was so personal that the adjacent group stopped reading in order to listen to Veronica. The energy in the room was dreamlike: a group of sixteen people let go of fears, misconceptions, judgments, and thoughts beyond the present moment. We all focused on this opportunity to learn from one another, to grow together and to begin to understand each other. When Veronica completed her reading, the look on her face was one of relief; she had had a cathartic moment indeed. In that instant she faced her demons, shared them with

the world, and let them go. Powerful. As a teacher I knew this would be the result, but it was up to Veronica to make the decision, to take the risk, and begin to heal. She did; and in that moment I witnessed her peers become her friends ... magic.

The next class, Theoni hugged Veronica and thanked her for being so very brave. Later, when Theoni and Veronica met one-on-one and talked about Veronica's story, Theoni began to cry.

> I wanted to meet with Veronica alone and after some time and space had passed through the experience. We talked privately in my office and I shared my perspective with Veronica. I explained to her that when students are brave enough to share the truth it facilitates the process I try to evoke through the assignment. When students seize the opportunity to enlighten others about personal obstacles it allows the entire group to grow and learn from one another. Moreover, it offers these pre-service teachers a chance to connect to experiences they may not have had in life and offers insights to what their own students might be going through. The assignment offers an opportunity for awareness, reflection and growth, all in preparation for developing powerful experiences for their own students one day. I shared with Veronica that without her candor and bravery the assignment would have limitations – the group grew together because of her actions and I will always revere Veronica for that.

Veronica, powerfully moved, went home and told her mother,

> I made my professor cry for the right reasons. Because of my negative experiences with teachers throughout grade school, I was genuinely surprised and moved that Dr. Soublis was moved by my story. I just never think I have that sort of impact, but that was my goal with sharing my story all along. I wanted to give others a window into my experiences.
>
> Dr. Soublis created a classroom environment so secure that I felt safe to share something so traumatic in my life. If it were any other teacher, I do not think I would have taken such a risk. She also never let me, or any of us, fend for ourselves; Dr. Soublis' gentle encouragement gave me strength and made me feel empowered. I liked and respected Dr. Soublis before that assignment, but now? I honestly see her as someone with great empathy, which I think is so important in teaching.

> I will definitely carry this experience with me throughout my life. I went into the teaching profession in large part because I saw a need for empathetic educators who cared for their student's emotional growth and well being as much as their academic education. I have had wonderful education professors, and the vast majority of them are kind and helpful, but I really see in Dr. Soublis that empathetic, emotional healer I want to be as a teacher. I hope all of this means I will impact my students positively and I am able to gain their trust by understanding and connecting with them. I will be here to reassure them and bolster their confidence by having high expectations, even when other adults in their lives may not.

Theoni adds,

> These enchanted moments do not last long, mere flashes in our overly-distracted lives; so I soak it all up as deeply as I can. It's the energy I use to get me through the rest of the semester; it sustains me and I know the energy has the capacity to sustain students through the pressures of the teacher-training program; it's the subversive curriculum in the class: mold opportunities for students to bond and relate to each other in a way that will propel them to persevere all obstacles together. And it works.

10   Final Thoughts from Theoni

> I started teaching high school seniors when I was twenty-one years old. My seventeen and eighteen-year-old students were in my same peer group. I needed to find methods for rising above the similarities in our interests and commonalities, yet continue to be relatable and approachable. It was important to me to be taken seriously, even as a brand new, young, green teacher. I found the recipe of being consistent, predictable, rigorous, yet reasonable to be a powerful elixir toward developing positive relationships with my students.
>
> They responded to my youthful energy, but appreciated my intelligence and ability to control the classroom. They respected my approaches to making literature and writing relevant to their lives; that relevance opened the door to building and maintaining a synergy that energized the teacher-student relationship.

My respect for their abilities as thinking human beings, my desire to get them excited about the curriculum, and my interest in their lives beyond the academic spectrum fostered a mutual understanding. I also believe that my youth worked more in my favor in that I acted as a role model to them; a young college graduate who succeeded and started a rewarding career. As high school seniors, they were on the direct path to make similar choices that could set up their futures. They were attracted to that success and regularly sought advice from "someone who had just been there."

I have always defined myself as a natural born teacher. I have always wanted to positively influence the lives of people; I am a humanitarian at heart. Therefore, much of my ability to connect with my students is a natural instinct to want to care, but I also believe that time and experience has honed that natural tendency into a nurtured skill. For example, when I first started teaching, my patience was limited. I had zero tolerance for late work, unexcused absences, and daydreaming students. But years of teaching brought with it a sense of tolerance for the teenage plight. I learned to choose my battles and keep the most important lessons in focus. With time, my management style shifted from one with strict rules and limited negotiation, to a style that allowed for flexibility.

When I stopped to listen to my students, when I allowed them to be human, and started to understand the insanity of their schedules, I became more patient. It took years, but it came, like a warm comfort of trusting to let go of the control of deadlines and assessments. If a student needed more time, I worked with that particular student, versus having a set policy for all students. If a student requested an alternative assignment, I considered it and we developed the assignment together; one that would better demonstrate the desired learning gains. Once I began to let go of *the one-size-fits-all* mentality, the doors to designing a caring curriculum opened. It changed my life. It changed the life of my students. I dare say, it saved the lives of many of my students.

The motivation that continues my desire to sustain a caring curriculum is the energy it gives back to me. Most religions and spiritual reading tell us that the more we give the more we will receive. I find this to be most true in the classroom. Yes, I have an academic curriculum I am required to teach, but the subversive curriculum is to nurture, support, cheer, challenge, and most of all listen to my students. This style of teaching takes time, a lot of individual attention and differentiated curriculum design, but the results are palpable and observable. When a student takes the time to write a thank-you note at the end of a course, offer a small gift, send emails long past graduation thanking you for your support, insight, and inspiration, what more is there? What other purpose is there? Then I receive a career update that they were admitted to law school, or started their own business, or got published; that is my paycheck; that is my benefits package.

I was motivated to be a transformative teacher because I was lucky enough to have a transformative teacher; a teacher that saw a lost teenager with unique potential. He took me under his wing, trained me, nurtured me, and challenged me. He helped me to set my path. I will happily spend my lifetime repaying that debt to the universe. Being a transformational teacher makes me feel like I have a life's purpose. I feel like I am contributing to the greater good of the community. I know I am positively influencing students every day. My job is more than a career; I get to make personal connections at very emotional levels with other human beings. I do not know of too many careers that afford that opportunity.

Veronica's experience in my class is not an anomaly. In fact, given this particular assignment, I have students every year who experience a transformation of some sort. Some become open to more personal peer relationships, others feel safer in taking risks in class by sharing their opinions and volunteering, and others have become avid readers always looking for inspirational literature that they can connect to. I learned over the years of teaching that the more I facilitate opportunities for self-expression, the more students will take risks. Some may test the waters and wait for others to take the lead, but most of the time, each will take on a challenge at some point. I have had students share some of the most personal experiences of their lives: abusive relationships, death of loved ones, sexual orientation, self-abuse, the pressure to be perfect, alcohol and drug use and so forth. When the facilitator of the class takes the time in the beginning of the year to model a caring disposition, to be an active listener, to take student concerns seriously, that facilitator is setting up the safe classroom atmosphere. All of this takes place slowly and subversively within and between the academic lessons of the day, but over time the stage is set to introduce an assignment such as this where students are ready to share at deep levels.

11 Transcendent Shamanism in the Everyday Context

In my experience, shamanic teaching more frequently does not lead to immediate and dramatic outcomes as did occur for Veronica and Theoni. Many shamanic events do not involve a catharsis as this one did for Veronica. More commonly the outcome of a healing shamanic teaching event, or of ongoing shamanic interaction, is not realized until later, sometimes many years later. Shamanic teaching is a process for which shamanic teachers work to maintain a response-able stance in their interactions with all learners.

Shamanic teaching capacities build as teachers and learners come to know each other on a variety of levels. Shamanic teachers create opportunities for shamanic interaction and prepare to respond as opportunities arise for shamanism.

The example of Veronica and Theoni is important because both teacher and learner were able to verify that a shamanic event had taken place immediately afterwards and to identify the powerful transfigurative effects of the event. Both certainly felt the power of the event even as it occurred. The enormity of the experience was comprehended, analyzed and evaluated.

For other shamanic teachers and learners, the awareness of a shamanic event or ongoing shamanic interaction may be peripheral, subtle or unnoticeable for a time. Again, the impact of shamanism remains whether or not it is consciously recognized. The shamanic teacher's work is sophisticated, the results of which may be subtle or striking depending on the people involved, their needs and their style of interaction. Learners may feel buoyed up by the shamanic event but may not be aware that healing has occurred or that they have been mobilized by the encounter.

Again, such realizations occur later for most teachers and learners. Shamanic teachers may sense that their efforts are powerful but frequently cannot verify the transfigurative extent of those efforts. Nonetheless, they do recognize that an exchange of power has occurred.

Once again, it is critical to note that as the shamanic teacher heals others, she also heals herself in ways that may be subtle or striking depending on the circumstances involved. Shamanic teaching begins with transcendent teaching, that is mutually rewarding, mutually healing and mutually transformative. Thus, what one gives, one also receives and that is yet another indication of the rewards and gratifying nature of teaching. Theoni as example, speaks of the encounter with Veronica as an *enchanted moment* that she avidly soaked up so as to sustain her over the long haul.

As a transcendent teacher, Theoni creates a safe, non-judgmental atmosphere and interaction where learners and the teacher enjoy mutual care, mutual trust, mutual respect and take risks together. Theoni's shamanic capacities, like those of Anne are reflected in a variety of ways as they deliberately chose activities that delve deep into her learner's psyche. They prepare the learning environment carefully in a way that leads to healing. They act in a manner that shows degrees of omniscience, tapping into the deepest needs of their learners and intervening at critical moments with enormous sophistication and grace. Theoni and Anne shape events in such a way that are, for Veronica and Helen in particular, uplifting, healing and mobilizing. Veronica's colleagues are also transformed by her story, the stories of her other colleagues and by Theoni's masterful shamanic prowess of facilitating the shamanic event. Throughout the shamanic process, Veronica and her colleagues accept Theoni's challenge that involves significant risk. As a result, all of those present are liberated and encounter poignant moments. All, including Theoni, are ultimately transformed by the risks they shared.

12   Questions for Thought

1. Citing particular terms and concepts identified in Chapter 2, how can Anne be characterized as a transcendent shamanic teacher?

2. How is Anne considered to be a miracle worker and how are other transcendent shamanic teachers, such as those you may have known, also miracle workers?

3. Define O'Hara's transcendent shamanic teacher. What guides the transcendent shamanic teacher?

4. Discuss O'Hara's glamour and how it is an essential component of the *transcendent* shamanic teacher.

5. Define O'Hara's merger. How do transcendent shamanic teachers merge with the learner and for what purpose do they merge?

6. Define O'Hara's uplift. How do transcendent shamanic teachers uplift the learner?

7. How do O'Hara's transcendent shamanic teachers heal the learner?

8. Define O'Hara's mobilization. How does O'Hara's transcendent shamanic teacher mobilize the learner?

9. Drawing from specific concepts and terms in Chapter 2, how is Theoni characterized as a transcendent shamanic teacher?

10. How does Theoni heal Veronica?

11. How is transcendent shamanic teaching an extension of transcendent teaching?

12. How do O'Hara's transcendent shamanic teachers differ from what are called good teachers?

CHAPTER 3

Portrait of Transcendent Shamanic Teacher

Peggy (*Mrs. Pridemore*)

> I get scared sometimes later, but at the moment I don't think about it if it feels right and it's not harmful .... To me it's intuitive .... It has to be done or we're going to lose a kid or we're going to lose this opportunity.
>
> PEGGY

∵

As a high school student, I was addicted to the atmospheres and encounters Mrs. Pridemore created. I knew I wanted to become a teacher who could create such moments for others. My interest in this teacher continued to build over the years. Years after I graduated from high school, Peggy described her life as a learner and then as a teacher.

Peggy has large expressive eyes that flash and fill with passion when she talks. Her laughter is raucous and engaging. She is a study in contrasts and unpredictability. Her speaking voice is soft, round and lilting or boisterous, depending on the situation. She appears at times to be shy and withdrawn but at other times she is regal and commanding, drawing every eye and ear in a crowded room. I interviewed her in her Victorian voice studio in Charleston, West Virginia situated between her baby grand piano and her tower window.

1   Peggy the Learner and Her Transcendent Teacher Mr. Santon

As a young woman, Peggy said that she remembered being somewhat overwhelmed by a new young drama teacher when she was a junior in high school. He came to her hometown from New York and everything about him seemed bigger than life. His style and personal qualities attracted her from the beginning.

> He represented a world that I had not experienced, but wanted to experience. It was most attractive. He represented a world that I'd only read about or seen in magazines, like *Life* magazine, for instance when it used

to have the big color pictures, you know, when they really did it big. And he spoke so quietly and with such command that you found yourself straining to hear him. He had worked as a stage manager of Broadway shows and he had sophistication about him. He was very slick, full of culture, style and taste. So I felt very flattered that he even knew I was in the class. And this wasn't a schoolgirl crush. It was never anything like that. It was much bigger than that, and I thought, "oh, I want to know everything this man knows. My God, this person, this teacher, is just fantastic and he cares what happens to me!"

Mr. Santon's caring about Peggy made her feel special. "It made me feel worth something." He said that he was lucky to be her teacher. He made her feel good about herself. Peggy notes,

> If you don't care about me, then you don't care what happens to me. I'd always heard that expression, you know, the links in a chain? But when he used that expression, it took on a whole new meaning. Mr. Santon explained that each one of us are links in a chain of humanity and the way I treat you and the kind of link that I make to you determines how you will link to others. I never thought about it the same way, not after I heard this version! I never thought about a chain of humanity, I only thought about a chain – you know, literally.
>
> He complimented us when he talked like that to us. He was saying, "you're not dumb kids because you're from the coalfields and the hills, you're not dumb. You're just another nice person that we're very lucky to know," and he was constantly saying "how lucky I am to be your teacher." And, oh, my gosh, we would kill for that man. I mean, it wasn't a cult. It's just that I wanted to be around him all the time because he made me feel good about myself. Now as a teacher myself, that's the most marvelous compliment when kids want to hang around you!

Mr. Santon had high expectations for students and he challenged them.

> We were doing a spring Thespian Review in my senior year. We were going to a speech competition and I was doing some kind of a reading from Sandburg about Abraham Lincoln, and he said, "what really means a lot, what will have the most lasting impression on us is going to this speech meet and doing our best rather than competing." So he said "you're going to have to do preparation on your own." He said, "don't bring me your recitation if you haven't memorized it; don't even bring it to me for my

critique. Don't even start to do it for me." That's all he said. There were fifteen of us going and we had our recitations all memorized within three days and we had rehearsals going on until 11 o'clock p.m. for the Thespian Review.

So what happened inside?

Oh, my gosh, the word trust. He trusted me. Well, he didn't need to hold my hand. He made it quite clear that I had to do this on my own. So I did. And he polished – a little inflection here, a little reflection there. And as each person would walk up on the stage with no book and no notes, he would stand up and say, "thank you, Miss P." I couldn't help but do my very best.

And then?

This is weird. I felt like I was in the spotlight. But there was no spotlight – just the overhead lights in the auditorium. I felt like I had an aura. I didn't know that was the word at the time, but it was a shimmer, and at that moment, I couldn't do anything wrong. I really couldn't. And I didn't. It brought me dignity, grandeur. He made me feel like the most beautiful, the most intelligent, and the most wonderful person in the world.

Mr. Santon's creation of this atmosphere was pivotal for Peggy. The atmosphere and his affirmative remarks to Peggy, by her own admission, signified a turning point in her development.

Until then I felt that I could have just dropped in a hole somewhere and wouldn't have been missed. But he made me feel that I mattered, as if the world would have missed out if I weren't a part of it. This is the type of human interaction that causes one to forget negative and sometimes even suicidal thoughts. If he were sitting right here and I'd tell him these things, he'd probably be modest about himself, and he would say "oh no, Peggy." I wonder if he knows what he did, not just for me. He did it for all of us. Humility is an integral dimension of fine teachers.

Mr. Santon worked with students in a way that Peggy felt transformed her, and enabled her to acquire new perceptions of herself. His belief in her gave her a new confidence. His very personal and complimentary approach allowed her to see herself differently. She could believe in herself if he believed in her.

Mr. Santon never berated Peggy for any reason, but instead only accentuated her strengths and he believed in her capacity to grow in every way. Peggy said he loved his students, and that they would have died for him. She emphasizes repeatedly that he made her feel that she mattered, an ability that can even prevent teenage suicide. Twenty-four years after her classroom association with Mr. Santon, Peggy was at a point in her life at which she considered suicide. More than even her parents, Mr. Santon came to mind at that time. He had taught her to take responsibility for her life and she thought of how disappointed he would be in her. And so she was able to move on.

Mr. Santon and Peggy still remain in contact, more than thirty years later.

> His voice sounds exactly the same over the telephone, because I still talk with him. I want him to know what he did for me. That's the least I can do. That's the only way I can say thanks, because of you, I'm the kind of teacher I am.

2   Peggy the Teacher

As a teacher, Peggy is profoundly concerned with the impact of caring for others. Real teaching she says,

> just doesn't happen unless the teacher cares. And that's why I get really fired up about huge classrooms, because I don't care how much you care as a teacher, if you're so horribly outnumbered, you just can't do it for the kids. You can't. So in those groups where I had 95 or 110, like one school year, it was so draining and I always was afraid that some child was going to think, "God, I'm nothing." And I thought, "how would I feel?" I mean, that's the worst thing in the world – you don't know my name. Then I'm not important to you. So I can be less than I am. I can forget to turn in my homework or deliberately slack off. What are you going to care?

For Peggy, it is critical that the teacher has personal contact with the student in a way that the student feels as though they are an integral part of the classroom community.

Knowing their names, looking them straight in the eyes and saying "hey, couldn't have done this concert without you," is an example of a way a teacher might approach a learner so as to invite their participation in community.

For Peggy, "Just because they exist they demand my respect and they demand to be treated with dignity. And it's such an exhilarating experience that they just start giving it back to me."

Peggy believes in honesty and truthfulness in her interaction with students, even when it comes to her own shortcomings.

> For instance, when I taught elementary school, in one fourth grade class, I said, "How can you all stand me today? Come on, tell me." I said "I'm awful today. I'm sorry. I just feel horrible. And I didn't mean to take it out on you and I just now did and there's no excuse for what I did, and I'm sorry, and will you forgive me?" And that class ran and grabbed me, and you know, they said as they went out the door, "Well, tomorrow will be better." I said, "Well, it's bound to be after what you did." I mean it was immediately better because they said it was okay to be me. They had so many problems, that particular class, and for that moment, they just put away all their problems and just nurtured me. It was wonderful. I just didn't feel deserving of that kind of magnanimity or gesture. That's what's so great about kids.

Peggy talked of going with her intuition especially when she's uncertain or knows she must take a risk.

> I get scared sometimes later, but at the moment I don't think about it if it feels right and it's not harmful. To me it's intuitive. It's acting in the moment, but not being rash or panicky. It's just so right at this moment that it *has* to be done. It has to be done or we're going to lose a kid, or we're going to lose this opportunity. And I don't know how to develop that – that's just something I do. People do other things that I don't do well, but this is the thing that I do and I've really started appreciating it.

As a teacher, Peggy perceives herself to be a catalyst, a person who causes something to happen within the learner, just as Mr. Santon was a catalyst that enabled her to have faith in herself. "You've got to cajole and persuade people to get out there and risk." But the teacher must undergird that persuasion by trusting and having faith in the learner.

Peggy believes the learner's freedom is essential to their growth and development, but at the same time the learner must develop discipline. One must be disciplined so as not to be uncaring about others. Freedom allows for discipline, and vice versa.

To me discipline is a moral thing, you know. I'm not going to tread on you because I care for you as a human being. All our problems are caused because we don't care about each other; war is an example of that. If I respect you, your rights and your right to be, I have freedom, true freedom, to do whatever I like. But I will qualify it in a positive way so that it's not destructive or harmful. I have to discipline my desires, my wants, so that I don't infringe on you, and yes, I still exercise my freedom and it's limited as to where I begin to infringe on you. I have discipline. Therefore, I can act in freedom.

3 Charley

Peggy talked of a transcendent relationship she developed with a fifth grade boy, Charley. His peers perceived him as nerdish, and they rejected him in various ways. Although Charley drove Peggy "nuts" at times as well, she describes him as being "very mannerly, considerate and polite. He's very mature in many ways, and in other ways, he's got some real hang-ups." Charley seemed to respond positively to Peggy immediately, and it is likely that it was because she was able to respond to him in a way that met his needs.

Peggy commented,

It's just that nobody makes Charley feel good but me. I found that out. I knew it the first day I met him. And the first three months of school, Charley would run in at break time and plant a big smooch on my cheek, and I wasn't uncomfortable, and he was so cute. He was in the fifth grade and he was so uninhibited and he expected me to accept it in the way I accepted it. I know he trusted me. He thought I was fun. That was the first thing. I think humor got to him and made him comfortable.

Peggy and Charley continued to share a mutually rewarding relationship until Peggy left that school the following spring.

Peggy described what is for her the reciprocal nature of teaching.

Teaching is like a light that shines back and forth from teacher to student, and then from student to teacher, and so on, depending on the situation. Rigidity prevents that shifting, a rigidity that comes when teachers assume an all- knowing, attitude. The way, for example, the word "professionalism" is used bothers me. Professionalism is not something one adopts, such as a briefcase, an expensive dress or mega-syllabic words. It is instead a matter of being all that one can be by being the genuine you. My approach is one of "what you see is what you get." I accept you as you are and you must accept me. I tell my students, "for the next forty-five minutes, nothing, nothing in this world exists but you and me."

Again, Peggy believes that what she calls "real teaching" does not happen unless the teacher cares for the learner. The teacher must have a personal, felt contact with the learner, a contact characterized by non-pretentiousness. The teacher must take risks that are frequently based on intuition alone. Freedom, supported by discipline, is an important theme for teacher-learner interaction. That discipline comes from caring for the other. The teacher's role is to act as a catalyst to enable the learner to feel good about him or herself, and to take measured risks in a safe environment.

Peggy works against the distance that the traditional teacher and learner relationship imposes as she moves toward a goal of reciprocity and unpretentiousness between teacher and learner. She finds that in return her learners offer her support, humor, enthusiasm, and dependability.

A decade before Charley, a tall, skinny and insecure me entered Peggy's senior high vocal music classroom. A transformation was to occur in my personal and artistic development because of her.

4 Peggy and Hunter

At first, Peggy said she saw me as Joe Btfsplk in Al Capp's "Li'l' Abner" comic strip. Btfsplk always had a sour face and a thundercloud over his head. She said I was negative and complaining. She said I surprised her when I began to become sunny as I progressed and was successful in her class. Important to her as well was my "zany" sense of humor and my dependability. She noticed that I took responsibilities seriously and fed off her excitement.

Difficult to convey is the power Peggy has as a teacher. Her dramatic flair tends to fuse learners to whatever she is teaching and you become a part of her organic, creative whole. You see the enthusiasm in her face and then you feel it in yourself.

For Peggy, a vocal music teacher, musicians are sophisticated people called upon to communicate a musical idea with dramatic flair. In my classes with her, she modeled drama even when she was not singing. She took great pains describing, demonstrating and discussing musical feeling and meaning with us. Each word sung had to be fused with shape and purpose. We laughed with her, I sometimes cried for happy reasons, as we talked about meaning in music and life.

She conducted music with her whole body. Her face was a stage and we soon we found ourselves drawn into her theatre and swept up in the music. She knew just what to do to move and inspire people. The high school existence, with its dingy dark halls, pale walls and lifeless faces, was transformed for me. School had a new and irresistible meaning for a formerly disenchanted learner.

I recall one particular class in which we were rehearsing a work that was composed about Joan of Arc's life. We had already learned the music, notes, rhythms and text and were in the process of developing our musical interpretation of the work. She told us a story about Joan. Peggy's face was so alive, as if she were living the story herself. Her eyes were large as saucers. I remember feeling the power of Joan's life at that moment. Immediately after the story she asked us to stand and channel that power into our voices as we sang the piece. The adrenaline surged in me and a chill spread from my spine to my neck and face. I felt electricity in the air during the performance. My heart beat rapidly as the class was charged with excitement.

Peggy had managed to accomplish her musical objectives brilliantly. I was mesmerized by what we had created. I could think of little else for several hours. I felt more alive in those moments with her than I had during most of my life.

Then, as now, I view that class as a supreme example of teaching and learning against which all others I attend or teach, are measured. My life was changed and would continue to change by the inspiration I derived from this teacher.

5 A Moment of Peggy's Teaching: An Act of Glamour and Power

Each spring the high school gymnasium served a rather theatrical, unintended purpose. It was converted into a stage and theatre for four days and four nights allowing for one dress rehearsal and three performances of *Opus,* an annual presentation of the music department. The gym floor was the stage, choral risers with sound shell at one end and band chairs and stands at the other. The gym floor between the chorus and band areas was the center of our stage, used for dancing and various production numbers.

I preferred this alternative purpose for the gym. Usually, I felt uncomfortable and alienated in my physical education classes. I had never enjoyed public school athleticism, where amiable classmates became adversaries. I disliked competition, and the fear I experienced in competitive games made me shiver. But now, for one brief shining moment, the high school music community of several hundred filled the room with visual and sonorous beauty. I was in my element. My life was to change during that first *Opus* show.

I played trumpet in the Band when I was not singing with the Chorus. The house was dark, serving as a stage curtain as the Girl's Chorus took their place on the risers. The audience made the only muffled noises. I was nervous for the singers. They were to sing two selections. A few more moments passed in the dark and suddenly the lights flooded the chorus of fifty young women in floor length burgundy dresses with white opera gloves, stunning. They were striking, lovely as they stood with dignity, composure and regal posture. The audience seemed transfixed, and the singers had not made a sound.

Peggy, the conductor, embraced the mood, and controlled it. She always told us that singing was an intellectual as well as a spiritual endeavor, and so she stood, as Athena, the goddess of intellectual pursuits, with chin up, waiting for the best moment to begin. Finally, with all eyes looking into hers, all minds and hearts of one accord, the downbeat was given. The sound wafted across the warmly lit floor and began to spin. The singers' song and ambiance projected such intimacy. Listeners seemed breathless.

> He's gone away for to stay a little while, but he's coming back if he goes ten thousand miles.

They sang tenderly, thoughtfully. Their faces were glowy and angelic. The conductor shaped every phrase with her entire body, particularly her eyes. The singers responded to every nuance with sophistication and poise. Peggy ended the piece with a tiny bow like gesture of two fingers. The audience and the chorus were quiet, motionless. Something pure and seemingly effortless, something larger than life engulfed us. The second selection was a Shaker hymn.

> Tis a gift to be simple tis a gift to be free, tis a gift to come round where we ought to be, and when we find ourselves in that place just right we will be in the valley of love and delight.

That was it. We were in the place just right. I was in the valley of love and delight. I never wanted to leave. We were the music. My throat had that tight, speechless feeling. For me, Peggy was a heroine. She and her students had delivered a prize of incomparable worth to the audience. She was a star and she was also my teacher. She was mine to learn with and grow with. She had changed that gym and she had changed me. My life had a new purpose, although as yet I could not begin to understand where it would lead. She was an artist, and I wanted to be an artist, to transcend time and space as she had. Together we would become co-creators, magic makers. I did not know then that I was experiencing a transcendent shamanic teacher at work.

Maxine Greene, an existentialist philosopher of education is generally regarded to be the spiritual heir to John Dewey (Levine, 2014). As a champion of aesthetic education she describes her impressions and reactions to Peggy's teaching as an example:

> of people really, really inspired. The description of the costumes, those glowing faces, the sound of the Shaker Hymn, the way the teacher stood up, the way the people responded, not only the relation with the teacher, but medium, color, atmosphere, plus her presence – it's paradigmatic. Not just because she's powerful in that way, but it's the situation that she created. Dewey used to do that. Then you ask, what does it mean? Also I suppose, where could it lead? Such a thing is always a possibility, but such occurrences are seldom. This is not what has to happen, this is the highest possibility. I have a feeling that in the pursuit, in the striving, you may never reach it, but, the pursuit itself makes you a little more than you were. (O'Hara, 1991)

To summarize, as a learner, several themes emerged for Peggy in her relationship with Mr. Santon. Those themes include care, trust, and his belief in or faith in her. Mr. Santon's affirmative style created an atmosphere in which Peggy felt that she mattered as an individual who felt she was worth something. Mr. Santon always focused on her strengths, not her deficiencies, but at the same time he challenged her. Because of him, Peggy was transformed so much that he ultimately enabled her to choose life over death. Peggy finds that when she opens up to her learners they respond in a gracious manner. Peggy tries to remain faithful to all that she learned from Mr. Santon whenever she enters a classroom, and she finds that serves her well.

6   Questions for Thought

1. Who was Mr. Santon? What was he like? Why was he important to Peggy?

2. How did Mr. Santon convey high expectations for his learners? What spell did he recast on his learners?

3. What qualities of Mr. Santon would you want to have as a teacher and why is that so?

4. How might Peggy's life have been different if Mr. Santon had not been her teacher?

5. As a teacher, what are Peggy's beliefs? For Peggy, what kind of risks must a teacher take?

6. How was Peggy important to Charley?

7. What is the reciprocal nature of teaching?

8. What is the nature of Peggy's relationship with Hunter?

9. What are some examples of transcendence in Peggy's work?

10. What about Mr. Santon's manner complimented his learners?

11. How are Mr. Santon's remarks complimentary to his learners?

12. How did Peggy invite learners to reach out to her?

13. What are the characteristics of Peggy's interaction with learners?

14. Describe how Peggy's teaching impacted Hunter's teaching.

15. What characteristics of Peggy's teaching did Hunter want to be reflected in his own teaching?

16. How are Mr. Santon and Peggy transcendent shamanic teachers? Use concepts and terms from Sections 1–5.

17. How is teaching a glamorous act for Mr. Santon and Peggy?

CHAPTER 4

An Ethic of Care, Tact and Tone

> ... and I thought, oh, I want to know everything this man knows.
> My God, this person, this teacher, is just fantastic and he cares what happens to me.
> PEGGY

∴

As a learner, I sensed that Peggy cared for me. Her persuasive approach led to an internal overhaul, or transformation, of my outlook on life. Peggy's power was due to particular characteristics of her ability to relate in precise ways to learners. In this chapter I will identify and discuss several of those ways in an attempt to clarify their nature.

1   An Ethic of Care

Throughout my experiences as a learner and a teacher, I developed a philosophical orientation that took into account the importance of extraordinary teaching and learning and how that occurs. My sentiments in that regard were strong, but I kept them to myself. I always tried, however, to be true to them in my teaching. It was not until I was in doctoral school that I read the words of prominent education philosophers, psychologists and theorists. Many of my deeply-held convictions were confirmed as I read their works. My studies led me, in particular, to Nel Noddings. Formerly a high school math teacher, as a professor at Stanford University, Noddings received awards for teaching excellence. She was the associate dean or acting dean of the School of Education for four years. Noddings is past president of the Philosophy of Education Society and the John Dewey Society. She has been Lee L. Jacks Professor of Education, Emerita, at Stanford University since she retired in 1998. Noddings has 10 children, 39 grandchildren, and over 20 great-grandchildren, many of whom are highly educated and educators themselves. In 2012 she lost her husband of over 60 years to cancer.

I met Nel Noddings at the end of one of her presentations at the Annual Meeting of the Education Research Association (AERA) in 1991. After standing in line to greet her, I asked her if she could spare me a few minutes. Without dropping a beat she pointed to an empty table and we sat down. As we chatted, I told her how deeply her published works had affected my personal philosophy, my teaching and how her work reinforced many views that I came to have as a teacher and later as a professor. I spoke of her assertion that giving learners grades negatively impacts the quality of the relationship between the teacher and learner. I told her that her claim was very important for me and for my research because I shared the same sentiments. I asked her if she still stood behind her claim. She replied emphatically that not only did she stand behind it, but that she had taken considerable amount of "flack" for making the claim. We talked comfortably for a while and, for me, it was as if I had always known her.

In her book, *Caring: A Feminine Approach to Ethics and Moral Education* (1984) Noddings says, "teaching involves two persons in a special relationship" (p. 195). That special relationship, she explains, requires that the teacher *care for* the learner. "I care for someone if I feel a stir of desire or inclination toward him. In a related sense, I care for someone if I have regard for his views and interests" (p. 9). Caring is a belief that one must care for the other and assist the other in the removal of barriers. "Caring involves two parties: the *one-caring* and the *one-cared-for*" (pp. 49, 68). The caring process serves both the self and the other individual. The one-caring (teacher) listens to, and feels for, the other cared-for learner. As with transcendent teacher learner relationships, Noddings' *caring* ethic may lead to the removal of barriers that have often prevented the teacher from fully receiving the learner.

Noddings' ethic of caring involves looking at and *"feeling with* 'the other'" (p. 3, emphasis added) as in the example of Peggy feeling with Charley. The one-caring (teacher) must accept the cared-for's (learner) learning problem as their own, must receive and respond to it holistically by immersing themselves in the learner's problem. The cared-for learner, who may be having difficulty, is dealt with in a personal manner with warm acceptance and trust. The cared-for learner's unique talents and ability levels are respected by the one-caring (teacher). The one-caring teacher makes it safe for learners "to risk themselves in new and difficult situations" (p. 189). The reader will recall how Mr. Santon created a warm atmosphere by caring for his learners and making them feel valuable and capable. He demonstrated his belief in learners and built their confidence with his sophisticated yet subtle approach.

1.1   *Attributing the Best Possible Motive*
The cared-for learner must be able to trust the one-caring (teacher). In the process of building a trust dynamic, the one-caring (teacher) must always

attribute the *best possible motive* to the learner's behavior toward the one cared-for (learner). To interpret this as it seems to relate to transcendent relationships, if the one-caring (teacher) takes a risk to send a cared-for (learner) to the office with a note to be delivered to the principal, but the cared-for learner does not return in the expected amount of time, the one-caring (teacher) does not presume that the cared-for learner is not behaving responsibly or is behaving inappropriately. Instead, the one-caring (teacher) continues to attribute the best possible motive about the cared-for learner until the learner returns. Once the cared-for learner returns, the one-caring (teacher) does not begin the dialogue in a manner that does not attribute the best possible motive by saying, "Why are you late? I thought I could trust you." Instead, when the cared-for learner returns, the one-caring (teacher) displays authentic concern for the cared-for learner and may say, "I was worried about you. Did you have difficulty getting the note delivered?" The cared-for learner is then called upon to rise to the trust that the one-caring (teacher) demonstrates and to respond accordingly and truthfully.

Recall that it was this type of caring that Mr. Santon demonstrated with Peggy in Chapter 3, in addition to his high expectations for her that enabled her to transcend her feelings of inadequacy and to succeed so remarkably well. Mr. Santon never deigned to presume a negative, or even marginally negative, motive on the part of his learners. Mr. Santon, or any teacher practicing Noddings' ethic of care, attributes the best possible motive to the learner's behavior.

Attributing the best possible motive is *not* to be confused with giving the learner, what is commonly referred to as, "the benefit of the doubt." Rather the teacher practicing Noddings' ethic of care steadfastly avoids doubting the learner. For the one-caring (teacher), *no negative presumption* may exist. Because the caring teacher attributes the best possible motive to learner behavior rather than doubting or blaming the learner, a foundation of trust is laid that continues to grow, and to undergird, the caring relationship. The caring teacher's mindset of consistent attribution of the best possible motive does not suggest that the caring teacher is naive to the possibility that a learner may take advantage of such an attribution. Moreover, despite that possibility, the caring teacher is aware, that their trust of the learner will indeed ultimately be transformational for that learner because of the learner's natural inclination to live up to the teacher's trust. Attributing the best possible motive to learner motivations and behavior is worth the risk involved because the myriad benefits that such an attribution, in the context of a caring and trusting relationship, extend not only to the learner, but the teacher as well.

AN ETHIC OF CARE, TACT AND TONE   65

1.2   *Engrossment and Motivational Displacement*

The one-caring (teacher) is characterized by *engrossment* and *motivational displacement*. "By engrossment I mean an open, nonselective receptivity to the cared-for" (Noddings, 2011, p. 211). "When I care, I really hear, see, or feel what the other tries to convey" (pp. 211–212). The one-caring (teacher) listens and responds in a way that the cared-for learner fully receives and recognizes. When the cared-for learner receives the caring effort, the caring relation is completed. In Chapter 9, Leslie describes how such a process unfolds in her work with her learners:

> ... a special bond develops between the two of us. It sounds kind of arrogant, but it's a communication just the two of us have in some way. I try to find out what their background is and then say "OK, what do I have today, how can I move myself to that place, into that mindset, so we're in sync, on one kind of wavelength?"

In Chapter 13, transcendent shamanic teacher Laura describes how she unwittingly practiced engrossment with her learner Melinda by remembering when Laura, as a young woman, experienced the same emotions that her learner Melinda, was feeling.

> ... [Melinda] hated wearing dresses. She felt awkward in them. I understood that. My relationship with Melinda was tied-up in my own background. When I was young, I hated the fact that dresses called attention to my body. People noticed my body when I wore a dress. I was very self-conscious and like many young women I had a pretty unhealthy view of my own appearance. When I taught school, I wore dresses all the time, so Melinda couldn't believe it when I told her I understood how she felt about "girl clothes." When she wore a skirt to school on game days because they were supposed to, everyone pointed it out and made a "deal" about it. I never did. In fact, I never mentioned it. I knew that what she needed was time to get comfortable with herself.

In addition to Laura and Leslie, recall Chapter 2 and how Anne practices engrossment by using personal and ongoing struggles with her own eyesight, and even more her second sight, her intuition, to inform her strategy to facilitate the unfolding of her solitary vision for Helen's transcendence and transformation.

Motivational displacement occurs when the one-caring (teacher) sets aside their own professional or personal project and begins instead to focus on the cared-for learner's project, responding "in a way that furthers the other's [that is the cared-for learner's] project." Here is an example. The one-caring (teacher) is on their way to pick up their mail, but is stopped by the cared-for learner, who asks the one-caring (teacher) for assistance carrying in a class project. Motivational displacement occurs when the one-caring (teacher) willingly chooses to set their mail run aside and helps the cared-for learner carry in the class project.

My example above is devised based on my interpretation of Noddings' work. Noddings asserts that engrossment and motivational displacement as constructs do not specify what is to be done. Instead they "characterize our consciousness when we care" (Noddings, 2011, p. 212). Caring is not, she explains, a series of steps that one follows. "Caring is a way of being in relation, not a set of specific behaviors" (p. 213). And so it seems that because each opportunity to care may be new and different, carers develop a consciousness that helps them determine how to care in a particular situation, that is *a way of relating in the moment.*

Noddings further explains that as the relationship matures, the one-caring (teacher) and the one cared-for (learner) may exchange places as opportunities present themselves. That is, the cared-for learner may become the one-caring and the one-caring (teacher) may become cared-for.

Additional components of caring, indeed of moral education as well, are the attitudes and processes that follow. The one-caring needs to *model*, or show, how caring occurs in their relation with the cared-for on a regular basis so that, among other reasons, cared-for learners may elect to become carers themselves.

1.3   *Dialogue*

The one-caring (teacher) creates and provides opportunities for *dialogue* with, and amongst, cared-for learners that are genuine and open ended. Dialogue is "a genuine quest for something undetermined at the beginning" (Noddings, 2011, p. 217). Dialogue, "is a common search for understanding, empathy, or appreciation" (p. 217). When the one-caring (teacher) engages in such a genuine dialogue they, of course, cannot know they outcome in advance.

The one-caring (teacher) *practices* caring themselves and provides opportunities for the cared-for learner to practice caring. Experience provides a process for which attitudes are shaped. Moreover, the practice of caring, "should transform schools and, eventually, the society in which we live" (Noddings, 2011, p. 218). Noddings nevertheless does caution that current school atmospheres inhibit the implementation of the teaching of caring.

1.4 Confirmation

The one-caring (teacher) *confirms* and thereby encourages the best in cared-for learners. "When we confirm someone, we spot a better self and encourage its development" (Noddings, 2011, p. 219). "Confirmation cannot be done by formula. A relation of trust must ground it" (p. 219). Confirmation is "a loving act founded on a relation of some depth" (p. 219). The confirmation process, in some respects, parallels the transcendent shamanic emotional, spiritual, social as well as intellectual, *uplift* of the learner. In Chapter 15, Beth describes, in emphatic terms, how she approaches confirming her learners who have been de-confirmed by their past teachers:

> In the past, teachers have told my students that they are stupid bums who can't do anything. Then they come to me and say "I'm too stupid, I can't do this." I say, "I don't believe that for a minute and neither do you. I can see in your eyes that you have the intelligence of a genius." If they feel that you truly believe in them, they can do it, but the fear and the emotional rape that has been put on them by those teachers, or whomever, has kept them from letting out their true selves and thereby their capacity to learn well.

In chapter 13, Laura's teacher confirmed her, in life changing ways. When she was an undergraduate education major, her Sunday school teacher identified one of her talents. The teacher said that Laura had a unique ability to befriend people who, for one reason or another, were shy, hurting, or not likable. She said that Laura had the capacity "to look inside and see the worthy person," the capacity to nurture those individuals and bring out their very best. The teacher called this "frog kissing." The teacher's revelation had a significant impact on Laura's development. Prior to her teacher's observation, no one had ever said that there was anything special about Laura. She explains, "I still remember that like it was yesterday. You want to live up to expectations and when you can see a unique feature that you can contribute, you practice it. It was really significant to me that she saw it. She saw my compassion." And so, Laura became a teacher with compassion who continued to confirm her learners as the one-caring (teacher).

2 Obstacles to Caring for the Learner

Obstacles to caring may be created by the very structure of learning environments. For example, Noddings (1984) observes that the caring relationship may be damaged or destroyed when teachers issue grades. Regardless of what has gone before, the teacher who gives grades is compelled to apply the measuring stick to the student as if the student were an object without feeling. With grades, teachers are frequently called upon to grindingly wrench themselves from the relationship and ultimately say, "I have decided thus and so." Such a demeaning and distracting process is "a fundamental violation of the relationship" (p. 194). Whatever trusting relationship that exists prior to grading may be destroyed in the grading process. For so many, grades are an artificial measure of performance that intrudes on the teacher learner relationship.

Rather, according to Noddings (1984), the one-caring must be prepared to take risks for the cared-for individual. Conceivably, when it is mandatory to give grades, the one-caring finds avenues to minimize the damage that grades can cause. Otherwise, learners feel violated, and frequently they do not feel cared for, when teachers are vague about requirements for grades or when expectations for their performance are otherwise vague. When the teacher's instruction does not prepare the learner for examinations, it suggests to the learner that the teacher does not care enough to provide adequate instruction to ensure the learner's positive development and success.

When I am in the one-caring (teacher) role, I attempt to provide absolute clarity in terms of expectations for learner development and performance. I also offer multiple honor-system-based projects, non-graded assignments and regular opportunities for learners to re-submit assignments without penalty. The motivation behind my honors systems projects and grade-free assignments is for learners to trust that, as the one-caring, I have their personal development at heart foremost and that I will not impose an artificial timetable on their development. In over four decades of practicing trust for my learners, rarely have I seen learners who were unworthy of my trust.

As I grapple with Noddings' caring ethic and the obstacles that may emerge with its implementation, I think about the impact of testing. I ask how testing serves the learning experience or long term memory of the learner. Consider for example, the short-term effect testing has on learners who must prepare for the tests that are then used to justify grades. When learners discuss their teaching/learning stories included in this book, they report that they frequently forget much of what they studied for tests within one or two weeks of writing the test. For them and so many others, it is clear that the learning and evaluation process has not been deep enough or intense enough for them to connect with content in a meaningful way. The expectations for the learner become broad and so vague as to be amorphous, unmanageable or unwieldy. The learner is not enabled to accommodate and assimilate content in a way that has a deep cognitive, affective, and psychomotor impact.

Contrast this scenario with the extraordinary and powerful learning scenario that Peggy generated during *Opus* and in her classroom. She was able to use drama, wit and an innate understanding of development to create learning encounters that can still be vividly recalled by her learners over forty years later (O'Hara, 1995). The one-caring facilitates learning experiences effectively by making the learner's problem own.

The one-caring teacher, therefore, establishes learning objectives and learning expectations that are crystal clear and manageable for the learner. It cannot be denied that when instruction and tests are poorly matched or incongruent, the grades that follow the test frequently intrude on the teacher learner relationship. Benign terms attached to grades like "Good" or "Average" that are used to describe a very complicated and ongoing process of learner development are also damaging to the relationship when learners believe that their actual performance has been undersold, undervalued or inaccurately reflected. The developmental process is minimized and the powerful bonds that are needed between teacher and learner to sustain caring and transcendent relationships are severed or at least strained.

3   Tact

Closely related to Noddings' one-caring is Max Van Manen's (1991) conception of *tact*, that refers to relating to others with thoughtfulness, openness and togetherness. Mr. Santon interacted with learners in a way that made them feel good about themselves by tactfully affirming them and complimenting them. On a regular basis he said to his learners, "I'm so lucky to be your teacher."

Tact is a characteristic that is part of Van Manen's (1991) description of a *new pedagogy*. Van Manen's new pedagogy, a new way of relating, replaces what has been the educator's authority and governance over the learner with something that is more powerful. Van Manen, an educator, phenomenologist and founding editor of *Phenomenology + Pedagogy: A Human Science Journal*, calls for "a new pedagogy of the theory and practice of living with children" (p. 3). Rather than to govern learners with discarded values, fixed impositions and old rules, the new pedagogy "recognizes" how to stand in a relationship of thoughtfulness and openness to children and young people (p. 3). "A certain encounter of togetherness between parent and child, teacher and pupil" must exist (p. 30). Teacher and learner mutually share the learning experience. The pedagogical relationship involves personal kinds of relating. In Van Manen's words, "Regardless of what we think parents or teachers do precisely, pedagogy is cemented deep in the nature of the relationship between adults and children" (p. 31).

Van Manen defines pedagogy as "the art of tactfully mediating the possible influences of the world so that the child is constantly encouraged to assume more self-responsibility for personal learning and growth" (Van Manen, 1991, p. 80). Tactful meditation is facilitated by love, care, qualities that make "a pedagogical relationship possible" (p. 80). Also, the pedagogue's, or teacher's, attitude must be one of "watchful encouragement" (p. 38). The reader will recall how effectively Mr. Santon and Peggy were able to demonstrate tact in their relationships with learners and the remarkable results that followed.

When teachers show learners they care *for them* and believe in them, learners do their best to succeed and meet their teacher's expectations. Teachers show care and confidence in learners by "teaching in a personal manner" and by "setting challenging expectations" (Van Manen, 1991, p. 58). I found, for example, that it was Peggy's genuine approach, including her candor about the dynamics impacting her own life, that drew me in and captivated me. Her chain-analogy discussions convinced me that all of us together could meet the challenging expectations that she set before us and that we would miss out on so very much if we did not rise to the occasion. In such a process, the teacher may also need to restore some of life's difficulty to learning opportunities they design and implement.

The teacher may deliberately create additional challenges to learning encounters that facilitate positive risk and adventure, so that learners come to terms with extended consequential questions and human issues that are imbedded in a particular lesson. In Chapter 9, Leslie's challenging professor, moved her to an entirely new level of performance:

> He took me into the room and said "don't ever play the piano like that again in your life." I was devastated, because at the time I played most of the right notes, and I did it all. But now I realize exactly what he meant; don't ever play without any commitment. Your whole object in life must be to make this come alive and be real. I knew what he meant ...

Her professor wanted to challenge Leslie and his challenge payed off. Leslie's pushing professor "wanted to see how far he could push you and see if you would turn lazy, or see if you would quit. For me, as a female, that would be his test, to see if I would quit. I'm sure he wouldn't have it any other way."

Van Manen's tact enables transcendent teachers to identify when learner's are ready to share their perceptions and relevant personal information related to a given topic at hand. One of the outcomes of such student sharing is that the teacher learns ever more about the learner, thereby equipping the teacher to better teach that learner. In Chapter 9, Leslie explains how she practices tact.

AN ETHIC OF CARE, TACT AND TONE　　　　　　　　　　　　　　　　71

> ... Whenever students encounter a problem I will try every approach until a solution to the problem is found. There is never one solution for all learners. I find out what works best for them. I always try to do it with some sense of humor so it's not a really serious "this has to be done," or "this has to be accomplished" situation. Also I tell them "it's OK" and "it's no big deal that we are trying to fix this." Performing ... becomes very serious business for the performer and some ... teachers escalate that seriousness ... with their teaching style. I try to downplay the seriousness. I try to say that it's not that they're having problems or there has been a mistake or anything. Rather, I say "let's just try to find a way to make it easier or do it better or make it sound better. Whatever it has to be to accommodate their needs is the way we will do it."

When interacting tactfully, transcendent teachers should avoid inclinations that may predispose them to believe in any one learner less than another. As is the case for transcendent teachers as well as tactful teachers, "It is anti-pedagogical to assume that by some criterion or other, some individual or group is somehow superior or inferior to others" (Van Manen, 1991, p. 211). The teacher remains hopeful for each learner's success and demonstrates trust in all learners as they move through the developmental process.

As Noddings (1984) discerns, when learners are trusted by teachers they are heartened to trust themselves. It is the teacher's responsibility to establish a trusting relationship with the learner. It is that trust that enables the learner to trust in his or her own potentiality for development. Again, it was Mr. Santon's trust of Peggy that allowed her to trust herself enough to move to a new level of performance. Underlying the teacher's hope for, and trust in, the learner is the teacher's ability to respond to the learner or to be "response-able." The response-able teacher therefore is thus morally accountable to the learner to provide the learner his or her unique, optimal, learning environment and related support for positive development.

The response-able teacher does not at any time, dispense with pedagogically appropriate structure, limits, or boundaries, nor does the teacher proceed blindly in her trust of the learner. Instead, the teacher takes measured and incremental risks designed to elevate the quality and level of trust in the relationship.

Tact, it is clear, has to do with being attentive to the other, *observing as the learner observes* and *listening as the learner listens*. The teacher puts his or herself in the learner's place."Tact as a form of human interaction means that we [educators] are immediately active in a situation: emotionally, responsively, mindfully" (Van Manen, 1991, p. 122).

Tact is not a skill set. Rather, tact refers to grace in dealing with others. Grace is demonstrated by Jean in her interaction with her children as she created learning experiences that seem to flow like silk fabric over the fingertips. "Tact is improvisational" (Van Manen, 1991, p. 146), and cannot be planned. Even though tact cannot be planned, one can prepare the heart and mind for the regular implementation of tact. As is the case with Noddings' ethic of care, tact requires that one have "a generally trustful, sympathetic attitude toward young people" (p. 123). Tact is not obtrusive; rather it is subtle, hardly noticeable.

Tact feels, hears, and respects the dignity, subjectivity, and uniqueness in others and "attempts to enhance the uniqueness" in them (Van Manen, 1991, p. 169). The tactful individual, through sensitivity, is able to interpret the other's inner thoughts, feelings and desires from indirect means such as gesture, body language, expression and demeanor. The tactful teacher is "able, as it were, to read the inner life of the other person" (p. 125). The reader will recall that reading the learner's inner life is a fundamental characteristic of the transcendent shamanic teacher. Tact implies "a fine sense of standards, limits and balance that makes it possible to know almost automatically how far to enter into a situation and what distance to keep in individual circumstances" (p. 126). Tact allows one to know when to step in, when to pass over or not notice something, and when to remain silent. Tact is discerning and the tactful individual perceives the positive in others, even when that positive is first construed as weakness. Tact also implies strength, and that strength is active when a situation calls upon a teacher to be direct or candid. "Tact can indeed be firm," decisive, and open (p. 143). The reader will recall that tact is demonstrated effectively by Jean and Peggy. In Chapter 1, I quote Helen Keller (1988, pp. 29–30) and the tact her teacher, Anne Sullivan, demonstrated:

> It was my teacher's genius, her quick sympathy, her loving tact which made the first years of my education so beautiful. It was because she seized the right moment to impart knowledge that made it so pleasant and acceptable to me. She realized that a child's mind is like a shallow brook which ripples and dances merrily over the stony course of its education and reflects here a flower, there a bush, yonder a fleecy cloud ....

Tact can result in learner transformation as tactful teachers transform "an unproductive, uncompromising or even harmful situation into a pedagogically positive event" (Van Manen, 1991, p. 130). Tact is also the ability to "create a warm social atmosphere" through gesture, posture, smiles, winks, etc. (p. 131). Recall Chapter 2 in which Theoni, guided from within by understanding and awareness, shares, "I leaned in very close to Veronica and I said, 'you *can* do this, *you need* to do this.'" For Veronica, "When Dr. Soublis said that, it felt like more of a reassurance than a demand ..."

Tact, as Van Manen identifies it, means "that the teacher is there in a personal way for those students" (p. 78), trusting, open and expectant of the learner's positive development. The teacher looks past the learner's outward persona and ostensible maturational level to identify hidden capacities and inclinations thereby identifies them for the learner, as well as for themseves.

4   Tone

Van Manen also conceptualizes the role of tone in teaching and learning. Tone is the learning, social atmosphere that is created by the teacher. *Tone* is a "... special quality in human interaction that allows a person to behave with sensitivity and flexibility toward others" (Van Manen, 1991, p. 131). The teacher creates appropriate tone through the use of the voice, through humor, and through standing for something. Clearly, Mr. Santon and Peggy stood for high expectations for learners as is demonstrated by their careful efforts to establish fine performance standards and to enable learners to feel worthy to meet the challenges set before them. The teacher's presence demonstrates, in a personal way, that a strong loving relationship exists between him and the subject to be learned. The teacher *embodies* the subject and that embodiment is apparent to the learner via, as Jean describes in Chapter 5, "... the expression on your face and your body movements ...."

Because classrooms are inhabited by people who carry their biases and expectations about teachers with them to the classroom, tone exists whether the teacher deliberately creates it or not. The teacher, therefore, needs to actively create a culture that transforms the preexisting tone, laden with traditional impositions and "the authoritarian discipline of formal coercion, to [one of] living vibrancy and spirited animation" (Van Manen, 1991, pp. 183, 200). In Chapter 2, Veronica describes Theoni:

> Dr. Soublis' tone was even and there was a soft strength to it, ... She seemed sure in her words, and that transferred to me, making me feel sure. Most importantly, there was no negativity in her voice, no demand, just support ... Dr. Soublis created a classroom environment so secure that I felt safe to share something so traumatic in my life. If it were any other teacher, I do not think I would have taken such a risk.

Recall in Chapter 2, Theoni's description of the process of creating tone that includes the physical environment:

> To get the magic to happen, several ingredients must be used on behalf of the teacher: (1) the initial decision of what one would like to occur as a result of the lesson, the planning – select the appropriate materials to foster the desired effect, (2) atmosphere – one must pre-determine the setting. This means moving furniture, adjusting lighting, perhaps using props and (3) the ability to be silent. Teachers often feel the need to jump in, change the conversation, and rescue a drowning student. But we must trust in the well-constructed plan and be patient.

Sarcasm, ridicule, rejection, humiliation have no place in the transformed atmosphere. In such a negative atmosphere, learners are not tempted to behave negatively. At the same time, however, the teacher carefully works to strike a healthy balance between freedom and control. This process will be discussed later in this book.

Also crucial to teaching is the teacher's understanding of a child as a learner. To teach effectively, the teacher must find a way to connect whatever background and prior experiences the learner already has with what is to be taught. To accomplish that goal the teacher must first familiarize him or herself, as fully as is possible, with the learner's biography and/or background and experiences as is demonstrated in the stories that follow.

5   Questions for Thought

1. How does Nel Noddings' define her ethic of care? In your answer, use specific concepts/terms from Noddings's work. Avoid references to care as care is generically defined and conceived. How does Nodding's ethic of care function?

2. Cite two examples in your own life of Noddings' ethic-of-care interaction.

3. What is Noddings' *engrossment* and how does it function in her ethic of care?

4. What is Noddings' *motivational displacement* and how does it function in her ethic of care?

AN ETHIC OF CARE, TACT AND TONE

5. What is Noddings' *confirmation* and how does it function in her ethic of care?

6. How does a teacher practice Noddings' ethic of care with learners?

7. What barriers exist to practicing Noddings' ethic of care in a classroom?

8. What does Noddings mean to "attribute the best possible motive?" How is attributing the best possible motive different from giving the learner the benefit of the doubt?

9. What damage is caused by grades and how can that barrier be transcended, beyond teacher clarity with assignments, support, encouragement and fairness?

10. If grades must be given, what must teachers do to protect their relationships with learners?

11. What is Max Van Manen's tact and how does it function?

12. What is Van Manen's tone and how does it function?

CHAPTER 5

Portrait of Transcendent Relator
Jean

> Freedom is good. But as far as I can tell, you and the child have to know the limits. And then you just try to work between them.
> JEAN

∴

1   **At Home**

Jean has subtly expressive facial features and a quiet but discerning presence. Her family is of Irish, Welch, French and Cherokee descent. As a result of that heritage, she has developed a special way of saying a great deal with few words.

Jean's father died when she was eight years old and her mother was left to raise Jean, her older sister Ann and younger brother Sonny. Her grandmother kept the house and children during the day and her mother, Mary, kept books for the general store located nearby. Money was tight for the family during those days of the depression.

Most everyone knew everyone else in the small Appalachian town of Buffalo, West Virginia. People in the community led rich and colorful lives. These "characters," as Jean describes them, were fine storytellers and Jean was fascinated with their tales of life in Buffalo and other places. They were sincere people, witty and very much alive. Life in Buffalo was enviable despite the dark shadow of the Depression and later World War II.

One can appreciate Jean's style as a mother only by understanding her interaction with the maternal figures in her childhood. In fact, Jean's mother was loving, sweet and kind; a good mother who read to Jean and held her close. Their relationship was different from the one Jean shared with her grandmother, with whom she experienced more relational distance. During the daytime, Jean's grandmother was her guardian. Her grandmother Annie was intimidating and temperamental and could be quite domineering. Her grandmother's frequently repeated phrase, "little pitchers should be seen and not heard" penetrated Jean's psyche. Jean understood that phrase to mean that children should only speak when spoken to and should never present a bother to adults. Her grandmother's attitude and her use of that phrase and other restrictive phrases, impacted Jean in profound ways, so much so that even today Jean has difficulty speaking before more than one or two people at a time. She can do this only if the atmosphere is warm and welcoming.

Later in her life Jean would grow to appreciate the role her grandmother played in her life and how giving and kind her grandmother had been to her entire family. Jean's grandmother loved her very much and did her utmost to care for Jean the best way she could manage.

2   Frances

A friend's mother, Frances, created a very different atmosphere from the one Jean's grandmother created. Jean admired the virtues of directness when it was tempered with care. Frances was very direct, at times blunt, but she was motherly toward Jean and encouraged Jean to be open with her. Jean felt safe with Frances as she discussed personal issues, ones that Jean could not discuss with her mother who was very bashful about personal topics. With a warm, pretty smile, Frances talked openly, particularly for a woman of her generation, with Jean about sex and other taboo subjects. She was also a fine cook and she often invited Jean to dinner. When Jean visited, Frances treated her with respect and regard and so Jean learned to trust Frances deeply. Frances' approach with Jean was to have significant influence on Jean. As a teacher/mother Jean would emulate Frances' style of openness, candor and respect for others, particularly respect for children.

3   Ms. Nettie

Another friend's grandmother, Ms. Nettie, treated Jean wonderfully as well. "My father died when I was eight years old and Ms. Nettie always talked to me about him. She said he was the finest man she ever knew, even if he drank. She said 'he was so mannerly,' and he was. I think she meant that he had good rearing. He was nice to her, very nice. 'A fine looking man,' Ms. Nettie said."

Jean loved those moments because she missed her father so. She knew that Ms. Nettie held high regard for him and that helped Jean to have good feelings about her dad.

4 The Pedagogy of Manners

Jean's family practiced good manners and they believed in the importance of them. Manners and courtesy continued to be very important for Jean as an adult and as a teacher. She began to teach them to her own children nearly as soon as they were born. For Jean, of course, manners go beyond holding the door for someone or saying please and thank you; manners are procedures for relating well to another individual at all times.

Manners are the foundation of the pedagogy Jean developed for her children. But in order to teach with such pedagogy, she knew that an individual has to *live* manners, to practice and model them for children. An approach to teaching, built around kindness to others, requires one to treat the child or the learner with the same regard, respect and love one would any other adult individual.

Like her mother, Ms. Nettie and Frances, and in defiance of her grandmother's highly assertive caregiving style, Jean's pedagogy of manners involves decorum, openness and receptivity in conversation. Jean relates to her young children by talking to them as one would any other adult individual in general conversation. Even the preverbal child, she believes, has the capacity, the intuition and the empathy to interpret the meaning of spoken language even though such children are not, at first, able to decode each word. "They know – I'm telling you. It is that they are told in a warm and intimate way. You have to start teaching kids early," Jean says.

5 Being Open

Jean, like Frances, believes in the importance of being open with children, responding to all of their questions with honesty and thoughtfulness. Like Frances, Jean is comfortable discussing the topic of sex, in an informational way, openly with children and young adults by responding comfortably and naturally to their questions; refraining from offering more information than is needed or requested. Jean is also free to say to children "I don't know," or "what do you think?" affording them the same types of interactional regard she would adults. She is not loud and forceful with children. Any approach which would impugn the dignity of the child would be inconsistent with the pedagogy of manners, and would be too close to the tone of phrases like "little pitchers should be seen and not heard."

6   The Art of Conversation

As a teaching mother, Jean believes she was able to develop her children's ability to converse very quickly, an accomplishment that afforded a deepened rapport between Jean's children, other children and herself early in their childhood. For Jean, conversation removes barriers that frequently typify the relationships between adults and young children. A conversational, reciprocal kind of interaction not only contributes to the healthy development of the child's capacity to speak their mind but it also affords many rewards to the parent as well. Of course, the adult must always remain cognizant of extra time a young child requires to formulate conversation and complete tasks. Jean said this about her approach as a mother, "For instance, if I asked them to put something up, and they didn't do it the minute I said to, I knew they were little. They had to have time. Little minds aren't that fast." Often adults may be heard ordering children about punctuating the directive with 'Now!' An impatient approach that demonstrates little to no regard for development is also inconsistent with the pedagogy of manners. Non-mannerly demands are rude and do not take into account the cognitive and physical developmental level of the child. In contrast to her grandmother, Jean would avoid any approach that tends to silence children or inhibit their capacity to express themselves freely and openly. For her, little pitchers will be heard as well as seen.

> I didn't try to be a domineering kind of mother because I'd been through that with Grandmother. We were never allowed to "talk back" or to be honest about our concerns or emotions. I always felt children should be allowed to express their feelings. With Grandmother, when company came you couldn't join in a conversation. You just had to sit there ... and not even meet anyone.

Jean was able to pass the art of conversation with any individual, regardless of their personal background, onto her children. Within that context, she emphasizes the importance of the ability to really listen to the other, not interrupting, looking them straight in the eye and responding to their remarks authentically and with sincere questions. Of course, conversation is not limited to words. "People do communicate in lots of ways. I think it is in the expression on your face and your body movements that really matter." People also communicate with song and Jean finds song to be a powerful mode for communing with children. Jean sang and taught simple songs to children such as "You Are My Sunshine" as a channel for sharing joy and delight.

> For example, if we were riding along in the car and the children started to bicker in the back seat, I started singing. And they started to sing too. They liked it and the bickering stopped. Singing focuses the mind and frees it at the same time.

Jean always prepares young children for social interaction. She talks with them about the people to be visited, what they are like, both as adults and when they were young children, if she knows. As a result, she found her own children were appropriate, and even precocious in their interaction with adults. "It was natural. They knew how."

Jean is very aware of the power of creative experience and endeavor. She goes out of her way to dream up special moments for children on holidays, or any day. Cloud watching, sardine and cracker picnics in the back yard or going to hear the high school band rehearse are some examples.

> The kids pick up on your enthusiasm. They don't say, "Well Mom, do you really want to take us out Trick-or-Treating?" for example. They must *know* you want to go with them. It comes from a real, honest interest in being and doing with them.

The parent's enthusiasm is critical in facilitating the child's development and it becomes obvious to the child as long as the parent's effort to interact and engage with the child is sincere.

Jean met my sister Mary Ann's and my own needs well because she cares deeply for children. She is affectionate with children and really listens to them when they speak. She looked at my sister and me intently when we talked. She questioned us and related her life to our stories. Lying on a picnic blanket we watched Sputnik above, identified faces in the clouds and experienced the joys of sardines, crackers and iced tea in the backyard. She was fully present, smooth and natural at her job as a teacher. We enjoyed her and the atmosphere she created.

During our childhood, my sister and I were entranced by the colorful characters we saw in fantasy films, on television and in theaters. Halloween offered an opportunity to *become* those characters. It was not Jean's way to buy costumes or to sew them. Instead, the three of us went to the closets and drawers to create our own costumes. One of my Mom's aprons with stripes and rickrack became an exotic frock for my sister. With a little brass costume jewelry, a bandana and blush, my three year old sister became a convincing, if only thirty-six inch tall, stereotypic gypsy. After opening and experimenting in three or four more drawers and with the application of a fake facial scar, I became a pirate. None of this was hurried. After forty years I can still recall this image and feel how swept up we were in this collaborative process that my mother facilitated so effectively. I still see her putting the final touches on us just before we went out the door into our fantasy.

7   Freedom and Affection

Jean seeks to free children from restriction and constriction. But freedom is possible only when interactional limits are clearly established. Limits specify what is acceptable and what is not in appropriate mannerly ways. Limits contribute to a child's awareness, self-discipline and a sense of feeling protected. Important as well is the creation of an ambiance of intimacy and holding one close.

> The main thing, I think, is to be affectionate. You don't necessarily have to hug to be affectionate. You can do it with words. The way you look at them, the way you treat them; a child knows when they're loved by the way you treat them. They know.

To summarize, several characteristics of Jean's style as a mother emerged from the transcendent relationships she had with the maternal figures in her life. Those included openness, receptivity, enthusiasm and manners. In reaction against her grandmother's restrictive style, Jean offers freedom to children within clearly established limits. The expression of intimacy and affection are also primary characteristics of her maternal teacher style. Those qualities paved the way for the transcendent relationships she established and has maintained with her children.

8   Questions for Thought

1. How were Frances and Ms. Nettie role models for Jean as a mother and teacher?

2. How is their behavior contrasted with Jean's grandmother's behavior?

3. What is Jean's "pedagogy of manners"? How is such pedagogy significant?

4. How are conversation manners and openness important when dealing with children and other learners?

5. How does Jean relate openly to learners?

6. What qualities or characteristics of transcendent shamanism exist in Jean's portrait, if any? Refer to Sections 4–7 to answer this question.

CHAPTER 6

Trust, Freedom and Mother Love

> I think [he] gave us a lot of responsibility and I think that in order to give us that responsibility, [he] had to respect us to a certain degree. The fact that [he] trusted me enough to give me responsibility and let me perform them my way, as long as I got the results that were needed, I respected [him] for that.
> KATHY

∵

The transcendent teacher learner relationship is characterized by the *trust* the teacher has for the learner. Trust is a central, foundational component of the transcendent relationship as can be seen, for example, in the relationships between Jean and Frances.

If the teacher trusts the learner, the learner is free to approach the teacher in a way he or she would not be inclined to in the context of the traditional teacher learner relationship. As a result, there is the intimacy in the connection Jean felt when she had her talks with Frances and the confidence Frances inspired in Jean. Trust spawns approachability and frees the learner to reach out to the teacher in personal ways. Learners are liberated to convey their needs to the teacher without the fear of retribution, and to confide in the teacher. Because of the security trust provides, the learner feels safe to experiment and to pursue difficult and challenging work all while knowing that the teacher is steadfastly there for them. Trust in transcendent teacher learner relationships goes beyond trusting the teacher or the learner to be honest and certainly beyond the learner trusting the teacher to be fair with grading. Learners must be able to trust transcendent teachers to create and maintain a safe, warm, social, nurturing and loving environment.

Chapter 5 identifies the role of trust Jean's relationship with Frances. Frances treated her with respect and regard and so Jean learned to *trust* Frances deeply. Jean felt safe with Frances as she discussed personal issues, ones that Jean could not discuss with her mother who was very bashful about personal topics. With a warm, pretty smile, Frances talked openly, particularly for a woman of her generation, with Jean. Frances' approach with Jean was to have significant influence on Jean. As a teacher/mother, Jean would emulate Frances' style of openness, candor and respect for others, particularly respect for children.

1 The Facilitator

In his book, *Freedom to Learn* (Rogers & Freiberg, 1994), Carl Rogers conceives of the *facilitator*, as one who creates a non-threatening learning atmosphere where risk-taking and trust can develop. Rogers's facilitator has become a standard construct in teaching, learning research and best practice nomenclature. For one to become a facilitator, Rogers believes that the traditional image of the teacher as information giver, evaluator of products, expert, keeper of order, etc. is in need of overhaul. At the same time, the learner is not a fact absorber. The facilitator creates circumstances that *allow* the learner to learn, as well as to discover how to learn. The facilitator's task is a delicate but demanding one. There is no room for the authoritarian style of Jean's grandmother, for example, so often seen in learning environments of the past as well as many in the present. Recall from Chapter 5 that Jean's inclinations as a facilitator derived from Frances' interaction with her, and in part, as a reaction to her grandmother's authoritarian style of interaction with children and adolescents:

> I didn't try to be a domineering kind of mother because I'd been through that with Grandmother. We were never allowed to "talk back" or to be honest about our concerns or emotions. I always felt children should be allowed to express their feelings. With Grandmother, when company came you couldn't join in a conversation. You just had to sit there ... and not even meet anyone.

For Rogers, when the facilitator and learner establish a genuine relation, there is no longer room for the facilitator to act as know-it-all, and the facilitator no longer relies on the authoritative sway of the official. Significant learning may be facilitated by the personal relationship between learner and facilitator. Again, avoiding the know-it-all approach, Jean is free to say to children "I don't know," or "what do you think?" affording them the same types of interactional regard she would adults. She is not loud and forceful with children. Any approach which would impugn the dignity of the child would be inconsistent with Jean's pedagogy of manners, and would be too close to the tone of phrases like "little pitchers should be seen and not heard."

Rogers' facilitator creates the classroom climate with their attitude. As facilitators begin the process of creating such a climate, Rogers directs them to ask these questions. How can they create a climate in which learners feel free to be curious and free to learn from their facilitator as well as other learners? How does the facilitator restore the learner's inborn excitement for learning (Rogers, 1969)? As a facilitator, Jean seeks to free children from restriction and constriction. But freedom is possible only when interactional limits are clearly established. Limits specify what is acceptable and what is not appropriate, mannerly ways. Limits contribute to a child's awareness, self-discipline and a sense of feeling protected.

Facilitators may develop an atmosphere and a particular quality of personal relationships with learners that allow these natural inclinations to reach fruition. In such an atmosphere, learners are enabled, and freed to reach out, to risk and bridge the gap that so frequently has existed between learner and teacher.

In Chapter 15, Beth finds that conversation with her learners facilitates the bridging of gaps and increased understanding. She attempts to create an environment of open and honest dialogue. She wants her learners to feel free to discuss whatever they will as long as it does not denigrate others. Beth shares, "There was no embarrassment on my part with them, or them with me. I think that through discussion ... you can really open up on a lot of levels. Everyone feels perfectly free to ask questions." Beth believes such an approach provides a way for learners to become informed and expand their awareness. Beth shares, "I accept what they say and use it or go beyond it. The other students identify with each other [and] work together. We have a mutual respect for each other. What I try to do with my students is to make things open enough that they can come forward, and empathize ...."

2 Three Essential Attitudes of the Facilitator

Rogers (1969) posits three essential characteristics that the facilitator of learning needs to possess to remove relational distance and barriers that so frequently have existed between teacher and learner. Those characteristics are:
1. realness/genuineness (pp. 106–108)
2. the most basic attitude, prizing/unconditional positive regard (pp. 109–111)
3. empathetic understanding (pp. 111–112).

Rogers defines *real* in this context. "When the facilitator is a real person, being what she is, entering into a relationship with the learner without presenting a front or a facade, she is much more likely to be effective. She comes into a direct personal encounter with the learner" (Rogers & Freiberg, 1994, p. 154). The encounter between facilitator and learner is direct and authentic. The encounter is *real*. The encounter lacks artificiality. When relevant to the teaching and learning context and in the process of emerging as direct and real, facilitators share what makes them 'tick," what they personally value, what is sacred for them, what made them the person they have become as well as the person they want to become. Recall Peggy in Chapter 3, "It is ... a matter of being all that one can be by being the genuine you. My approach is one of 'what you see is what you get.' I accept you as you are and you must accept me."

The facilitator does not deny their authentic self, conveys their authentic self to learners and offers their unique perspective to learners when they, as facilitators, are internally guided to do so (p. 154). The facilitator comes into direct personal encounter with the learner, meeting them on a person-to-person basis. For Jean, being authentic is a matter, in part, of being genuinely enthusiastic about the task at hand:

> The kids pick up on your enthusiasm. They don't say, "Well ... do you really want to take us out Trick-or-Treating?" for example. They must *know* you want to go with them. It comes from a real, honest interest in being and doing with them.

Realness lacks a peculiar pretense that somehow these two people are at opposite ends of the human interpersonal continuum and therefore unable to relate directly with each other. Facilitators who lack realness are part of Freire's retrogressive banking education. Rogers admits that this realness is most difficult to achieve, and it must be acquired slowly because the preexisting interactional culture established in many learning environments may be contradictory to what the facilitator wants to achieve and to express. Thus, realness is difficult to achieve because the process of becoming real requires the facilitator to break with the *status quo* and to draw out, and draw from, their authentic self.

Certainly Frances broke with the *status quo* with Jean, with powerful results. The facilitator interacts with learners in a way that is natural for that individual rather than fall back on facilitator interaction models that one has seen others apply, that no longer seem valid or appropriate. Non-real approaches include stale and commonly spoken adages such as teachers should not develop friendships with learners, should not smile until after the winter break and so on. The facilitator again, relies on their intuitive, authentic "gut" feeling about what is right or appropriate in a particular circumstance and responds to the learner in an authentic manner. When facilitators fall back on convention, on a prefabricated "recipe" approach for human interaction, they must ignore their internal direction and risk losing their credibility with learners by appearing phony to them. The choice that leads to phoniness is made because teachers believe that a generally accepted, externally imposed "axiom" or platitude is necessarily superior to their own inner direction or inclination. Thus, in the process of avoiding a risk, facilitators take negative risks, risks that emerge as phony to learners.

Real facilitators learn to respond to individual people, to individual groups and circumstances in ways that are tailor-made by that facilitator for that particular moment and individual(s). Peggy alludes to this when she says "I get scared sometimes later, but at the moment I don't think about it if it feels right and it's not harmful. To me it's intuitive. It's acting in the moment, but not being rash or panicking. It's just so right at this moment that it has to be done. It has to be done or we're going to lose a kid, or we're going to lose this opportunity." While realness stimulates learning it also improves communication and encourages teacher and learner self-understanding and acceptance. Rogers does not distinguish, in this sense, between facilitator and learners in terms of age. Facilitators are to approach learners at any age *without artificiality*. In Chapter 13, Laura shares,

> Once you shed your pretense and meet your student as another human being, that's when genuine power begins, power to become and to transform lives. I think a lot of it has to do with our interaction with learners. It depends on how we perceive their nature. We must perceive them as people first. I see my students as inherently good. In fact I used to *want* the "trouble-makers" because I knew that inside they were good people.
>
> When you use humor or give them a chance to back down instead of having a mouthy confrontation, it gives them a chance to save face. I looked at them. I made eye contact. When I was teaching, the kids used to come into the class and they would say right out loud, "I just love coming in this class, you know I just look forward to coming in this class." When I asked why, they would say, "I just came out of calculus and I just hate the last class, but I look forward to this class," and I would say "Why?" They would say "I can just be *myself* in here." I think that came from the fact that I was always myself in there. I just never could figure out how you could be different than who you really are, whether you're with a bunch of high school kids or people in a seminar or your family. I think that sets a certain tone in the class and maybe kids feel comfortable to be themselves.

In Chapter 9, Leslie describes her very real facilitator:

> She was a very strong female model for me, of a different kind. We have a wonderful relationship that's lasted for all these years. She's the most blunt, forthright, honest, direct person I've known. She's very assertive by most people's standards .... If she believes something, she just comes right out and says it. She's an outrageous person.

Again, in Laura's words, "I see my students as inherently good." The facilitator's attitude of *prizing/unconditional positive regard*, involves respect as well as caring for the learner in a non-possessive way, "a belief that the other person is somehow fundamentally trustworthy" (Rogers & Freiberg, 1994, p. 156). "I think of it as prizing the learner – prizing her feelings, her opinions, her person. It is caring for the learner, but non-possessive caring" (p. 156). Frances was a model of prizing Jean as she her interaction with Frances made Jean feel valued and valuable, comfortable and quite capable. In Chapter 9, Leslie explains as well, "My grandparents are the only people who treated me like I would have liked to have been treated. They seemed to care about me regardless of what I did, without putting all the limitations and restrictions on me. To me it was unconditional love."

The facilitator's attitude of empathy/*empathetic understanding* has to do with the ability to "understand the student's reactions from the [the student's] inside, a sensitive awareness of the way the process of education and learning seems to the student" (Rogers & Freiberg, 1994, p. 157). Such understanding on the part of the facilitator increases the likelihood of significant learning because the facilitator's instructional approach benefits from putting themselves in the learner's place, feeling what the learner may be feeling, imagining the thoughts the learner may be thinking, all of this before, during and after the teaching-learning encounter. Those learner thoughts and feelings are integrated into the facilitator's design, implementation and evaluation of learning encounters, a process that not only leads to superior instruction, but improved human interaction, as well. For Frances to become the very powerful model of empathetic understanding that she became for Jean, Frances had to, on a regular basis, put herself in Jean's place, to feel what it was like to be Jean, to feel Jean's frustrations and joys. Through practicing empathy/empathetic understanding with Jean, Frances was able to know, in precise terms, just what Jean needed to hear so Jean could overcome her frustrations and life impediments, and feel far more fulfilled as a young adult.

Rogers does not suggest that all improved interaction between teacher and learner will be harmonious. The facilitator-learner relationship, as with all human relationships, involves at least some disharmony.

Empathetic understanding increases the likelihood of significant learning. Rogers observes "that when teachers are empathetically understanding, their students tend to like each other better. In an understanding classroom climate, every student tends to feel liked by all the others, has a more positive attitude toward self, and a positive attitude toward school" (Rogers & Freiberg, p. 161). For Rogers, when facilitators model understanding attitudes in the process of interacting with others, that demonstration of understanding helps learners develop the capacity for empathetic understanding as well. Frances' modeling of empathetic understanding helped Jean to develop her own capacity for empathetic understanding that she then shared with young children. When learners practice empathetic understanding in their interaction with their peers, the entire community is elevated. All begin to have feelings of validation and worthiness. Teachers, applying a model of empathetic understanding, may reverse negative classroom behavior and relationships as they model better and more effective ways of relating. Negative interaction with learners may be avoided if facilitators collectively practice this approach.

3   A Bit on Trust from Rogers

The facilitator must trust the learner's capacity for development (Rogers & Freiberg, 1994). The learner's trust in the facilitator enables the facilitator to provide many opportunities that guide the learner in the process of choosing their own way, or their own direction in learning, as is the case with inquiry or project–centered learning. Likewise, the facilitator's attitude enables the learner to trust the facilitator, both as a facilitator and as a person. Again, the key is the facilitator's attitude because that attitude allows the cycle of trust to begin. Because the facilitator has traditionally had a dominant role, trust must emerge with the facilitator who must trust *and* also be trustworthy in the eyes of the learner. To be really effective, the facilitator must trust and be trustworthy, *at the first moment of interaction* with the learner. In this way, the facilitator initiates the cycle of trust that transcends the uneasiness and fear created by past, negative learning situations. In Chapter 7, Kathy shares about the first moments with her facilitator:

> The first day that I came into [his] class, [he] said to everyone "This is Kathy," and everybody said "Hi!" And, I thought, "What is this?" … I thought, "Wow! This is a family oriented class, and we're all going to be friends." I got that impression from the very beginning ….

If there was something that we needed help with, we could come to [him] and [he] could at least point us in the right direction. If [he] also saw a person needing a little morale boost, [he] asked other people to bring them in under their wing and take care of them, help them out, and include them. That struck me as being something most teachers don't do. If someone was out on their own, most teachers just let them be out there, on their own. They don't try to bring them in.

4 The Move toward Freedom

As the facilitator transcends long held learner fears, a subtle atmosphere in which the learner, operating in good faith, is made aware that they will not be dealt with unfairly or in a way that is threatening. The environment created by such facilitators is one of acceptance, as evidenced in the example of Peggy and Mr. Santon. Rogers and Freiberg (1994) explain:

> I only came into the attitudes I have described and the trust in the individual that is implicit in them because I found that these attitudes were so much more potent in producing learning and constructive change. Hence, I believe that it is only by risking herself in these new ways that the teacher can *discover*, for herself, whether or not they are effective, whether or not they are for her. (p. 160)

Essentially, the facilitator must be committed to caring more about the learner than the course content, and must value human beings preeminently over academic curricula. In Chapter 15, facilitator Beth's approach aligns beautifully with Rogers' perspective:

> To tell you the truth, more than even their ability to read, I am most concerned with their emotional growth. I never felt the subjects I taught were the most important outcomes. Most of my students were very creative and that's why they ended up in trouble a lot in school.

The facilitator must have faith in the learner's ability to succeed, even to succeed after the original learning situation has passed. Similarly, it is certain that depending on the learner's personal predicament, an act of faith is required for the learner to *go beyond* in the developing relation with the facilitator. That is, the facilitator's faith and trust in the learner becomes a catalyst which sets the learner on a path to freedom, thereby providing the opportunity for the learner to learn and transcend in profound, meaningful ways. It is that freedom, sustained by faith and trust that affords what Rogers refers to as *magnetism* between the learning experience and the learner.

One's freedom to choose how one will learn heightens the process of positive change. Freedom generates the context upon which discovery and transcendence are nourished. For freedom to emerge, a profound partnership between the facilitator and learner must exist, which is why Peggy, in Chapter 3, facilitates that process by telling her learners, "for the next forty-five minutes, nothing, nothing in this world exists but you and me."

Confidence and trust in the learner seem to go hand in hand in transcendent teacher learner relationships. If one is inclined to trust the other, it follows, at least for teachers and learners whose stories are chronicled in this book, that one has confidence in the other. When confidence in another's ability to succeed is expressed, that confidence has a marvelous affirming and enabling effect on the receiver. Having confidence in the other enables the other to envision circumstances as they could be otherwise and to subsequently pursue them. Peggy describes the impact that Mr. Santon's trust and confidence had for her:

> This is weird. I felt like I was in the spotlight. But there was no spotlight – ... [there] was a shimmer, and at that moment, I couldn't do anything wrong. I really couldn't. And I didn't. It brought me dignity, grandeur. He made me feel like ... the most intelligent, and the most wonderful person in the world.
>
> Until then I felt that I could have just dropped in a hole somewhere and wouldn't have been missed. But he made me feel that I mattered, as if the world would have missed out if I weren't a part of it. This is the type of human interaction that causes one to forget negative and sometimes even suicidal thoughts.

5 Mother Love

For philosopher and educator Theodore Klein (1989), the ideal for teaching is a non-genderized *mother love*. He explains that expressing trust and confidence in the learner undergirds a developing relationship. In an article entitled, "Teaching and Mother Love" Klein posits *mother love* as "a normative ideal for teaching" (p. 373). The mother love Klein refers to is motivated by, but not limited to, three concerns:

1. preservation/protection
2. growth
3. attentiveness (pp. 376, 377).

The reader will note below how *distancing* and *fairness* are also components of mother love.

The first of these, *preservation/protection*, refers to the effort to keep the child protected from harm on the part of the one practicing mother love. Such an attitude of concern is responsive to the child's vulnerability. Likewise, the teacher, motivated by mother love, commits to support the learner's "fragile confidence" (p. 377).

Klein's preservation and protection however, within the context of mother love, is balanced by an emphasis on the *growth* of the child. The vulnerable learner needs a degree of protection, but that protection also supports the learner's freedom. It is a type of protection that welcomes change (p. 377). Therefore, the teacher must nudge and release the learner to develop on their own accord. The reader may recall Peggy's struggle to move beyond protection in an effort to help them learn to "fly."

With Klein's mother love, the learner is not treated as a being to be shaped or molded. Rather, the child's ability to develop and flourish, presumably even to take ownership and direct much of her own development, is supported and nourished by the teacher. All of this occurs as part of the balance of protection that is achieved, or can be achieved, when appropriate protection is provided. Balance emerges again as a critical component of the relationship fine tuning process. The focus of the practitioner of mother love is on identifying limits that assist in the process of achieving balance. In Chapter 5, Jean protects the child as she and the child work between clearly established limits during the fine-tuning process of balancing freedom with the development of self-discipline. The practitioner of mother love avoids placing *limitations* on the learner. Limitations include any actions that inhibit development such as labeling, denial of opportunity on the basis of test scores or other limiting, potentially debilitating actions.

Attentiveness "involves seeking to understand what the child is going through" (Klein, 1989, p. 377). Consistent with Van Manen's tact, Klein's attentiveness has to do with "sensitivity and delicate timing" (p. 378), sensing when to intervene and when not to intervene. It involves staying close, supporting and being engaged with the learner who may be fearful of the process of change or of learning. Attentiveness also involves taking steps back, letting go, and waiting for the learner, who otherwise may not be confident enough to proceed (p. 378). Attentiveness enables the teacher to know when attachment is appropriate, and when detachment is appropriate. Attentiveness involves the teacher's capacity to fully perceive the learner's situation and to respond to it appropriately. Thus again, attentiveness in Klein's mother love is similar to Van Manen's tact, Noddings' engrossment and Rogers' empathetic understanding. If for example, a learner's parents are going through a divorce, the teacher, practicing attentiveness through sensitivity and delicate timing, watches and listens for the learner's grief and how that learner interacts with others. That is, through careful watching and listening the teacher may, with sensitivity and delicate timing, extend additional support, additional delicacy, and additional tenderness to that learner, continuing to do so throughout the crisis.

Through attentiveness the teacher is enabled to communicate effectively with the learner. The teacher, motivated by mother love, attends to the learner's present skills and feelings. The teacher seeks to increase the learner's confidence, and to decrease their self-consciousness. On the other hand, the attentiveness Klein (Klein, 1989) proposes, "cannot be captured by any formula, principle, or set of principles" (p. 378), but is instead a matter of tuning in closely and responding to the learner in such a way that comes through heartfelt understanding. Again, the congruence between attentiveness, Van Manen's tact, Noddings' engrossment and Rogers' empathetic understanding is apparent. In Chapter 9, Leslie shares how attentiveness emerges in her relationships with her learners:

> It sounds kind of arrogant, but it's a communication just the two of us have in some way. I try to find out what their background is and then say "OK, what do I have today, how can I move myself to that place, into that mindset, so we're in sync, on one kind of wavelength?"

In Chapter 2, Anne [Sullivan] ... [practices attentiveness by calibrating] Helen's myriad capacities and designs a plan to operationalize those capacities. Anne uses her personal and ongoing struggles with her own eyesight, and even more her second sight, her intuition, to inform her strategy to facilitate the unfolding of her solitary vision for Helen's transcendence and transformation.

Throughout this process of attentiveness, Klein emphasizes that the teacher, fully practicing mother love, must remain whole, not engaging in excessive self-denial or excessive self-sacrifice as a show of mother love. Such an approach of self-denial or excessive self-sacrifice is the opposite of mother love. While well practiced mother love "... directs attention clearly and fully to the child or student" (Klein, 1989, p. 378), it also involves a kind of relational caring for oneself that "contrasts with self-indulgence and extreme self-denial" (p. 378). Unlike "predominantly one-way nurturing relationships," practicing mother love involves "receiving as well a giving nurturing, [wherein] a person is in a better position to nurture well in mothering or in teaching" (p. 378).

Caring is, of course, a core component of mother love. Moreover, Klein's (1989) approach involves more than caring. Indeed, "mother love presupposes and specifies a kind of caring as an ideal" (p. 379). The teacher motivated by mother love recognizes the learner's vulnerability, avoids harshness because harshness "discourages further efforts and reinforces feelings of failure" (p. 380). Again, Klein does not advocate "excessive protectiveness" (p. 380). When mother love is practiced well, the practitioner recognizes when a learner "may need to be dependent up to a point and [the teacher] accepts that. But the same teacher searches out avenues for helping the learner to grow beyond dependence and for building confidence in the learner" (p. 380). Caring for Jean helped Frances grasp Jean's sense of vulnerability. Once Frances was fully aware of Jean's vulnerability, Frances was able to support Jean by providing the necessary messages for Jean to *overcome* those vulnerabilities.

Distancing also plays a role in mother love. Klein's (1989) connotation of distancing is unique as his mother love involves *distancing from oneself*, in the moment, rather than from the other. "Distancing from self involves stepping away from oneself, and one's own feelings and needs so that one can attend clearly to the child or student" (p. 380). In this sense Klein's distancing parallels Noddings' motivational displacement. With Klein's *temporary* distancing process (not to be confused with the extreme self denial referenced above), the teacher's attention moves from that teacher's own reality to the reality of the learner. For example, if the teacher is going through a serious illness, that ill teacher, as a practitioner of mother love, must rise above this personal crisis and meet the needs of each learner with the same determination they would use if no crisis existed. The process of rising above one's own dilemmas does not preclude the teacher from sharing openly with learners about personal health struggles. Rather, the teacher's practice of distancing enables them to rise above their personal dilemma, in this case a serious illness, thereby empowering the teacher to provide learners whatever they may need to assure their optimal development. The process of distancing may also have a healing effect on the teacher, as has occurred in my own practice of distancing. Because I practiced distancing from my own dilemma, my students were able to help me overcome my inability to feel authentic joy.

Fairness is another component of the practitioner of mother love. The teacher practicing mother love makes sure that no student is left out of consideration; no one student is favored over another and no one is neglected. Fairness is the practice of meeting every learner's needs, however divergent those needs may be. Klein (1989) recognizes that "a teacher may personally like some students more than others" (p. 381). Nonetheless, each student is to be extended "a love that nurtures them as they learn and grow" (p. 381).

Such a loving approach involves, for example, taking extra time to talk outside of class or during transitions with quiet or shy learners, exceptional learners who perhaps require more one-on-one conversations, or more attention and guidance on a given day than others may require. Therefore, the practitioner of mother love and fairness, on subsequent days deliberately acts to extend their attention and guidance to learners who were less needy on the previous day.

The extra conversations with more demure learners aid in giving them confidence to venture more into class participation. Klein identifies conversation between a teacher and a learner as a valid and powerful way to ensure that no learner feels left out. Philosophers and theorists cited in this book indicate that conversation, referred to by many as dialogue, is a foundational component in the teacher's work in terms of going beyond with learners, beyond the ordinary or what has heretofore existed. Any attention given to one learner, again, does not involve favoring that student at the expense of others (p. 381).

Concerns for the vulnerability of the learner, for fairness, for distancing, and for including each learner are all essential aspects of the disciplined practice of mother love. According to Klein (1989), mother love can energize and animate teaching. Moreover, he asserts that practicing mother love well "involves the strongest kind of motivation for teaching well ..." (p. 382). Practicing mother love satisfies and benefits the teacher as well as the learner.

Klein notes that the teacher's practice of mother love plays an important role in the students' learning to love and care for others, their peers for example, in attentive ways. For Klein, "A foundation for teaching students to love and care is provided by teachers themselves practicing love and caring. Children need to learn [this] not only for intimate situations, such as home and friendships, but also for a range of public activities extending to large societal and global concerns" (Klein, 1989, p. 382).

Although Klein recognizes that "realities in families often go against the ideal of mother love" he describes (Klein, 1989, p. 383), he emphasizes that mother love has been undervalued "in this society and the concept itself has been destructively connected with gender and sex roles" (p. 383). Klein endeavors to "free the term from limiting gender associations" (p. 379). Maternal practice *can* inform the development of educational models as well (p. 383). Klein acknowledges that schoolroom realities may include many obstacles to the practice of mother love, but mother love, nonetheless represents an *ideal* for teaching (p. 383).

In his book *Mothering* (1977), professor of psychology Rudolph Shaffer concurs with Klein that mothering skills, attitude and affection are not gender restrictive.

> The ability to rear a child, to love and cherish and care for him, is basically a matter of personality. There is no reason why the mothering role should not be filled as competently by males as by females. (pp. 103, 104)

Mothering, according to Shaffer, is a matter of mutual involvement, reciprocity and partnership. The one who assumes the mother role allows for reciprocity by personalizing new experiences and information for a particular child or learner. The mother ensures that the new stimulus connects with the child's *internal state*, the child's inclination to attend and willingness to reciprocate (p. 58). Changes in the learner, then, are not imposed from outside. Rather as the connection is established, the child chooses to respond positively. Ultimately however, both caregiver and learner are engaged in a process that changes them, even as they change each other in a joint venture (p. 77).

> [The mother's] relationship with the child is rather that of a partner, though a senior partner by virtue of being more experienced, more powerful, and more likely to have consciously formulated ideas about the purpose and direction of their interaction. The fine degree of interpersonal synchrony that is so particularly evident when we study interactions microscopically, a highly intricate pattern of interaction that subsequently develops the sheer experience of mutual contact. (p. 77)

As Klein (1989) and Shaffer (1977) have suggested, the key to the parent or teacher's relational success is the capacity to see the child's experience from the child's point of view. For Klein, sensitivity underlies this capacity. Shaffer emphasizes that insensitivity, on the part of those who assume the mother role, are the "greatest obstacle to the child's developmental progress" (p. 86).

Shaffer (1977) also concurs with Klein regarding the importance of the child receiving love from the caregiver. As a child receives love, he develops a capacity for returning it and giving it to others. Without receiving love, the child's ability to love fully will be stunted. He or she becomes what has been called an "affectionless character," one who cannot love later in life because he or she had never known love as a child" (p. 96).

6   Questions for Thought

1. How does Carl Rogers define the facilitator and how does the facilitator function?

2. How does Rogers' facilitator differ from a traditional teacher?

3. Define Rogers' three essential attitudes of the facilitator. How do they guide the facilitator?

4. What is most significant about Rogers' notion of freedom?

5. Condense Theodore Klein's mother love as a model for teaching into one paragraph.

6. What are the primary concerns of the practitioner of Klein's mother love? How does each concern guide the practitioner of mother love?

7. Identify three teachers who practiced Klein's mother love in your K-12 education.

8. What evidence of Klein's mother love exist in those examples?

CHAPTER 7

Portraits of Transcendent Relators
Lauren and Kathy

> It makes you feel like someone. It's being around somebody and talking and sharing feelings, and knowing that somebody else is caring.
> LAUREN

∴

1   Portrait of Lauren

One year, shortly after her high school classes began, I mentioned to another faculty member that Lauren was in my class. Lauren has cerebral palsy and was virtually wheelchair bound. She had short dark hair, and large dark eyes. The teacher I spoke with immediately began to comment about Lauren's wonderfully positive attitude and her strong commitment to learning. The teacher's comments, however, were no surprise to me after having had just one interaction with Lauren. I immediately found her to be personable, thoughtful and inspiring. She was enthusiastic about our class.

As the days passed, Lauren was quietly supportive of my work as her teacher, but never demanding. Her expressions and manner reflected her very serious contemplation of important issues in class. Her questions were fresh, thoughtful and responsible. During class, she provided a second conscience for me, reminding me of details and significant information I may have neglected, or not even considered in the spin of teaching. Lauren's perceptions as a differently-abled person gave her a unique frame of reference. In her talks with her colleagues and teachers, she suggested alternatives and options to them that they had previously never considered. She always thought ahead. Our developing relationship provided an open door for her to offer contributions. Lauren was absolutely dedicated to our class efforts.

Lauren was there for me, as I tried to be there for her, day by day. The confidence Lauren had in me, I believe, helped me to be a better teacher. When people believe in you and you know very well they do, you rise to the occasion and your performance improves. Clearly the same dynamic is in place as that supportive energy flows from the teacher to the learner. Because she was inspiring and very capable, she was highly respected by her peers, she provided a strong role model for them, influencing them and spreading a spirit of collaboration.

2   Lauren's School Experiences

Even though Lauren offered a model of collaboration to her peers, she did not learn that model in her childhood experiences at school. As a child, Lauren was never able to play with other children or interact with them much. She also felt rejection from school authorities. Lauren could sense the fear many teachers had when they were called upon to work with people who were handicapped. Some would have nothing to do with her.

> I went to Edgewood Acres until the third grade, and then they mainstreamed me in a school which was right around the corner. But the principal didn't want me there because I required an aide, and so my Mom said, "Well, I can come and take her to the bathroom." But they didn't want me. They transferred me to another school before my mom even knew about it.

The older Lauren became, the more she felt separated from her peers, and the walls between them seemed to grow higher. Because of her physical situation, she was excluded from the thick of activities. She was isolated. She was not afforded a chance to reveal what she *could* do. Lauren talked of how the relationship between her and me began.

> During registration, the counselor said, "We are now going to be offering a chorus class." I was excited because that was the first extracurricular activity that I could participate in. And I thought, "Well, I can sing, so I can participate." And so I was thrilled to death, because finally, it was something that I could do, which meant the world to me. I mean, everybody else was out there playing, and this was something that *I* could do.
>
> It wasn't that I was insecure or anything, because I didn't have that. This was my chance to be involved in extracurricular activities. That was the key thing that pulled it all together. I was ready for the chance to excel in something else besides schoolwork.

To Lauren's delight, the class atmosphere in chorus was relaxing and fun for her, even calming. People laughed and interacted in class and were very familiar with each other. The tone was bright and homey. Lauren explained that "People were laughing and carrying on, like back home with your father, mother and relatives just laughing and having a good time together." She felt she was treated like an adult in that class.

She felt that I "was there" for her, whatever the need, whether it was educational or personal. Lauren described her first impressions.

> You just looked like a friend, or a student. I didn't realize you were a teacher. I just thought you were another student, but then, you were our teacher because you didn't allow any foolishness. You cut up and you joked, but it was in your own way. You gave us enough room, but you had discipline. You challenged me in a lot of ways, and I know that I hadn't been challenged before. But when you challenged and we didn't succeed, you weren't down on us. We learned through trial and error. You were full of energy and enthusiasm. That's what helped.
>
> There are some teachers that are so boring you hate to go in their classes. It makes me feel more comfortable if teachers are enthusiastic because they help me out more, they make me feel more at ease than, for example, when someone doesn't even know I'm there. You energized us and we took an interest. You had such a sense of pride about it; you wanted us to be the best we could be, and that made us work harder. And then we had a sense of pride about our choir. We were motivated and excited about what we were doing. I respected you because of your honesty, what you stood for. You never gave me any reason to question your judgment or put down anyone for any reason. You gave me encouragement, advice and feedback, and allowed me personal and mental growth. You helped me explore alternatives in my life, without being pushy. Your insight was very important in my case.

3 Lauren's Connection with Her Teacher

Lauren felt freer to talk because I took an interest in her, and wanted her to be the best she could be. She was included in everything we did. Lauren believed that I looked out for her, and she could rely on that.

I was very conscious of Lauren's needs in this respect because as a child, I was awkward with sports and suffered a great deal of humiliation in physical education/gym classes. I knew what it meant to be left out, disregarded or looked down upon because of things I had no control over. I was determined that, in every way within my power, Lauren would be fully involved, fully assisted when necessary, and fully respected in my rehearsal classroom.

> When we had a performance, you didn't leave me out. You always included me. You were the only teacher that did that. Some other teachers didn't want the trouble, or the bother. You didn't discriminate against me because I was in a wheelchair. There were some teachers, for example, that no matter how good you are, if you're in a wheelchair they put a label on you, but you didn't do that. I was thankful that you took the time with me to help me in any way that you could.
>
> When you said you would do something, I knew I could depend on you to do everything in your power to get it done. I did not have to keep asking you whether a location was accessible for wheelchairs. This is where the trust came into our relationship. The worry of "will I be able to get into a place" was dismissed from my mind because I knew that it was taken care of.
>
> I felt I could come to you and talk about anything, about everyday things like what I would talk to Mom and Dad about. I don't really know if I would have felt comfortable around you had I not had been helped the way I was, because I have to get to know somebody well before I start sharing. You just don't walk up to somebody and start telling them your whole life history. And it wasn't that I didn't find it in other teachers, it was just that other teachers didn't take the time for me to really see what I could be outside the class, outside of my little classroom.

With a breaking voice she said, "you'll never know what it did for me."

It was so important that Lauren's needs be met in an individualized, personalized way. At the same time she was very much enabled to feel like "one of the kids." Lauren felt uplifted in chorus. When the teacher set an example, Lauren believes other students looked "beyond" her wheelchair and saw the person inside it.

Lauren emphasizes the importance of the learner's self-esteem, which she believes can be nurtured by the teacher in positive, caring ways. Self-esteem, motivation, freedom and discipline go hand-in-hand for Lauren. Without support, many learners like Lauren, encounter despair and see no reason for moving beyond where they are. Lauren said,

> It doesn't have to be hugging, touching, or even praise. It could be just through the teacher's words and how they express themselves and act. It

> makes you feel like something. It's being around somebody and talking and sharing feelings, and knowing that somebody else is caring.

To summarize, Lauren makes very clear the essential roles insight, dependability and trust play in her transcendent relationship. Equally important are conversation and the sharing of feelings, in a way that is possible only because the teacher first drew her out and made her feel comfortable, not someone to be pitied. Her teacher's encouragement and enthusiasm challenged her in ways she had not encountered before. Within a personalized relational context, self-esteem, motivation, freedom and discipline work in tandem.

4   Portrait of Kathy

> I seem to function better, in whatever I'm doing, if I'm on a more personal level with the person I'm dealing with.
> KATHY

Kathy's braces and rubber bands did not distract from her big adolescent smile. She was a generally quiet but powerful influence in the learning community. Her affect was always businesslike, but full of good cheer. The tone of our interaction was collegial. Kathy's belief in my efforts was invaluable. Through supporting me, she helped me facilitate positive group psychology. She was absolutely dependable, like my own arm.

I was impressed with the comfortable quality which surrounded our interaction before, during, and after class. Her sense of humor, her earnestness, maturity and sophistication appealed to me. I think most teachers enjoy such qualities in learners. Her hearty laughter uplifted, freed and reassured me.

Like Jean, much of Kathy's personal style can be traced to her childhood. As a child, her mother treated her as an equal, interacting with her as someone would with another adult. Kathy's mother asked Kathy's opinion on various issues that arose in home life. She reasoned with Kathy about her concerns, examined possibilities with her and then left many decisions up to Kathy.

> We worked together a lot. She always asked my opinion on everything, the furniture, the paint, and the car that we bought. It was always, "Well, what do you think? Do you like the color? Do you like the style? Do you think we ought to go with something just a little bit bigger, or something a little bit smaller?" There was always a real equal relationship there.

5   Kathy in High School

When Kathy was in high school she developed a personal relationship with an English teacher. That teacher responded to Kathy as if she understood her, trusted and respected her. The two had a kind of empathic communication. The relationship went beyond what the teacher, or Kathy, seemed to experience with other students and teachers. Kathy spoke of an encounter she had with that teacher.

> A close friend of mine left the area the day after graduation, and came to see me the morning that he was flying out. He was going to Florida, and I was in the hall talking to him. The bell rang and I didn't go into my class. My teacher knew I was out there, and she came out, looked at me, and saw tears running down my face. She'd seen the two of us get together from the beginning of the year. She didn't say a word, turned around, and went back in the classroom. It was because of the relationship that we had that she understood, and she seemed to be saying, "Okay, just take the time you need. I know you're going to come back, and I know you're going to do what you need to do, but I also know that you need to do this now." She was a very personal kind of teacher.

As a new learner in my class, Kathy quickly felt at home. It was her place, a warm place. I had auditioned Kathy and she noted that I knew her by name.

> The first day that I came into your class, you said to everyone "This is Kathy," and everybody said "Hi!" And, I thought, "What is this?" I'd never seen that before. Usually you walk into a class and you hear "This is so and so," and you take your seat and you go on. But I thought, "Wow! This is a family oriented class, and we're all going to be friends." I got that impression from the very beginning. I thought, "everyone is treating me like I'm supposed to be here, and this is my place." That was unprecedented.

Kathy noted that I was available and accessible to her, not only for classroom matters, but for life matters. She was struck when I asked certain students to take their peers under their wing, and to give them a lift.

> If there was something that we needed help with, we could come to you and you could at least point us in the right direction. If you also saw a person needing a little morale boost, you asked other people to bring

them in under their wing and take care of them, help them out, and include them. That struck me as being something most teachers don't do. If someone was out on their own, most teachers just let them be out there, on their own. They don't try to bring them in.

Kathy felt we had an intimate sort of relationship, like the one she mentioned with her English teacher, in which much could be said without a lot of words.

> I remember we used to go to your office in the morning before school, we'd sit out and wait for you to get there and eat breakfast in the hall, and then go into your office. I don't know if we ever did anything constructive while we were there. It was more personal, more than just going down for classes. It was having a personal contact with the teacher. It helped to build the bond. I don't know exactly how to explain it. It reaffirmed, in my mind, that you were more of a personal type, that it wasn't just a strict role. I think that was important for me because I seem to function better in whatever I'm doing if I'm on a more personal level with the person I'm dealing with. I think I function better when I have a friend-friendship instead of a teacher-learner friendship or relationship. I think it goes back to respecting each other and having that loyalty and the honesty, and, at the heart of it all, it is a matter of being friends.

Kathy believes in respect, loyalty and honesty as being powerful elements of the teacher learner relationship.

> I think you gave us a lot of responsibility and I think that in order to give us that responsibility, you had to respect us to a certain degree. The fact that you trusted me enough to give me responsibility and let me perform them my way, as long as I got the results that were needed, I respected you for that.

She felt that I pushed her, but she was assured that it was because she knew that I wanted the best possible experience for her. She relished being treated, as an adult. It was a give and take.

> Your approach was, "I'll treat you like an adult but you have to act like an adult in order to receive that." I went into that thinking, "Well, I'm mature, and he's going to treat me like I have something important to give and I'm going to give him what he wants."

She appreciated the non-competitive classroom atmosphere where people could work together *as a family*, as equals in what she refers to as a *respectful community*. In respectful, community-oriented families, people do not compete with each other.

Kathy was impressed as well with the informal singing "tests" we had. I asked Kathy to describe.

> The singing exams for grades that we did; for example, some would be sitting, and some would be standing. Sometimes I'd get up and start singing, and get real shaky and real scared, and all we had to do was look at you and it was like automatic – everything that you taught, all of it would come back to me. We'd get right back into it. I haven't had that kind of relationship with any of my teachers. We had a good time in class. I can go to another instructor for, say, like a reference or something, but that level just isn't there.

Kathy felt that she had a kind of empathy, a deep understanding of my efforts as a teacher.

> When we were practicing, I would get to a point where I would know what you were going for before you got there with the music. I think, in a way, I could see where you were going a lot of the times when you would tell us that we needed to do a certain thing. It seemed that some others couldn't see past just the action. If I know what you're going for, it makes it easier to get there. It was real positive, because I knew why I was doing everything I was doing. I think it depends a lot on the learner too, because a lot of people just can't see past what they're doing right now.

Kathy supported me, so much so that she was able to act on my behalf when I was placed on administrative transfer due to the school's declining enrollment. Kathy explained.

> Because of the relationship I felt we had, I didn't want you to go anywhere else. So I wrote my letter to the Superintendent. It was the first time that I had actually taken steps and actively done something because of something I believed in. It brought back everything that I'd learned at home: to stand up for myself, to take action and to play an active role. I'd never had to do that before. It was just something that I believed in, so I went with it, full force.

6   Kathy at College

That decision and her subsequent efforts were a turning point in her development. Later, she attended a large university with large classes and little personal attention from instructors. Recognizing her need for more personal interaction, Kathy felt confident to transfer to a smaller institution at the end of her freshman year. Many freshmen do not possess the maturity or initiative to make such informed choices at the end of their first year. Kathy's good judgment and courage at an early age could arguably be attributed to the skills she developed at an early age under her mother's tutelage.

> It got to the point that I didn't want to be there, and I felt like my teachers didn't want to be there. I actually had one professor sit there and tell me "I don't like being here at eight o'clock in the morning either. I don't want to be here." Everybody knew that he didn't want to be there, and *everybody suffered because of it*. I don't see how a learner can get anything out of the class if the teacher doesn't want to be there. I think there are too many teachers who look at teaching strictly as something they have to do, but not because they want to. The student can tell when a teacher doesn't want to be there, and I think that a teacher not wanting to be in a classroom negatively affects the way the student performs.

For Kathy, there is a great contrast between college professors who, for example, admitted they do not want to be there, and those who talk to her, create a relaxed environment, and relate to her on her level. She believes that when a teacher creates a personal environment, one in which the learner is treated with regard, that discipline and commitment become automatic. The teacher is not required to enforce rules because the learner responds, as Palmer (1983) has suggested, with "glad obedience." To summarize, Kathy's relationships with her mother and the teachers discussed were personal ones in which care, equality and mutual regard were demonstrated. She has highlighted the deep understanding and empathy that exists in those relationships. Her mother and her teachers demonstrated faith in her, gave her responsibility and challenged her. Important also for Kathy is the presence of a family oriented type of community environment, in which people respect each other in a way that is not possible in competitive arenas.

7 Questions for Thought

1. How did Kathy's English teacher demonstrate that her philosophy was transcendence-oriented?

2. How did Kathy's mother demonstrate that she was a transcendence-oriented parent?

3. How did Lauren help her teacher?

4. How would you describe Lauren's self-concept, and its evolution?

5. How can transcendent teachers facilitate learners with special needs to be successful in their classes?

6. Identify five factors that enabled Lauren to become part of the class community.

7. How did teachers in Lauren's past fail to meet her needs?

8. What does Kathy need and expect from teachers and professors?

9. How do teachers make all learners comfortable in class?

10. What kind of colleague and friend do you expect that Kathy would be if you knew her?

CHAPTER 8

Risk, Authority and Trust

> And, oh, my gosh, we would kill for [Mr. Santon]. I mean, it wasn't a cult. It's just that I wanted to be around him all the time because he made me feel good about myself.
>
> PEGGY

∴

Peggy is committed to taking risks for her learners in the same way Mr. Santon took a risk that his learners might not come through each time he challenged them to move to the next distant level of development. He did all of this while doing everything he could to express his confidence and trust in them. And that is why Peggy is so committed to doing the same for her learners. Jean is devoted to Frances because Frances made Jean feel safe to take risks in her own life. Both Lauren and Kathy speak of the family atmosphere in their class and how that atmosphere helped them to feel safe to take risks, even during test taking.

Like Peggy, Jean, Kathy and Lauren, existentialist philosopher of education and voluminous education writer, German Otto Bollnow (1972) is concerned with creating secure learning atmospheres that facilitate risk-taking as well as trust and approachability to emerge in teaching and learning relationships. Such qualities, he believes, create an atmosphere of security such as has been demonstrated above. Bollnow describes and analyzes below what must happen for such atmospheres to emerge.

1   Authority and Corresponding Risk

For Bollnow (1972) teachers need to release their grip and dependence on their *traditional authority* over the learner. *Traditional authority* is operationalized in a climate wherein the teacher talks and the learner listens; the teacher chooses and enforces their own choices while students must adapt and comply with those choices; the teacher disciplines and the students are disciplined, according to Paulo Freire.

Rather for Bollnow, a different dynamic, another way of perceiving authority, a *new authority dynamic* is needed. The teacher, applying a different type of authority, indeed a new authority dynamic, may well know that the order cannot be forced when the order is given. Nonetheless, Bollnow (1972) says,

> I cannot limit myself to cases in which my orders are certain to be followed, for in such cases, my orders are merely carried out in a mechanical nature and would lack any educational value. I have to give those orders that I cannot be sure will be carried out. From this uncertainty arises the real risk of giving orders, a risk that educational responsibility requires me to accept. (p. 528)

The learner needs to be called upon to submit voluntarily to the teacher's demand. Meaningful education begins when the teacher orders something that cannot be fulfilled by forcing or coercing the learner. For example, when the teacher holds a grade over the learner's head to achieve learner compliance, taking little or no risk on the learner's behalf, the field of possible learning opportunity is constricted. The teacher must, instead, find ways of risking for the learner without the security that a grade may provide for the teacher. The risk-taking teacher, while closely monitoring the learner's developmental process, may demonstrate trust in the learner by facilitating projects that involve honor systems and by providing opportunities for learners to resubmit assignments without penalty, in order to facilitate the learner's deeper and more meaningful development. This also demonstrates the teacher's non-reliance on grades as motivators. Occasionally the learner may take inappropriate advantage of such opportunities but that inclination decreases as the teacher continues to demonstrate trust in, and care for, the learner.

I may, for example, give learners an assignment that has no grade attached. I call upon them to do their very best because of the important nature of the assignment. I then explain why the assignment is so important even though no grade will be given for the assignment. And yet as their teacher I am taking a risk that my learners may not comply with my requirements and take advantage of no grade for the assignment. I risk that learners will take advantage of whatever honor system we put in place, but they never have and the outcome has always been positive for all concerned. Instead, I find that my learners recognize my risk and delight in cooperating with me. For over four decades, I have never regretted the risks I have taken with students.

Bollnow suggests that the very anticipation of a particular grade forestalls the potential to create a deep, meaningful learning experience because the learner is attached to the grade more than the quality of the learning experience. For teachers to force the learner's obedience through physical might, grades, or school regulation is not enough to accomplish the task Bollnow recommends. Again, teachers must risk that compliance might not occur.

Teacher risk-taking on behalf of learners may seem questionable for teachers who are unwilling to take such risks. Nonetheless, in the process of rejecting the temptation to coerce learners, new authority dynamic teachers risk themselves and in the process champion the learner's welfare.

Assuming that I have created well-developed and clearly articulated assignments and group learning projects, I take the risk and trust that my learners will work diligently to complete those projects, even when I am not directly overseeing them. I anticipate fun and laughter *even as* I have confidence that learners will complete the task well. Teachers must take such risks to build trust with learners. Otherwise, long-held cultures of mistrust, or non-trust, re-emerge that are firmly established in the learner's past. The teacher who risks to trust reverses such cultures.

Recall that Kathy describes her experience with her teacher's risk-taking behavior and trust this way:

> I think [he] gave us a lot of responsibility and I think that in order to give us that responsibility, [he] had to respect us .... The fact that [he] trusted me enough to give me responsibility and let me perform them my way, as long as I got the results that were needed, I respected [him] for that.
>
> [His] approach was, "I'll treat you like an adult but you have to act like an adult in order to receive that." I went into that thinking, "Well, I'm mature, and he's going to treat me like I have something important to give and I'm going to give him what he wants."

From the teacher perspective in Chapter 9, Leslie explains her risk-taking and the result she derives from it:

> "I take risks in everything. It seems like the risks I take in teaching are much more successful than any of the risks that I take in non-teaching relationships. Whenever students encounter a problem I will try every approach until a solution to the problem is found. There is never one solution for all learners. I find out what works best for them. I always try to do it with some sense of humor so it's not a really serious "this has to be done," or "this has to be accomplished" situation. Also I tell them "it's OK" and "it's no big deal that we are trying to fix this." ... I try to downplay the seriousness. I try to say that it's not that they're having problems or there

has been a mistake or anything. Rather, I say "let's just try to find a way to make it easier or do it better or make it sound better. Whatever it has to be to accommodate their needs is the way we will do it."

To accomplish her goals, Leslie must also present herself as a figure who is much different from a traditional authority model.

New authority, for Bollnow (1989), is to be mediated through attention and care. That is, through attention and care, risk is managed and learners respond positively to that care and attention with gratitude and obedience, even adoration and love. A trusting love emerges that is a fundamental desired condition of life. That condition of life is expressed in the learner's special kind of *upward glance*. Learners begin to *obey* because of a *sensitive communion* they feel with a teacher (p. 32). Thus, the teacher is able to assume appropriate non-traditional, new authority and is liberated from relying on sanctions, force or other artificial measures to coerce the learner. The reader may recall my reference to the artificial nature of the coercion that grades yield in the opening chapter.

2   The Dilemma of Building a New Authority Dynamic

In the atmosphere described, learners respond to "a positive order of things," a *new authority dynamic* (Bollnow, 1989, p. 32). That is, through attention and care, as well as the reassurance that such approaches afford, the positive order Bollnow recommends is achieved. In some initial circumstances, the educator may repeatedly face resistance, disorder or even injustice from the learner as indicated in my own example at St. Albans High School. Teachers like myself in such situations attempt to model a better order, an order that is larger than one's self. The better order in essence, refers to *power with other rather than power over others*. I try to facilitate the development of a community wherein I *share* authority with learners. A culture of shared power in classrooms remains exotic and very new for most people. Indeed, the facilitation and maintenance of a dynamic of shared power occurs over a period of time and cannot be rushed. The successful development of any culture must occur gradually.

At St. Albans High School, a culture ultimately emerged in which order was maintained by all members of the learning community even as I endeavored to express and demonstrate to learners my confidence in them. I explained Mr. Santon's chain analogy to my learners, wherein each learner is led to understand that the chain, in this case the class, is only as strong as its weakest link, or individual. Such an analogy, when understood by the learner, situates him in a powerful way and invites him to contribute only his best effort to the experience at hand. The learner understands that their effort *will* strengthen the chain. As the learner endeavors to strengthen the chain, and makes an investment in the enterprise, the learner encourages and cajoles others to do the same, even as others are responding in a similar fashion. The realization of the chain analogy therefore, leads to the maintenance of order at the individual and at the collective levels. That is, because *all* are contributing to the order and quality of the enterprise, the whole-is-greater-than-the-parts-it-is-made-of axiom is operationalized. Thus, a new authority dynamic culture is constructed and maintained over a considerable time period. The learner "buys into" an order that is unlike many other learning orders of the past. The teacher facilitates the learner's trust throughout the process. When learners understand and commit to the principle expressed in the chain analogy, the order that emerges becomes larger than the teacher, leading to teaching and learning vistas that were previously unimaginable.

Bollnow likewise recognizes that learners may not, at first, respond with gratitude to the teacher's risk to establish a new kind of authority and order. The learner's potential ingratitude and resistance may also interfere with the teacher's efforts to care for the learner. Nonetheless, the teacher must forge onward with the risk taking process because it ultimately offers the only avenue to authentic educational success. The only genuine support the teacher has, particularly at the onset, is the power of her personal ethical conviction to create appropriate order. The learner's obeyance ultimately arises as a matter of course in an atmosphere of accommodation. The obeyance that emerges is quiet and natural and may even have a spiritual character. Such a spiritual character is evidenced throughout Peggy's interaction with Mr. Santon, particularly in the example of her competition speech. In that experience, Peggy was elevated to see a grand side of herself that was heretofore unknown to her. "I felt like I had an aura. I didn't know that was the word at the time, but it was a shimmer, and at that moment, I couldn't do anything wrong. I really couldn't. And I didn't. It brought me dignity, grandeur."

From the teacher perspective, in Chapter 15, Beth describes how she achieved a new authority dynamic:

> ... I never saw myself as the big boss because we all talked about things and all accomplished things. I was really aware of that. I didn't want to go in there dressed in a suit; I didn't want to make myself seem better

than them, look better than them or act superior to them. I would try to talk more on [the learner's] level. I didn't want to be above Alexander, for example, *I wanted to be with him*. You see, that's how we could get through things. (emphasis added)

James MacDonald (1974), as well as Bollnow (1989), is concerned with the issue of authority in the classroom. For MacDonald, educators must look beyond, or transcend historical hierarchical dominance and submission patterns long established for human relationships, in particular teaching and learning relationships. Such patterns, or structures, effectively serve to "alienate the person from his own activity in work and from other people" (p. 89). Again, it is the transcendence process, freed of human hierarchy that dissolves learner alienation and estrangement.

With risk as a permanent component of teaching, education becomes a daring process. Willful and active resistance to the teacher's intention is always a possibility as the teacher accepts the learner in his freedom. Nonetheless, the teacher who does not risk trusting the learner and does not dare to trust the learner, offends the dignity of the learner as well as "the dignity of education itself" (Bollnow, 1972, p. 523).

Genuine risk in education should not be confused with adventurousness, recklessness or lack of appropriate direction. The teacher never becomes passive within the context of maintaining appropriate order. The teacher must accept responsibility for the outcome of risk taking (Bollnow, 1972, p. 528). Bollnow nonetheless reassures teachers that failure is the exception rather than the rule in the educative risk taking process. In rare examples when risk fails, however, the teacher experiences it in her "innermost core" (p. 525) and Bollnow refers to that experience as "… the painful and shadowy side" of teaching (p. 521). Again, risk and potential failure are viewed by Bollnow as a critical parts of the teacher's evolution as she refines the risk taking, decision-making process. Teachers need to pursue new approaches to accommodate the ever-changing requirements of learners, regardless of the possibility of personal failure and pain.

3   Trust

Trust [people] and they will be true to you; treat them greatly and they will show themselves great.
RALPH WALDO EMERSON (Transcendentalist, 1983, p. 365)

Bollnow (1972) suggests that *trust* may be defined as a firm belief in another's reliability, abilities and capacities to grow in positive ways. Trust is a particular kind of risk that also requires "ethical courage and strength of souls" (p. 530). Trust involves the risk of yielding oneself into the hands of the one trusted (p. 530). Trust is absolutely "necessary to the healthy development of human beings" (p. 529) as was demonstrated in in the examples of Peggy and Jean. An absence of trust or directly not trusting the learner is particularly damaging to learners because the learner relies on the teacher's positive faith in them to provide the security they desire. When trust is withheld the learner loses the positive interpersonal traction that has been established or could have been established with a teacher while also damaging the faith and confidence the learner has in himself. On the other hand, the learner detects an insincere demonstration of trust instantly. Such demonstrations are not recommended because they damage the learner's capacity to trust the teacher. No demonstration of trust is preferable to false demonstrations of trust.

The teacher must trust the learner to keep his promise. Nothing is colder, more discouraging and destructive for learners than an educator's declaration in plain words that he cannot trust the learner's promise after so many unkept promises, that he is convinced that the learner involved will retrogress despite all good resolutions. The teacher's skepticism, no matter how much it is grounded in past experience, has destructive effects because it deprives the learner, despite all his honest intentions, of the will or strength to carry out his promises. When teachers explicitly proclaim that a learner is untrustworthy, the learner can only assume that their attempts to improve are pointless in light of the teacher's bias. The educator needs to constantly renew his capacity to trust the learner (Bollnow, 1972, p. 530) and to take *measured risks* with tiny steps when a learner's trustability record has not been good in the past. Throughout the process, the teacher recognizes the learner's current reality but continues to hold the vision and anticipate positive change. Recall that Peggy describes her risk taking in the process of building trust for the learner in Chapter 4:

> I get scared sometimes later, but at the moment I don't think about it if it feels right and it's not harmful. To me it's intuitive. It's acting in the moment, but not being rash or panicky. It's just so right at this moment that it *has* to be done. It has to be done or we're going to lose a kid, or we're going to lose this opportunity. And I don't know how to develop that – that's just something I do. People do other things that I don't do well, but this is the thing that I do and I've really started appreciating it.

In Chapter 7, Lauren describes the importance of the role of trust from the learner's perspective:

When [he] said [he] would do something, I knew I could depend on [him] to do everything in [his] power to get it done. I did not have to keep asking [him] whether a location was accessible for wheelchairs. This is where the trust came into our relationship. The worry of "will I be able to get into a place" was dismissed from my mind because I knew that it was taken care of.

4 An Atmosphere of Security

Trust, like risk, is a prerequisite to the establishment of what Bollnow (1989) calls an *atmosphere of security*. Such an atmosphere, secure in it's of freedom from fear, anxiety and a variety of dangers including emotional, spiritual, and social as well as physical danger, is the only medium in which the learner can "grow in the right direction, and only in this medium does the world reveal itself to the child in all its reasonable order" (p. 12). Without the atmosphere of security that trust provides, the world emerges to the learner as threatening and shocking, as an encroaching negative power.

In Chapter 9, Jerry described one of his teachers who was autocratic, power wielding, rude, cynical and cold. That teacher acted as if she were impervious to error, fear, insecurity, and nervousness. She seemed devoid of feeling, could not empathize with learners, nor ever begin to think of them as equal to her. He would always remember her for the many ways in which she managed to make him and his peers feel *badly* about themselves.

When an atmosphere of security is not afforded the learner at school, like the example of Jerry's teacher, or at home, "the child is refused the will to life, and he or she withers emotionally" (Bollnow, 1989, p. 12). Again, the atmosphere of security, provided by the parent's or teacher's trust, leads to an internalization of security within the learner. Security must be externally present if it is to be internalized by the child. Security is an "indispensable condition for the healthy development of the child" (p. 12). Recall how Theoni, in Chapter 2, deliberately and strategically generates an atmosphere of security:

> I weave around the two circles, listening to the personal reflections of my students. I stand close to a student who I know is struggling; I rest my hand on the shoulder of a student who may begin to cry; I make eye-contact with a student after the story is over and mouth the words thank you; I kneel down next to a student and whisper, "that was the bravest thing I have ever heard." I am there to support, encourage, promote, and challenge. I know the magic that will reveal itself if the atmosphere is tended to appropriately. I intuitively make these connections with stu-

dents; it may be experience, it may be my desire to make meaningful connections with these young adults, it may be my compassion for their situations that allows me to interact in such a way with my students. But because I take the risk to interact with them, they feel safe enough to continue and take the risk.

Bollnow adds to the vision for what Klein has since called mother love. Bollnow (1989) is very clear regarding the importance of the child's relationship with a beloved person in which a secure "trusted and sensible world" can be revealed to the child (p. 12). Indeed, a trusted and sensible world reveals itself to the child fundamentally only in the trusting relationship with a certain beloved person. From the beginning, the common tone of security is tied to such a beloved person.

It is the mother who usually first establishes the atmosphere of security as she humanizes the world for the child. Through caring love, the mother provides a secure atmosphere and removes the threat of invasion, strangeness, and darkness. She familiarizes that which is unfamiliar and renders what is unfamiliar harmless. The mother creates "a space of trustworthiness, of dependability, of purity" (Bollnow, 1989, p. 13). Within that space, things seem "to belong, to have sense, to be alive, trusted, close, and approachable" (p. 13). Moreover, the mother establishes what Bollnow calls the *glowing region of trust*, which stands stark "against the background of darkness and mystery" (p. 13). Only this kind of parental love, and later "the common trust of other caring adults" can provide the glowing region (p. 13).

The glowing region of trust is at the heart of the relationship between two individuals, most particularly between parent and child. The power of trust is demonstrated throughout this book. In preceding chapters, trust was demonstrated in the relationships of Jean and Hunter, Jean and Francis, Hunter and Peggy, Peggy and Mr. Santon, Peggy and Charlie and the others. In those examples, it was the glowing region of trust that facilitated powerful learning, substantial development and enabled sparkling relationships to occur. Recall Lauren in Chapter 7 describing the glowing region of trust wherein, "People were laughing and carrying on, like back home with your father, mother and relatives just laughing and having a good time together."

Veronica's encounter with the atmosphere of security in Chapter 2 was possible because of trust:

> Dr. Soublis created a classroom environment so secure that I felt safe to share something so traumatic in my life. If it were any other teacher, I do not think I would have taken such a risk. She also never let me, or

any of us, fend for ourselves; Dr. Soublis' gentle encouragement gave me strength and made me feel empowered. I liked and respected Dr. Soublis before that assignment, but now? I honestly see her as someone with great empathy, which I think is so important in teaching.

The atmosphere of security, then, has to do directly with the quality of security of the relationship with the beloved other person who, after the mother, may be the teacher. Bollnow (1972) observes that the quality of security is "related to the quality of protectedness we feel in a sheltered domain" (p. 522). Within such a domain the teacher must take the risk of challenging the child. One takes such a risk to challenge the learner toward further development. That is to say that the teacher must expect more from the child than their ostensible level of development or strength would otherwise suggest. "Children have to be given more than they are prepared for or are capable of receiving at their respective level of development" (p. 522). In so doing the teacher creates a "tide of development that pulls the child forward" (p. 532). The risk involved is that too much tension may be applied by that tide so that the child fails and becomes discouraged. Despite that possibility, the tide of development must be created. Decidedly, part of the purpose of the atmosphere of security, of understanding and caring, is that it enables the learner to flow more easily with the tide of development. The teacher must perceive as the learner perceives, must feel as he feels. Proceeding with that shared feeling of awareness, the teacher can best determine how much tension to generate in the process of pulling the child forward.

Particular attitudes such as trust and approachability determine the nature of the learner's relation with the pedagogue or teacher. At the same time, attitudes are formed by the relationship. Such a pedagogical relation involves the interaction of general atmosphere and particular affections. Because of the interaction, the atmosphere and affection realms are difficult to separate. For Lauren,

> It doesn't have to be hugging, touching, or even praise. It could be just through the teacher's words and how they express themselves and act. It makes you feel like something. It's being around somebody and talking and sharing feelings, and knowing that somebody else is caring.

5 The Revelation of the Teacher's Innermost Self

Part of the dynamic involved in the development of the relationship between the teacher and learner lies in the *teacher's revelation of his innermost self*

(Bollnow, 1972, p. 533) to the learner. Aside from the teacher's emotional life, "the teacher is forced again and again to talk about [for example] the most sacred and fragile matters to persons who will accept them in a manner he cannot predict (p. 533). Thus, what is sacred to the teacher may not, at first, be sacred to the learner. Teachers must nonetheless talk sincerely with learners in a way that reveals their own feelings, what they value, love, is sacred to them, and how they became the person they are. The teacher's own feelings are "those feelings which are connected with his inner self "(p. 533). Such a phenomenon is apparent in the frank relationship and candid conversations between Frances and Jean in which Frances shared her own personal experience and wisdom in ways that validated Jean, thus enabling Jean to view her own life very differently than she had prior to her relationship with Frances. The type of risk that Frances took cannot be avoided if the teacher is to relate to the learner in an open way, a way that "brings things within reach of his students that they never would have gained by themselves" (p. 533). Without Frances taking the risk of acting in the role of Jean's mother and sharing her innermost self, Jean's developmental evolution might not have occurred. Another example is when Peggy, from Chapter 3, revealed her innermost self to her learners by sharing that she was having a very rough day. To her astonishment, her learners gathered around her and reassured her that tomorrow would be a better day. Peggy realizes how giving learners can be when the teacher reveals their innermost self, even when having personal struggles:

> … in one fourth grade class, I said, "How can you all stand me today? Come on, tell me." I said "I'm awful today. I'm sorry. I just feel horrible. And I didn't mean to take it out on you and I just now did and there's no excuse for what I did, and I'm sorry, and will you forgive me?" And that class ran and grabbed me, and you know, they said as they went out the door, "Well, tomorrow will be better." I said, "Well, it's bound to be after what you did." I mean it was immediately better because they said it was okay to be me. They had so many problems, that particular class, and for that moment, they just put away all their problems and just nurtured me. It was wonderful. I just didn't feel deserving of that kind of magnanimity or gesture. That's what's so great about kids.

The teacher's revelation of their innermost self becomes ever more vital to the learner as the learner grasps what has been revealed to them. Once the learner fully understands their teacher's revelations and what makes them "tick," the learner will be able to begin the journey of figuring out their own values, what they love, what is sacred to them, who they are and who they want to become.

6 Morning Spirit

The teacher stands to reap many rewards as a result of her relationship with the learner. The teacher benefits from what Bollnow (1972) calls the *morningness of youth* (p. 24). Morningness of youth refers to the youth's thirst for action, her open anticipation and readiness to proceed with new adventure. Morningness also involves an "attitude of joyful hope" (p. 25) and innocence. Each of these youthful learner characteristics is optimal because they predispose the learner to deep meaningful engagement in the learning encounter. The teacher also shares the youth's fresh dreams, dreams that have a rejuvenating and absorbing effect on the teacher. For Bollnow, the morningness of youth phenomenon needs to be the "precondition" of successful teaching and learning. In Chapter 7, I reveal how my learner Lauren expressed her morningness of youth coupled with a stiff dose or self-responsibility,

As the days passed, Lauren was quietly supportive of my work as her teacher, but never demanding. Her expressions and manner reflected her very serious contemplation of important issues in class. Her questions were fresh, thoughtful and responsible. During class, she provided a second conscience for me, reminding me of details and significant information I may have neglected, or not even considered in the spin of teaching.

The teacher may rely on their learner's morningness of youth as the teacher shares the learner's life and fresh dreams, which in turn rejuvenates the teacher's life. Bollnow (1972) quotes Friedrich Froebel, "Let them give back to us what we no longer possess: the stimulating power of the child to create" (p. 56). Correspondingly, the teacher is called upon "to spread [this] joy and encourage youth." For Bollnow, "only the joyful educator is a good educator" (p. 21). The act of spreading joy is not difficult, nor is a joyful atmosphere difficult to cultivate. It is not difficult because joy arises naturally out of the child's experience. Joy is innate in the child. Lauren describes the impact of the teacher's embodiment of morning spirit as well:

> [He] energized us and we took an interest. [He] had such a sense of pride about it; [he] wanted us to be the best we could be, and that made us work

harder. And then we had a sense of pride about our choir. We were motivated and excited about what we were doing. I respected [him] because of [his] honesty, what [he] stood for. [He] never gave me any reason to question [his] judgment or put down anyone for any reason. [He] gave me encouragement, advice and feedback, and allowed me personal and mental growth. [He] helped me explore alternatives in my life, without being pushy. [His] insight was very important in my case.

To characterize his overall conception of the teacher's relationship with the learner, Bollnow quotes philanthropist author C. G. Salzmann's (1785–1788) enchanting eighteenth century vision of a futuristic teacher.

> All teachers strove to remove their wrinkles which, since the beginning of time, had made their facial features so unfriendly and sullen, and their glances became bright as the sun. And they joined in the lives and activities of children, and played street games with them, chased after balls, and learned to whip and spin tops. The children were thrilled and threw their arms around their teachers' necks, squeezed them and kissed them. (p. 22)

7 Questions for Thought

1. Define Otto Bollnow's trust. How does it function in Chapter 8?

2. Drawing on Chapter 8 terms and concepts, how and why is trust so critical in the relationship between teacher and learner?

3. Why is trust so critical for any relationship?

4. Define Bollnow's obedience and how does it function? How should teachers work to get obedience from learners according to Bollnow?

5. Define Bollnow's new authority dynamic and how does it function? What does a new authority dynamic look like? Feel like?

6. How are risk and security reconciled in a transcendent classroom?

7. Define Bollnow's morning spirit, how does it function and how/why is it desirable?

8. How does C. G. Salzmann's quote from the 1780's describe the transformed teacher? How is Salzmann's teacher as valid today as his teacher was in the 1780's?

CHAPTER 9

Portraits of Transcendent Relators

Jerry and Transcendent Shamanic Teacher Leslie

> How comforting for a teacher to say "I don't know" or "What do you think?" What a welcome phrase.
>
> JERRY

∴

1 Jerry

Jerry is a warm person around whom people feel comfortable and relaxed. Despite having a tall, commanding appearance, he is very gentle. Unfortunately, his teachers were not always as gentle with him.

2 A Cold Teacher (Ms. Gilzenskolds [A Pseudonym])

In an interview with me, Jerry spoke of a negative relationship he had with a teacher who was autocratic, power wielding, rude, cynical and cold. That teacher acted as if she were impervious to error, fear, insecurity, and nervousness. She seemed devoid of feeling, could not empathize with learners, nor ever begin to think of them as equal to her. That teacher left Jerry with feelings of resentment and frustration. He would always remember her for the many ways in which she managed to make him and his peers feel *badly* about themselves.

3 Leslie, a Caring Teacher

Contrastingly, a year or so later, Leslie, a college professor, showed that she cared about him as a person. She took the risk to become close to Jerry. In the lessons that she instructed, she tried to teach what is referred to as the "whole learner." She offered condolence, empathy and sometimes advice. At a critical point in Jerry's emotional life, Leslie broke through barriers with him and she risked for him. Jerry said,

© HUNTER O'HARA, 2021 | DOI: 10.1163/9789004445321_009

> One day, I was so upset about personal things that I just told her about it. And then, I said, "Well, let's get on with the lesson, you're not here to hear my problems; we needn't take class time for you to hear them." Then, Leslie said, "No. Do you think all I care about is whether you learn a skill with your hands?" And then I wondered, should the teacher take the chance of becoming too personally involved with the student? Should they concern themselves with what is dysfunctional or non-productive with the student? But, there's an intimacy between she and I because she stepped in and offered a solution or a suggestion and whether I acted on them or not, I realized that I wasn't slapped in the face when I took a risk. I risked, and I wasn't threatened. I wasn't met with a brick wall. She tried to help. She was willing to offer a suggestion, empathy or some kind of condolence. She tried to associate, and I realized that she tried to help, or she cared enough to help. She was interested. I went to her and involved her. She chose to step in.

Leslie could alleviate Jerry's tension and pressure by telling him of her own personal struggles with learning because she trusted him.

> There is a feeling that we're in this together. I like the equality I feel with her. It's not that I'm as good a pianist as she is, or I know as much as she does, or that my knowledge is equivalent to hers. It's not that kind of equality. It's not so much she treats me like an adult, but that she treats me as an equal.
>
> Sometimes you find yourself concentrating and it is really hard, and you feel like "what's the point?" And she realizes, I guess, your frustration and your discouragement, and then she says, "I know this is one of the hardest things in the world to do. I fought this all the way through graduate school, and it still doesn't come naturally to me." I realize she is taking a risk because I could be the student that says, "Well, I'm not going to get it, and why should I attempt it." But, it alleviated the tension and pressure in me, and I said I don't have to get this just yet. I didn't feel a failure because I didn't get it.

4 Jerry at Saint Albans High School

I first knew Jerry several years prior to his undergrad and graduate school period. The remainder of this portrait focuses on his experience in high school as my music student. I remember when I met him. He was taller than most of his classmates, and soft spoken. He played the piano beautifully and he was auditioning to accompany our choir.

What an asset he would become. I remember thinking, "Wow, we have it made now." Even more significant for me was the quiet realization that a great alliance was being initiated. Consistent with what I would later recognize as his style, Jerry was already, and without bravado, deeply involved in pragmatic and holistic ways. He was quiet, and nurturing with his peers. I was happy to be included into the fold.

The exchange between Jerry and me was mutual, the kind of interaction that happens in some professional environments where individuals really have each other's best interests at heart. I have not found such a situation to be common in life. How important it all seemed, and the possibilities for creative pursuits were endless.

As accompanist, Jerry's instinct and artistry were well beyond his chronological age, and yet none of the arrogance that sometimes accompanies precocious students was present in him. Instead, his approach was one of concern, sincerity and quiet accommodation. He was receptive to my every effort to teach and his response contributed more than I ever could have hoped for. Teachers are isolated from other teachers, or even other adults, during the school day. This can lead to feelings of apprehension as they feel the tug of the learner's collective, receptive need, hour after hour. Teachers may be reinforced by the reassurance and support that some learners offer them.

When Jerry was there, I never felt the sense of teacher loneliness that so many teachers feel. It was as if there was another teacher in the room. At the same time, his contributions were selfless and quiet. Our interaction was collegial, supported by mutual respect, intent and purpose.

Jerry was looking for a teacher and peers who would value him, respect him, and not underestimate him. It was important to Jerry that I seemed genuinely interested in him, conversed with him, and was concerned about the non-classroom issues in his life. I had empathy for him and demonstrated more confidence in him than he had in himself. Jerry observed my interactions with others as well.

5   A Little Thing

Jerry discussed an incident that occurred when I was his teacher.

> I remember one day the class changed, the bell rang, and there was a flurry of activity as we all prepared for class: getting the piano, the folder

rack, the chairs, people coming in, etc. Several people came up to you during all of that. We hadn't settled into choir yet, and I heard you compliment a student. It was the things you said to people. All of a sudden, you just tuned into them like they were the only one there, despite the hustle and bustle around. I mean, it wasn't necessarily a haircut or a pretty shirt, but also the way you joked around, which for you to joke with them was just the attention they needed. The point is, whoever was in your space, happened to pass by you, or happened to speak to you, you keyed into them despite the hustle, despite the "I've got to get these kids to settle in here" and all the commotion. Despite all, you always did. You never shoved anybody off.

As he became more involved in the class, Jerry began to respond differently to those outside his immediate circle of friends. He began to notice that,

When you respond nicely to people, it's possible that they'll respond nicely to you. Well, I mean, I could sit and eat lunch with Becky, for example, in the lunchroom, or at least invite her to sit with Heather and me. I became less exclusive. It was just a matter of being nice to people.

It seemed that somehow because I wanted good things for Jerry, he could want them for himself. And because I as the teacher respected him, others respected him. Jerry said,

It is important for the learner to feel very individual, not separated, not delineated, but individual. The teacher has to be aware and open to the individual. Every person of the class is necessary. The community of the class is not threatened by a person's individuality. There can be a strong sense of community and equality, but at the same time, you feel respected for the individual that you are and what you have to offer the class. So somehow, you got us to compromise so that we could all function in this community, and let no one be more imposing than another. I remember that. I like that feeling.

6   Affirming the Learner's Individuality

Jerry believes that once the teacher has affirmed the learner's individuality, the learner feels enough confidence, trust and security to participate in the community. Within that community, he began to look out for his meek and timid peers. He could see them as individuals, sometimes needful individuals. Jerry talked of taking up the cause of the meek and timid, of upholding his classmates to others, and standing up for them and encouraging them to stand up for themselves.

Jerry changed the way he viewed others. He found others more approachable, more affable. He saw each person in the class as absolutely essential, and their individuality as something to be honored. Jerry emphasizes that community, equality and respect are critical if people are to work together.

To summarize, relationships in which Jerry and teachers work together as equals are very rewarding for him. Trust in the teacher learner relationship allows the teacher to risk for the learner. Correspondingly, Jerry finds he is enabled to risk as well. He is enabled and encouraged when teachers have empathy for him. He appreciates being drawn into conversation in a personal way that affirms his individuality. He finds that when the teacher respects him and has confidence in him, his peers do the same. Likewise, he feels respect, and can open up to them as well. This exchange of respect creates community which Jerry believes is critical if people are to work together.

7   Portrait of Transcendent Shamanic Teacher: Leslie (Jerry's Professor)

> I try to find out what the learner's background is and then I say, "OK, what do I have today, how can I move myself to the learner's place, into his mindset," so that we're in sync, on one kind of wavelength.
> LESLIE

One cannot help but notice Leslie's energy: her focused and organized approach to living. She is not tall physically, but her energy *is*. Leslie immediately inspires one to have confidence in her and to respond to her with sincerity. Leslie was raised by her grandparents who treated her in a way that seemed natural and comfortable to her.

> My grandparents are the only people who treated me like I would have liked to have been treated. They seemed to care about me regardless of what I did, without putting all the limitations and restrictions on me. To me it was unconditional love.

Leslie's grandparents accommodated her in every way possible, and collaborated with her in various learning projects.

> For some reason, I was always fascinated with Native Americans, and so they would take me to the library and get all the books on Native Americans. Then we tried to figure out how to make "Indian" headdresses. My grandfather painted a huge bulls-eye on the side of the barn, and made some slingshots and bows and arrows and wonderful, cute little pictures. And then my grandmother taught me how to cook, how to sew and she also taught me to appreciate arts and crafts.

Leslie's grandparents always demonstrated faith, both in Leslie and in her projects and whatever activity they were engaged in. They included her in an inviting, non-structured way. They never forced her to learn, but instead had a sort of graceful way of saying just the right thing to her when she needed it most. Subsequently, Leslie developed into a successful, freestyle learner who engaged in learning for the pure joy of it, to satisfy her curiosity and to follow her interest.

Leslie's family learning scenario changed at the age of five when Leslie's mother became her primary guardian. She took Leslie to live in a city, in a more structured environment. Leslie was physically separated from her grandparents. The school environment was equally structured and because of the approach to learning her grandparents had taught her, Leslie became a fish out of water. She kept getting into trouble.

> Now I know I was a successful free-styler, but nobody thought that was worth anything back in then. No, they didn't understand my way of doing, and I think they were either threatened or they didn't appreciate the fact that I was as smart as I was.

Leslie knew inside that she had the capacity to achieve at her new school. But it had to be in ways that were natural for her, ones devoid of unnecessary confining, restrictive structure.

Things changed when Leslie was in undergraduate school. Her college teachers trusted her as an individual. They also had a sense of humor. They were "sincere, they were there because they wanted to teach; they loved teaching." They always accepted her for who and what she was, just as her grandparents had accepted her.

8   Spiritual Professor

In the example of one college teacher,

> I suppose it was a psychic thing. With some people there is an immediate bond, and I accept that. I understand that. With others it has to grow.

That teacher seemed to drift in and out of Leslie's life serendipitously. For Leslie, he displayed a kind of pedagogical omniscience, or grace.

> He could always pinpoint something, one little tiny detail which would tell me a piece of the problem. I don't know if it was how he said it or that he just made me stop for a second and listen to that one thing, but everything would turn out to be all right. He was, I would say, one of the most spiritual professors we had.

Later, when Leslie had her first teaching job and things seemed really hard, she wrote him a letter and he knew exactly what to write back. He said the right things, and enabled her to work out her problem.

9   Direct Professor

Another of Leslie's university professors displayed an attractive characteristic for Leslie – directness.

> She was a very strong female model for me, of a different kind. We have a wonderful relationship that's lasted for all these years. She's the most blunt, forthright, honest, direct person I've known. She's very assertive by most people's standards, very rude. If she believes something, she just comes right out and says it. She's an outrageous person. I like being blunt myself, but it doesn't seem to be encouraged much.

Leslie enjoys being direct herself. Her mother, by contrast, could never be that way.

> My mother never says what she thinks. She even has my father saying "now what do you really want" when we are trying to make a simple decision, like "what are we going to eat" or "where are we going to go?" It just really wears me out since nobody tells the truth.

10 Beloved Professor

Another female university professor, on the other hand, showed Leslie an effective way of being direct. She was a model of success as a teacher, and was much loved by her students. "For me to see that she could survive at that age, still have a respectable job and have everybody love her, and be turning out phenomenal students, was wonderful." That teacher also taught Leslie how to listen. She, like Leslie's first professor, had the omniscient quality of knowing just what to say at the most appropriate moment. Leslie believes that sort of a phenomenon in a teacher occurs spontaneously.

11 Challenging Professor

In the example of a fourth teacher, the relational interaction seemed at first to be negative, but nonetheless had the effect of challenging Leslie to move beyond her performance level then as a pianist. This teacher was also very honest and direct with her.

> He took me into the room and said "don't ever play the piano like that again in your life." I was devastated, because at the time I played most of the right notes, and I did it all. But now I realize exactly what he meant; don't ever play without any commitment. Your whole object in life must be to make this come alive and be real. I knew what he meant, and it hurt me terribly.

Even though the incident hurt, Leslie felt that her teacher approached her the way he did because he had faith in her, not because he lacked faith in her. He wanted to challenge her.

12 Pushing Professor

The fifth teacher challenged and tested Leslie and all other students.

> It was an adversarial type of relationship with him that had quite an effect. He wanted to see how far he could push you and see if you would turn lazy, or see if you would quit. For me, as a female, that would be his test, to see if I would quit. I'm sure he wouldn't have it any other way.
>
> He was a wonderful history teacher. He showed me how all things were interrelated. He could speak a zillion languages. He knew everything

about costume, everything about history, everything about cooking, everything about all aspects of life, and no aspect was unrelated to him, at all. For him, everything is related in this incredible universe. All that is happening in the world and what you're going to have for dinner – all are related.

In the end that teacher was supportive of Leslie before other faculty members, and displayed his belief in her to them. She felt there was an empathic connection with him as well as the other professors and they felt about music in much the same way. He wanted people to grow, to expand and to do well.

13   Graceful Professor

Another teacher had the quality of being able to tell her the right thing to do at precisely the right time.

> I don't know if it was his expertise that astounded me or if it was because he was a very interesting person. If I was having difficulty he would always be there. I found out that he respected what I could do learning-wise.

That teacher also used humor well in conjunction with his quality of grace. He respected Leslie for her abilities and taught her important lessons about life.

> He also taught me how to survive in an academic world. You can't fight every battle that you come to. There are lots of things that you may disagree with, but you can't fight every single battle. You're going to have to pick one or two that are the most important to you and put all your energies into them, otherwise if you disagree every time, nobody will take you seriously.

14   Leslie the Teacher

Leslie is determined to pass on the quality of her college experiences to her own college students and to recognize her own creativity as a teacher. She attributes her success as a teacher to her capacity to come to know learners quickly, and to determine their strengths, weaknesses and interests. Leslie looks for a particular way to communicate with each individual learner. Subsequently, as she says, a special bond develops between the two of us. It sounds kind of arrogant, but it's a communication just the two of us have in some way. I try to find out what their background is and then say "OK, what do I have today, how can I move myself to that place, into that mindset, so we're in sync, on one kind of wavelength?"

15   Putting Oneself in the Place of the Learner

Leslie feels that she can achieve pedagogical success by avoiding instructional techniques that were unsuccessful for her as a learner. She feels that teachers can avoid negative pedagogy by putting themselves in the place of the learner. Leslie emphasizes that she has trouble separating the person from the task at hand. She believes that the teacher must address the total individual in learning. One must enter the learner's world in a way that could potentially backfire. For example, some situations may even require the teacher to "push" the learner, creating a situation from which the learner may even want to run away. Leslie is willing to take that risk, however, because she believes emotional blocks that go unchecked can prevent learning and that the teacher can assist in the unblocking of emotions. She spoke of an encounter with Jerry.

16   Jerry (Prior Portrait) and Leslie

I just knew Jerry was hurting a lot. I mean, he told me some of his problems and yet our biggest thing beyond that was that it was all held in. There was no emotion coming out in his playing. Finally we got to the place where he was playing the piano and I was singing in my usual off-key way and stomping, anything to get some emotion to come out. I was pushing him, all through the whole piece. He allowed me to make him really mad. I kept telling him musical things to do. I was pushing him that way until he was so furious with me, I knew he was mad and yet, I knew he wasn't really mad at me. He was mad at everybody but he was taking it out on me, so that's why I kept pushing. It was a real chance; I knew I was taking a chance. He could have put his arm up to my face in a second, but I had to take the chance. When we came to the biggest musical spot, the last page, which is just humongous, I just touched him and said "this is the spot where you let it out. You just let us know, let us know how much it hurts. I want you to say to me right now all those things you wanted to say to your parents; you release that." Jerry was able to release all of his pain, a wall of pain, into the music. It was amazing. I knew that if you can't express yourself and you're not living as a human being, and you are totally distraught, then how in the world can you make sense out of something as emotional as music? The private and the personal are ultimately the music the person makes.

17   Risk

"I take risks in everything," Leslie explains.

> It seems like the risks I take in teaching are much more successful than any of the risks that I take in non-teaching relationships. Whenever students encounter a problem I will try every approach until a solution to the problem is found. There is never one solution for all learners. I find out what works best for them. I always try to do it with some sense of humor so it's not a really serious "this has to be done," or "this has to be accomplished" situation. Also I tell them "it's OK" and "it's no big deal that we are trying to fix this." Performing music becomes very serious business for the performer and some music teachers escalate that seriousness in rehearsals with their teaching style. I try to downplay the seriousness. I try to say that it's not that they're having problems or there has been a mistake or anything. Rather, I say "let's just try to find a way to make it easier or do it better or make it sound better. Whatever it has to be to accommodate their needs is the way we will do it."

Leslie feels she is able to excite the learner by being excited herself. Even so, there are some students, no matter how hard she tries, with which she cannot connect.

> I'm obviously not the right person, or it's not the right time, you know? There is no connection that is going to be made this semester, at this particular point. Often times in such situations, however, it helps to completely, radically alter the approach by asking the learner, as Leslie explains, to do something totally out of character and to do it in as many ridiculous ways as I can think of.

In the types of relationships Leslie depicts, distance between teacher and learner for both relators is removed by humor. The relationship goes beyond, or transcends, barriers in a personal way for both relators. The teacher still makes particular decisions, but she nonetheless is enabled to go beyond the traditional role and reduce the distance between them.

In summary, as a child, Leslie was treated by her grandparents with unconditional love and accommodation for her every need. They had faith in her and collaborated with her. Because of this, Leslie developed as a "freestyle learner." When she started school, she was frustrated by her teachers and the structured learning environments in which all students were expected to learn in the same way or with the same style and at the same chronological age. Leslie felt unappreciated and invalidated. But, when she entered college, she developed extraordinary relationships with her professors. The themes of individuality, trust, directness, serendipity and empathic connection were strong in those relationships. The most prominent characteristic her teachers demonstrated was grace. They seemed to know just the right thing to say to her at just the right moment.

As a teacher, Leslie wants to offer her learners what her college teachers offered her. Leslie finds that she must put herself in the place of the learner. She is able to do this by virtue of her intuition. She is able to risk herself in an effort to assist the learner in the unblocking of emotions that prevent learning. In the process, Leslie is able to remove relational distance.

18   Questions for Thought

1. How do you feel when you have a cold teacher like Jerry's Ms. Gilzenskolds?

2. How do you react to a cold teacher? What impact does such a teacher have on your ability to learn?

3. Describe five ways that Leslie was different from the cold teacher?

4. What does Jerry believe about the individual in the classroom context?

5. How did Jerry transform in class and why did that happen?

6. What qualities or characteristics of transcendent shamanism occur in Jerry's portrait, if any? Use concepts and terms from Sections 5–6 to answer this question.

7. How were Leslie's grandparents like her professors in terms of how they interacted with Leslie?

8. What do you think Leslie meant by "spiritual professor?"

9. When did Leslie behave like her pushing professor?

10. How does a graceful professor, or teacher, act?

11. What risk did Leslie take with Jerry?

12. What qualities or characteristics of transcendent shamanism are represented in Leslie's portrait? Use concepts and terms from Sections 7–17 to answer this question.

CHAPTER 10

Balance, Transcendence and Dispositions

> There is never one solution for all learners. I find the one that works best for them. I always try to do it with some sense of humor so it's not really a serious "this has to be done," or "this has to be accomplished" situation. Also I tell them "it's OK" and "it's no big deal we are trying to fix this."
> LESLIE

∴

1   Maxine Greene, Freedom and Negotiation

At her death in 2014, Dr. Maxine Greene was Teachers College's William F. Russell Professor Emerita in the Foundations of Education Department, Professor of Education, Columbia University. An existentialist philosopher of education and teacher, Greene was past President of the American Philosophical Society and the American Educational Research Association (AERA). According to her obituary on the Teacher's College website, she was "described by *The New York Times* as 'one of the most important education philosophers of the past 50 years' and 'an idol to thousands of educators.' Greene was regarded by many as the spiritual heir to John Dewey. Her work remains a touchstone for generations of [Teacher's College] faculty, alumni and students, as well as for scholars and artists around the world."

As a doctoral student, I was inspired by Greene's work enough to call her on the phone and ask her for an interview at the 1991 AERA Annual Meeting that spring in Chicago. She graciously granted my request. After my friend Laura Van Vorhis (see Laura's Portrait in Chapter 13) and I interviewed Greene in a hotel lobby about her work, Greene invited Laura and me to her home in Manhattan a few weeks later. We were able to arrange that meeting. At her home, she served Laura and me a chicken dinner prepared by her, even as we admired her view overlooking Central Park.

Greene invited me to lunch the next day. At that lunch, having read one paper that I had written about her work, she offered to serve on my doctoral committee without my asking her, otherwise I do not think I would have had the courage to ask her. I am indebted to Maxine Greene for her encouragement and guidance throughout that process as a member of my doctoral committee and throughout my friendship with her. Greene continues to have enormous influence on my work as a teacher, author and philosopher.

For Greene, teachers who are in search of their own freedom may be the only ones in a learner's life who possess the enthusiasms that are the very source of creativity, that can arouse young persons to go out in search of their own freedom (Greene, 1986, p. 16). Teachers must nurture the learner's capacity for freedom through creating conditions that enable learners "to act on their power to choose" (Greene, 1988, p. 18), to question, to resist, to have and to develop varied perceptions. Teachers provoke the learner to "reach beyond himself or herself" (M. Greene, personal communication, December 3, 1991), to pose questions, to wonder and imagine (Greene, 1988, p. 14).

Greene (1988) explains that learners are enabled to develop an awareness of something lacking in a situation, an awareness that is essential before the learner can begin to reach beyond the existing reality. Literature and the fine arts in school curricula play an essential, pivotal role in the process of activating or firing the imagination of the learner to dream, to see things as they could be otherwise. Once that recognition of how things could otherwise arise, vision emerges and the learner is able to identify the space that lies between the current reality and the learner's newly imagined dream. The teacher then releases the learner to act and overcome obstacles and transcend barriers that stand in that way of the dream. The learner's intellectual passion is aroused and is *onto something*: onto the pursuit of a dream, and is thereby liberated (Greene, 2011). The learner is free.

Of course, this does not suggest that teachers should, in libertarian fashion, "release people to act on their own" in a sort of directionless way or in a purely "self-involved way" (M. Greene, personal communication, November 1, 1991), (M. Greene, personal communication, July 26, 1992). Rather, freedom helps the learner act on their own initiatives, but with an informed perspective that is nurtured by the teacher (Greene, 1988, p. 43). Through the relationship of teacher and learner reaching beyond together, the learner's personal distinctiveness and uniqueness are upheld and the teacher's and learner's motivations are raised in a reciprocal manner (1984a). Teachers need to respect the intellectual integrity and the independent judgment of the learner (Greene, 1984a, p. 6) if intellectual passion is to be aroused. As teachers, in search of their own freedom, join in the process of removing obstacles and transcending barriers to what lies beyond (Greene, 1988, pp. 116, 128), teachers are freed as well as learners.

When teachers and learners choose to act on their freedom, however, there are no guarantees in terms of success, failure or interpersonal harmony

(Greene, 1988). "... Teaching has much to do with what Vandenburg calls the 'admonition,' striving to move students to act on their freedom, to reach beyond themselves, to become – even though their very reaching may defy and deny the teacher" (M. Greene, personal communication, December 3, 1991).

Each day, as I walk into a classroom and work to transcend educational barriers such as learner confusion and distraction, I must offer learners something better than the everyday, or the mundane. I must attract them to new territories, new landscapes. I must in Peggy's words, "cajole and persuade" them to desire to move in a new direction and to feel the winds of freedom at their backs as they do so. And when I do this, I am never guaranteed that learners will select paths that I had in mind for them. And yet if such a guarantee could exist, freedom could not.

When a teacher is defied or denied by the learner, the teacher may be inclined to respond by oppressing the learner. The teacher may make a request that is ignored. The learner may flatly deny or disagree with the teacher regarding how a project or event should proceed. But if the teacher responds in a punitive manner, the learner's resistance may increase and ultimately drive a wedge, perhaps a permanent wedge, between teacher and learner. In such situations, the bonds of mutuality and reciprocity are damaged or lost and the learning process is hampered. In every example, the teacher needs to act to reset and to reverse a negative or deteriorating interactional circumstance, to uphold the learner's dignity and to support their developing judgment and motivation. Better approaches for all concerned include those that allow *natural consequences* for actions to unfold, if in fact there are to be consequences. The teacher may say, "I'm counting on you, I know we can do this and we're going to work out the kinks together. Would it help if we pursued x course of action?"

At the same time that teachers avoid inclinations to oppress the learner, they pursue *their own motivation to be free* – to be in search of their own personal freedom. A teacher cannot liberate someone else if they are oppressed or not free. And to be free, the teacher must follow a path that inspires her or him. When teachers are "on fire" as they pursue their own freedom, learners can see it in their eyes, hear it in their voice and feel it "in their bones" as they interact with the teacher. The creative result is palpable and all are swept up in the power of the moment. Therefore if the teacher is not enthusiastic about the content or the projects set forth, the quest for freedom is likely lost for all concerned.

Both learner and teacher collaborate in the negotiation of meaning (Greene, 1986) so that authentic learning can take place (Greene, 1984a). The teacher actively challenges or directs the learner toward the "field of possibles, to what might be or should be, but is not yet" (Greene, 1988, p. 21). In this process, it is the teacher's care as identified by Noddings (1984) that enables the teacher to look through a student's eyes and to struggle with them (Greene, 1988), participating in the process of learning with the learner (Greene, 1989). Reverend Dr. Martin Luther King Jr., as example, inspired and taught his followers as he relied on their capacity "to look at things as they could be otherwise" (1988, p. 4). Freed of the handicaps of exploitation and oppression, people can become "authentically present to one another" (Greene, 1988, p. 16). Once again, they transcend the barriers imposed by roles or badges of office.

Through what Walt Whitman has called *loving comradeship*, equality and freedom are somehow harmonized (Greene, 1988). "Freedom has to do with coming together, the attainment of communion, imagining and then breaking through the structures of the world and creating something new" (1988, pp. 17, 34). It is then that a "community of equals" emerges wherein people learn to act in concert with one another (Greene, 1988, p. 46), in spaces open for possibility (Greene, 1982). Obstacles are transcended; understanding is gained (Greene, 1988). "Persons are enabled to see what they already know, somehow differently" (Greene, 1984b, p. 10). Projects for transformation are then invented and pursued (Greene, 1986). In that process, both teachers and learners are renewed, refreshed and redirected.

Leslie's grandparents always demonstrated faith, both in Leslie and her projects, and whatever activity they were engaged in. Her grandparents negotiated with Leslie and extended freedoms to Leslie that were not extended to Leslie by her parents. Her grandparents included her in an inviting, non-structured way. They never forced her to learn, but instead had a sort of graceful way of saying just the right thing to her when she needed it most. Subsequently, Leslie developed into a successful, freestyle learner who engaged in learning for the pure joy of it, to satisfy her curiosity and to follow her interest.

> For some reason, I was always fascinated with Native Americans, and so they would take me to the library and get all the books on Native Americans. Then we tried to figure out how to make "Indian" headdresses. My grandfather painted a huge bulls-eye on the side of the barn, and made some slingshots and bows and arrows and wonderful, cute little pictures. And then my grandmother taught me how to cook, how to sew and she also taught me to appreciate arts and crafts.

Martin Buber urges educators not to construe freedom as the precondition and the source of education. Teachers in particular, should strive to take individuals in the direction of freedom (Cohen, 1983, p. 36). Buber provides a definition of freedom wherein freedom comes about through tension and responsibility. Freedom is the goal and discipline is the strategy used to get to that goal (Friedman, 1976, p. 178). To fully engage the learner and to accelerate development, Buber believes that it is important for the teacher to place demands on the learner. In that process the teacher acts in the role of what can be called "critical guide and directing spirit" (Cohen, 1983, p. 32).

In Chapter 15, Beth realizes that unspoken communication, within a framework of limits, offers a powerful tool to balance self-discipline and freedom. Beth and Alexander worked together to create that balance. For Beth,

> We didn't have to talk. All I had to do if he wasn't doing something was just look at him and he knew exactly what I meant. It had all been worked out before. Dealing with him was more non-verbal than verbal. He was able to con the other teachers and principal pretty well, but he couldn't con me. He would try, but I would just look him in the eye and he would laugh and then tell the truth. He couldn't put anything past me. It was his habit to try that, to pull the wool over my eyes. It was part of his "street smarts." That was his way and he was fairly manipulative; I knew that. He realized that he couldn't manipulate me, so he relaxed in my room. I saw a change in the tension in his body and his face. He was more relaxed in my class. I argued with the principal, I'd say, "he doesn't have security if he knows he can manipulate the system or you." With other teachers, the problem was that Alexander did not know how far he could go, there were no limits. He kept on getting by with things with other teachers. I just think he needed some kind of security, and limits provided a kind of security for him. The lack of boundaries for him showed that nobody cared about him.

2 Freedom and Discipline

The portraits in this book reflect the need for freedom in learning that is reconciled with discipline, specifically learner self-discipline. The process of establishing a balance between freedom and *self*-discipline in learning environments is demanding. Teachers and learners may pass through a number of stages that involve negotiation and collaboration before balance is achieved. Throughout this balancing process, self-discipline emerges in learners as they become more self-aware of interactional boundaries and the necessity for those boundaries.

The point of balance between freedom and learner self-discipline shifts in response to learner development. Balance between freedom and self-discipline requires constant attention and adjustment on the part of learners as well as teachers. Achieving balance requires learners and teachers to focus on a wide array of issues and concerns on an ongoing basis. On a given day of the week, for example, a teacher may need to impose more structure than on another day. That is, the teacher establishes additional guidelines for interaction and may relax other guidelines on a given day. As example, learners may be tired or more distracted on Friday than they are on Wednesday, and so on such days, the teacher may be called upon to reshape limits and boundaries to provide more structure that may be needed. At the same time, as learners of their own accord take on more responsibility for contributing to the well run classroom, they will also work even harder than they did on Wednesday to attain commonly understood classroom goals on Friday.

Parker Palmer (1983) notes that teachers, like mothers, reconcile the demands of freedom and discipline on a regular basis, but that no solution or formula exists for that reconciliation. Achieving a balance between freedom and self-discipline is an art that requires a sophisticated level of thoughtfulness on everyone's part. Jean summarizes it this way. "You and the child have to know the limits. And you try to work between them." Again, a mutual understanding of limits is negotiated between the teacher and the learner, with the teacher maintaining oversight and coordination of classroom events. Beyond that, a higher force is brought to bear, a force that transcends what are otherwise oppositional viewpoints.

The teacher raises the bar of expectation for learners, thereby calling upon them to produce higher levels of performance than they heretofore thought themselves capable of achieving.

Peggy described her Thespian Review speech encounter. Pursuant to Mr. Santon's explicit belief in her aligned with his carefully designed and expressed demands and expectations, Peggy felt a shimmering sense of grandeur and dignity during her speech. She felt a confidence in herself that seemed miraculous to her. She could suddenly accomplish what had seemed impossible only moments before. I interpret Peggy's encounter to be an example of Palmer's (1983) straining to another level. Such an encounter occurred for Peggy's students in their Opus performance, as characterized by Maxine Greene. "Not just that she's powerful in that way, but it's the situation she created. Dewey used to do that. This is not what has to happen, [but] this is the highest possibility" (O'Hara, 1991).

Parker Palmer (1983) believes that freedom and discipline are reconciled best where there is an atmosphere of hospitality, a networking of relationships to form a community. For Palmer, an educator, sociologist and recipient of the Uhrig Award for excellence in teaching, such a genuine community is free of the tenuousness imposed by traditional roles. All truth is found and known in the particular qualities of our personal relationships of "personal responsiveness and accountability to each other" (p. 15), and "of careful listening and responding in a conversation of free selves" (p. 65). The teacher invites the learner into a full partner relationship and in so doing sees the learner as potential friend. Teacher and learner "pledge to engage in a mutually accountable and transforming relationship forged of trust and faith in the face of unknowable risks" (p. 31). Transcendent love reconciles opposites.

In my own teaching practice, I actively strive to establish a balance between freedom and learner discipline through facilitating, again, the development of the learner's *self discipline.* That is, with greater freedom for learners, and others, comes greater responsibility. Thus, as I actively and deliberately create circumstances that teach learners how to be free, I also guide them in the process of developing lifelong self-discipline skills that enable them to continue balancing freedom and self-discipline throughout their lives.

3 The Transcendence Space

The transcendent learning space may begin to arise if people do not feel threatened or judged. In Palmer's (1983) words, one "is not closed down by fearful emotions" (p. 74). Such a space enables teachers and learners to challenge information, to criticize and test hypotheses together. In such a space, an emotionally honest interaction occurs between teacher and learner. To create an "emotionally honest learning space" (p. 87), the teacher must risk, not run from, or resist the expression of emotion. The teacher must create "a place where it is safe for [one's] feelings to emerge" (p. 85). Although Palmer acknowledges that discomfort and pain may emerge in this process of the genuine expression of emotion, he believes that if emotion is accepted in the learning space, the learner can emerge a whole person. Such an authentic, whole person is filled with inner direction and purpose, freed of the interactional costumes one may wear in an effort to meet another's expectations for them.

For individuals to remain whole in a transcendent relationship, they need to gain "an inner understanding of the other, which comes from empathy; a sense of the other's value, which comes from love" (Palmer, 1983, p. 53). The need for deeper, more genuine relationships is desirable in the learning space. Palmer discerns, "as our capacity for conscious and reflective relationship increases, so does our knowledge" (p. 53). Palmer concedes that while "such involvement has its problems," he flatly rejects its polar opposite approach – detachment, as a viable solution (p. 34) to interactional dilemmas that occur in learning situations.

Such a transcendent space was created between Mr. Santon and Peggy and between Peggy and Charlie. In Chapter 13, the reader will see how Laura created the transcendent space with Melinda and in Chapter 15, how Beth did this with Alexander. Recall how Leslie created the transcendent space with Jerry in Chapter 9. When Leslie recognized Jerry's struggle, she worked to help him channel his pain into the music he was creating. Jerry describes how a transcendent space emerged between him and Leslie:

> One day, I was so upset about personal things that I just told her about it. And then, I said, "Well, let's get on with the lesson, you're not here to hear my problems; we needn't take class time for you to hear them." Then, Leslie said, "No. Do you think all I care about is whether you learn a skill with your hands?" And then I wondered, should the teacher take the chance of becoming too personally involved with the student? Should they concern themselves with what is dysfunctional or non-productive with the student? But, there's an intimacy between she and I because she stepped in and offered a solution or a suggestion and whether I acted on them or not, I realized that I wasn't slapped in the face when I took a risk. I risked, and I wasn't threatened. I wasn't met with a brick wall. She tried to help. She was willing to offer a suggestion, empathy or some kind of condolence. She tried to associate, and I realized that she tried to help, or she cared enough to help. She was interested. I went to her and involved her. She chose to step in.

4 Hospitality

The space for learning has three major characteristics, or essential dimensions: "openness, boundaries and an air of hospitality" (Palmer, 1983, p. 71). *Hospitality* refers to teachers and others "receiving each other, our struggles, our newborn ideas with openness and care" (pp. 73–74). A host receives and entertains guests or learners in this example. The learner is led to feel valuable while developing a transformative caring friend relationship with a teacher or other individual. Palmer believes that such hospitality is absolutely necessary to learning. Competition, on the other hand, is not only non-communal; it is anti-communal (p. 37). In many cultures, Palmer observes that when learners attempt to learn cooperatively, they are said to be "cheating." Teachers must instead endeavor to *create*, facilitate *and energize* the development of a harmonious, cooperative community in classrooms where cheating is not a temptation or a need.

BALANCE, TRANSCENDENCE AND DISPOSITIONS   143

Whenever new learners are brought to my class, acting as host I try to connect them with one or two particular other learners to help facilitate the building and the strengthening of the community and the beginning of new friendships as Kathy and Lauren mentioned in Chapter 7. For Kathy,

> The first day that I came into [his] class, [he] said to everyone "This is Kathy," and everybody said "Hi!" And, I thought, "What is this?" I'd never seen that before. Usually you walk into a class and you hear "This is so and so," and you take your seat and you go on. But I thought, "Wow! This is a family oriented class, and we're all going to be friends." I got that impression from the very beginning. I thought, "everyone is treating me like I'm supposed to be here, and this is my place." That was unprecedented ...
>
> If there was something that we needed help with, we could come to [him] and [he] could at least point us in the right direction. If [he] also saw a person needing a little morale boost, [he] asked other people to bring them in under their wing and take care of them, help them out, and include them. That struck me as being something most teachers don't do. If someone was out on their own, most teachers just let them be out there, on their own. They don't try to bring them in.

In an effort to create and build the hospitable community, I group learners for all projects randomly so that they have opportunities to interact with all learners in the community, one-on-one or in small groups, rather than with the peers they already know. Over time, such a process results in the breaking down of cliques and simultaneously builds the hospitable community.

A traditional notion of host is also helpful in an effort to characterize the teacher-as-host role. As was described in Chapter 2, the transcendent teacher/host acts to generate a glamorous atmosphere and space, one of excitement and appeal wherein the host figure acts to comfort, to reassure and to provide an air of optimism in interactions with others within her or his charge. The learner is received via attraction within a context of felt adventure that is created by the host. Recall Jerry in Chapter 9:

> I remember one day the class changed, the bell rang, and there was a flurry of activity as we all prepared for class: getting the piano, the folder rack, the chairs, people coming in, etc. Several people came to [him] during all of that. We hadn't settled into choir yet, and heard [him] compliment a student. It was the things [he] said to people. All of a sudden, [he] just tuned into them like they were the only one there, despite the hustle and bustle around. I mean, it wasn't necessarily a haircut or a

pretty shirt, but also the way [he] joked around, which for [him] to joke with them was just the attention they needed. The point is, whoever was in [his] space, happened to pass by [him], or happened to speak to [him], [he] keyed into them despite the hustle, despite the "I've got to get these kids to settle in here" and all the commotion. Despite all, [he] always did. [He] never shoved anybody off.

5   **Teacher Reflection**

Teachers in pursuit of their personal freedom and the freedom of their learners must ask themselves how effective they are at building supportive, cooperative environments. Freedom seeking teachers concern themselves with building community. They must consider whether they may sabotage efforts at building community by deliberately creating learning situations in which it is taboo (prohibited or restricted by social custom) to consult another person for information or assistance. Are collaboration taboos such as these really necessary for effective learning to occur or are they destructive of deep, meaningful learning? Is there a field of endeavor outside schools where cooperation and collaboration are not helpful? If not, what are the implications of the opposite state of affairs for schools? Teachers must consider how cooperation and collaboration could possibly yield a negative return if one's goal is for all learners to be successful in whatever field of endeavor with which they may choose to engage. I hope that schools will someday establish a consummate model for meaningful interactive learning, a model that has always existed in fine arts education, for example; a model in which concerns about cheating do not exist for teachers or learners because the atmosphere, interaction and teaching-learning methodologies in place do not put a learner in a position to need to "cheat." Classroom situations in which the need to cheat exists are artificial and unnecessary because they do not inspire, or fully support deep, meaningful learning.

Grades are a reality in the majority of schools. Teachers are compelled to assign them but it is the process for arriving at grades that needs to be revolutionized. If one's teaching goal is to facilitate optimal cognitive, affective and psychomotor development in learners, how can one from an ethical perspective declare that the only "rewardable" growth must occur before a particular date or under particular circumstances?

One must, as Noddings (1984) suggests get "in there" and make the learner's problem her own. The teacher may do this by putting herself in the learner's place and encouraging multiple opportunities for success and for resubmissions of assignments. Teacher feedback, at each juncture, puts control of grades in the learners' hands as they receive guidance over time from the teacher and are enabled to improve at their own speed without a grade penalty. The only relevant date becomes the very end of the learning experience between the teacher and the learner, i.e. the end of the evaluatory period when a grade must be submitted. In the meantime, learners must be given every possible opportunity to develop and achieve in the most comprehensive ways possible. Learners need to be empowered to take charge of their own developmental schedules, indeed even their own grade, through the provision of multiple opportunities for success including multiple resubmissions of assignments without penalty in the process of reaching optimal development, regardless of essentially arbitrary timelines. Tests, if they must be given at all, do not need to include surprises. Test content does not need to be a moving target, mysterious, unwieldy, amorphous or unmanageable if the goal is for the learner to master the required content rather than for the learner to outguess a teacher's unnecessarily broad, and frequently arbitrary, choice of test content.

The positive teacher learner relationship (Palmer, 1983), despite the absence of competition, does indeed sustain challenge and conflict. In non-competitive relationships, the tensions that arise in pursuit of a common goal are regarded as a creative opportunity. The teacher mediates whatever tensions may arise applying what Van Manen (1991) refers to *tact*. Tact is grace in dealing with others, improvisational and in many ways, unplanable. In Chapter 13, Laura is able to mediate Melinda's frustrations and tension through thoughtfulness and the careful application of tact.

For Palmer (1983), the learner that exists *within* the teacher is as important as the learner in the classroom. For teachers to remain inspired themselves and to inspire learners, they need to be engaged in the act of learning *with* learners as opposed to *over* them. When teachers fully engage with learners in the pursuit of projects, teachers find that learners affirm them and support them, thereby enhancing the teacher's growth alongside the learner. As teacher and learner overcome challenges and conflict and affirm each other, relationships move beyond or transcend barriers that would otherwise ruin transcendent possibility for all concerned.

6   Transcendence

According to Phil Phenix (1974), even though transcendence exists in many learning environments, it is frequently not recognized or identified. Moreover, it "is denied because it challenges the *status quo* of finite realizations"

(p. 122). Transcendence-oriented encounters may be viewed as strange, or even dangerous to unaccustomed individuals who have never experienced them. Transcendence is an expansive phenomenon that supersedes the artificialities of social constructs as race, class, nation, doctrine, tradition, institution and absolutism. Indeed, such limiting thought structures are evidence of the "flight from transcendence" (p. 122). Phenix provides a "set of criteria for a transcendence-oriented curriculum [that is] organized according to general dispositions" (p. 123). These are hope, creativity, awareness, faithful doubt, wonder, awe and reverence.

7   Hope

Hope refers to an expectation or desire for something to happen. The disposition of *hope* motivates, sustains and leads to transformation. Without hope "there is no incentive for learning, for the impulse to learn presupposes confidence in the possibility of improving one's existence" (Phenix, 1974, p. 123). Phenix submits that the loss of hope is a principle cause of educational problems:

> When widespread social dislocations, dissolution of customary norms, dehumanization, and other malaises of social and cultural life cause people to feel impotent, no technical improvements in the content or methods of instruction will induce people to learn well. On the other hand, those who are buoyed by strong hope can overcome substantial formal deficiencies in program or technique. The explicit acknowledgment of transcendence as a ground for hope may therefore contribute significantly to the efficacy of education. (p. 123)

Mr. Santon gave Peggy great hope. Prior to her encounters with Mr. Santon, Peggy explains, "I felt that I could have just dropped in a hole somewhere and wouldn't have been missed. But he made me feel that I mattered, as if the world would have missed out if I weren't a part of it. This is the type of human interaction that causes one to forget negative and sometimes even suicidal thoughts."

8   Creativity

The second general disposition is *creativity* or the use of one's imagination in the creation of original ideas. Many regard creativity to be the province of those who create via the fine arts, writing or other structured from of human expression.

But, despite this commonly held view, creativity is inherent in all beings. Whereas creativity is regarded to be the capacity for divergent thought as it relates to any realm of human endeavor, to create is "the normal mode of behavior for everyone" (Phenix, 1974, p. 124). In fact, "To be human is to create" (p. 124). If one recognizes transcendence as "inseparable from the human condition," (p. 124) one also recognizes that human beings are certainly disposed toward creativity. Environments without hope are also ones in which creativity wanes.

Habitual conformity and dehumanization, present in hopeless environments, act as the "prime enemy of transcendence" (Phenix, 1974, p. 124). Conformity of thought may be the very goal of the standardized assessment movement. The presence of conformity and dehumanization, suggest a "flight from transcendence."

> When [educators] presume to act as authorities dispensing to the young knowledge and values that are to be accepted without question, they act as enemies of transcendence. On the other hand, the educator who affirms transcendence is characterized by a fundamental humility manifest in expectant openness to fresh creative possibilities. (p. 124)

Leslie manages to inspire learner creativity by being excited herself about learning opportunities. Sometimes, Leslie says, "it helps to completely, radically alter the approach by asking the learner, as she explains, to do something totally out of character and to do it in as many ridiculous ways as I can think of."

For her learner Jerry, individuality lies at the heart of creativity:

> It is important for the learner to feel very individual, not separated, not delineated, but individual. The teacher has to be aware and open to the individual. Every person of the class is necessary. The community of the class is not threatened by a person's individuality. There can be a strong sense of community and equality, but at the same time, you feel respected for the individual that you are and what you have to offer the class. So somehow, you got us to compromise so that we could all function in this community, and let no one be more imposing than another. I remember that. I like that feeling.

Recall Chapter 2, Theoni describes the process of creating opportunities for creative self expression:

> I learned over the years of teaching that the more I facilitate opportunities for self-expression, the more students will take risks. Some may test the waters and wait for others to take the lead, but most of the time, each

will take on a challenge at some point. I have had students share some of the most personal experiences of their lives: abusive relationships, death of loved ones, sexual orientation, self-abuse, the pressure to be perfect, alcohol and drug use and so forth. When the facilitator of the class takes the time in the beginning of the year to model a caring disposition, to be an active listener, to take student concerns seriously, that facilitator is setting up the safe classroom atmosphere. All of this takes place slowly and subversively within and between the academic lessons of the day, but over time the stage is set to introduce an assignment such as this where students are ready to share at deep levels.

Had Mr. Santon not offered opportunities that affirmed the learner's capacity for creative endeavor, Peggy would not have had the profoundly positive encounters she had in his class. He demonstrated his humble nature by telling them that he was lucky to be their teacher and he set the stage for them to creatively express their unique selves with all the simplicity and elegance such an expression allows. Peggy's perspective is that, indeed, "Humility is an integral dimension of fine teachers."

9   Awareness

The third general disposition of transcendence is *awareness* (Phenix, 1974). Awareness includes empathy, sympathy, hospitality and tolerance (openness outward, as well as toward the future). The aware individual must liberate herself from perceptions of the unfamiliar or the unknown as a threat to be avoided (Phenix, 1974, p. 125). The aware individual adopts a positive attitude toward all beings, as well as toward nature and avoids "self-protecting isolationism" (p. 125). Meaningful education is not found in teaching methods or in content. Rather, meaning lies in the power that is generated by relationship between teacher and learner (p. 125). The teacher, who enables the learner to expand her awareness, creates "a strong catalyst for learning" (p. 125). Likewise teachers expand their own awareness when they share in the freshness of young learners "who affirm the world and celebrate the possibilities of ever-deepening relationships within it" (p. 125). In Chapter 9, Leslie explains how her professor "could always pinpoint something, one little tiny detail which would tell me a piece of the problem. I don't know if it was how he said it or that he just made me stop for a second and listen to that one thing, but everything would turn out to be all right ...." As a teacher, Leslies also notes that "a special bond develops between the two of us. It sounds kind of arrogant, but it's a communication just the two of us have in some way. I try to find out what their background is and then say 'OK, what do I have today, how can I move myself to that place, into that mindset, so we're in sync, on one kind of wavelength?'"

10   Faithful Doubt

The fourth general disposition, *faithful doubt* (Phenix, 1974, p. 125), has to do with the melding of doubt and faith. In transcendence, doubt and faith are intimately linked. Doubt, serious doubt, is only possible if one has a transcendent faith, or a confidence that "does not rest on any objectified security structures" (p. 126). Presumably, one can doubt well only when one is free intellectually, socially and spiritually by virtue of one's faith.

The educator in pursuit of transcendence does not run from doubt but approaches doubt as an opportunity to criticize constructively while being motivated by concern for improvement and a sense of responsibility to learning oriented cause (Phenix, 1974, p. 126).

> The teacher who is spiritually aware does not seek to protect himself from the insecurity of uncertainty, perplexity, and irremediable ignorance. He does not try to hide behind a screen of academic presumption and professional expertise, embellished with mystifying jargon. Nor does he confuse the role of teacher with that a presumptive or ostensible authoritative oracle. He does not expect or encourage his students supinely to accept his beliefs or directions. On the other hand, he shares with conviction and enthusiasm his glimpses of light. Such sharing encourages his students to do the same, resolutely resisting in himself, and in his students, the paralysis and sense of *futility associated with skepticism and indifference.* (p. 126, emphasis added)

As a teacher, I think about faithful doubt as doubt I may have in myself. And yet, I must also have faith in myself, a determination that I can, and will, see the task at hand through to its successful completion. In terms of faithful doubt, I try to be open with learners when I am not certain that a teaching/learning strategy or project will work effectively. I explain how I feel, if I am doubting myself, or even if I am experiencing uncertainty about content in a given example. I invite learners to work with me until doubt is set aside. I typically say, "I'm not sure whether or not this will work but let's give it a try anyway," and we do. I find that when I express my uncertainty, that relaxes learners and they respond by encouraging the effort. Because I am free to doubt myself or to be critical of myself, I also feel free to express my concern that my learners may, or may not, have invested all that needs to be invested to realize success even as I share my confidence in them. We collectively up our game by encouraging each other.

11 Wonder, Awe and Reverence

The fifth and final dispositions are *wonder, awe, and reverence*. Phenix (1974) describes wonder as a spiritual act involving the attraction one feels toward the unknown or unrealized possibilities (p. 126). Learners are attracted and inspired when teachers emerge as authentic, impassioned human beings who are in search of their own freedom to pursue unrealized possibilities. The teacher's quest for freedom is aligned with those of learners whose quest for freedom is also facilitated. Phenix defines awe as "the sense of momentousness excited by the experience of transcendence" and he adds that a sense of awe is the source of lasting interest in learning (p. 126). As teacher and learner approach transcendence their sense of awe creates a resilient, reverberant, motivating force for learning. Again in such a context, teachers and learners strive to realize a vision that does not yet exist. Veronica, Theoni and the rest of their class experienced such a context as Veronica bravely shared her story even as Theoni emboldened her to do so, thereby establishing a reverberant aura of wonder, awe and reverence.

Reverence refers to the recognition of one's participation in transcendence as a surprising and continually renewed gift. In this context, reverence refers to one's recognition and valuing of one's own capacity to transcend and to act on the capacity to transcend. Reverence also spares "one from the arrogance of self-sufficiency," characteristics that may prevent one from responding in an open way to creative possibilities that are ever present in learning and present with all of life's myriad opportunities (Phenix, 1974, p. 127). Arrogance, self-sufficiency and hubris impede development as well as one's ability to even dream of a world that could otherwise be.

With transcendence characterized by such dispositions, the teacher is enabled and mobilized to create curricula that are responsive to "the uniqueness of the human personality" (Phenix, 1974, p. 127). The transcendent teacher seeks, engenders and celebrates the learner's inner illumination. That celebration occurs not so much in terms of the official curriculum objectives, but more in terms of the atmosphere created wherein freedom and self-discipline permeate the environment and dreams are created and pursued. Once again, freedom is not to be misconstrued with anarchy, indifference or skepticism (p. 128). Rather, appropriate learner conduct, as well as learner awareness of the need for the conduct, is clearly established in transcendence-oriented learning environments.

In transcendence-oriented environments, learners frequently participate in the development of appropriate standards for conduct. In such a school, learners who are aware of the purpose of such standards are motivated to cooperate for the good of all persons involved in the learning community. Transcendent freedom involves "openness to fresh possibilities of insight, invention and provision. Freedom provides ample cultural and interpersonal resources for the formation of unique structure of existence" (Phenix, 1974, p. 128). Freedom, if you will, greases the sophisticated interplay of individuality and culture to facilitate a well functioning transcendent dynamic. A transcendence-oriented school is concerned with education for the whole person, indeed for "the lure of transcendence is toward wholeness" (p. 128) emotional, physical, social, aesthetic and cognitive wholeness. A transcendence-oriented-educator, therefore, is needed to meet the needs of the whole individual.

The transcendence-oriented educator also creates an atmosphere as an expectation for learners to share in the development of "more illuminating patterns of thought" which include viewing learning endeavors with an eye for the whole picture as well as for the specific (Phenix, 1974, p. 130). The directions of inquiry are not only multi-disciplinary; they are also interdisciplinary (p. 130). The various content areas are intermingled in a way that makes each area more vibrant. The study of history, as example, becomes even more compelling and vibrant when it is combined with the study of the language arts, literature, music, art, dance and drama since these disciplines emerge from particular historical contexts. See curricula in the school of transcendence, Chapter 17 for further discussion regarding the role of the arts in transcendence curricula. Regarding curricular integration, recall Helen Keller's words in Chapter 2:

> As my knowledge of things grew I felt more and more the delight of the world I was in. Long before I learned to do a sum in arithmetic or describe the shape of the earth, Miss Sullivan had taught me to find beauty in the fragrant woods, in every blade of grass, and in the curves and dimples of my baby sister's hand. (Keller, 2015, p. 13)

In Chapter 9 Leslie explains that, indeed, for her professor, not only the curriculum but the entire world is integrated:

> He was a wonderful history teacher. He showed me how all things were interrelated. He could speak a zillion languages. He knew everything about costume, everything about history, everything about cooking, everything about all aspects of life, and no aspect was unrelated to him,

at all. For him, everything is related in this incredible universe. All that is happening in the world and what you're going to have for dinner – all are related.

Transcendent curricula are made flexible and are taught with strategies that exploit the learner's innate interests so that what is taught is melded with the learner's background, experience, passions and dreams. Moreover, transcendence is characterized by the "perception of the central task of teaching and learning as dedication to the practice of inquiry" (Phenix, 1974, p. 130). The dedication and zeal for inquiry requires a critical examination of concepts, principles as well as efforts to conceive the gestalt. At the same time however, to assume "that anything is knowable with completeness and certainty arrests inquiry and closes the channels that lead on to deeper and wider insights" (p. 130). Hubris regarding what is knowable and how it is knowable stands at the heart of the argument against standardized testing because the very standardized curricula they force on the learner deny, certainly inhibit, the learner's capacity to perceive, consider or conceive what is knowable as a field of infinite proportions. The imposition of such finite standards stifles the effort to pursue inquiry even as they demobilize and defy the imagination of the learner. The mantle of standards has been touted as a way of ensuring that a minimum acceptable learning baseline is met. Actually, what frequently occurs is that the minimum is *all* that is taught.

And knowledge is not all. For Albert Einstein, "Imagination is more important than knowledge. Knowledge is limited. Imagination encircles the world" (Viereck, 1929, p. 117). Imagination ensures flexibility of thought. Imagination enables one to make connections, to grasp the gestalt. According to Phenix (1974) it is unrealistic to suggest that one can know all there is to know about any content area and correspondingly that a selection of core components of the whole is even desirable. To make such an assumption decreases the perceptual lens and distorts the very nature of inquiry.

The United States has been a model of innovation in education within the world context for decades. School curricula in the United States, prior to the for-profit assessment/standardized testing revolution, afforded great curricular and instructional flexibility that facilitated genuine inquiry as well as a decent amount of access to divergent, creative paths. A panoply of subject area options for inquiry was available in the curriculum. As the focus shifts evermore to what are called "core" content areas as well as the resultant standardization of that content, the options for what to study, as well as how to study it, are made less flexible and far less available. As teachers teach *to* the test, the test becomes *all* that is taught. Standardization of thought is the result, not thought for innovation or creativity, which until relatively recently have been the hallmarks of American public education.

12   Questions for Thought

1. How does Maxine Green conceptualize the role of freedom in learning environments? What is the impact of the freedom Greene describes?

2. How does Greene's freedom unfold in learning environments?

3. What does Parker Palmer say about balancing freedom and self-discipline in learning environments?

4. What does Palmer say about reconciling freedom and self-discipline? Why is it necessary to balance freedom and self-discipline?

5. Define Palmer's transcendent space. How is the transcendent space created and what role does the host play in such a space?

6. Beyond effective guidance, clarity with assignments and appropriate exams, how does a transcendence-oriented teacher meet the challenges of grades and competition?

7. What are Palmer's dispositions and how do they function? How and why are the dispositions essential to transcendence?

CHAPTER 11

Portraits of Transcendent Relators
Kellen and Dr. Ball

> When my father died I shook my fist at God. If I hadn't met Jan when I did, I probably wouldn't be here. I would have been dead. It would have been by my own hand.
>
> KELLEN

∴

1   Kellen

I met Kellen when I was in doctoral school and I noticed her small, delicate frame and charming demeanor. I also noticed that she is not a weak or a passive person; she is fiery. A full-blooded Cherokee, Kellen feels a strong connection to her heritage. She has learned that the Cherokee have always been lied to by the American government.

> Early on, the Cherokee tried to adopt the white man's ways, to try and get along. But if you know the history of the Native Americans, the government rounded them up and took them away from their families. They put them in boarding schools to keep them from speaking their language and to remove them from their culture.

To avoid teaching Native Americans

> inappropriately, don't try to remove their individuality, their tribal custom. Don't make them dress like you want them to, don't make them believe like you want them to as they did in the boarding schools. Don't ever lie to them, because they are expecting you to do that anyway. That's all they have ever heard from the white people, broken promises and broken treaties. The thing is to keep your word. Be honest with them, dead honest with them.

Kellen's demand for honesty that emerges from her heritage and life experience as a Cherokee woman has implications for how she has interacted with teachers throughout her life.

2 Kellen's Life

Kellen's personal life path has not been an easy one for many reasons. Her mother suffered mental illness that led to over thirty shock treatments. Kellen was present for her mother's shock treatments. Her father passed away when she was a young nursing student. Kellen experienced an abusive marriage, and was mother to a child born out of wedlock. She took care of her sociopathic brother, and has endured many physical difficulties of her own. "I have had eight strokes. I have emphysema and I had encephalitis as a child. I have a memory problem, and it takes a lot of studying for me to be successful in school. I want things to work out and so I plan things; I'm very organized."

Through the imposition of the difficulties described above, Kellen discovered that relationships are critically important for her, and so she has sought out "family" to be with throughout her life.

Kellen found it easy to bond with teachers. She made it her business to get along with all teachers, even the difficult ones.

> I was determined I was going to do it. Maybe I made the first effort. I think sometimes you feel challenged by something like that, but the difficult ones turned out to be my favorite teachers in school. And I don't know, maybe I do something to make these types of relationships occur. You see, I don't have any biological family; everyone is dead. My parents died. Dad died right after I graduated from nursing school, and then I lost my mother. But I have adopted family everywhere, grandparents, parents; I just pull them out of the woodwork. Sometimes they start out real difficult, and then I'll make an effort.

3 Jan

When Kellen was a student of nursing, her instructor Jan, took Kellen under her wing. "I met Jan in 1960 when I started nursing school. She was one of my instructors. She just took a liking to me, I guess because I was a good student. She took me home with her a lot and I knew her family, I babysat her children, grew close to them and loved them."

Jan "adopted" Kellen. She interceded for Kellen so she could be with her mother during her treatments. Jan made Kellen feel comfortable, and Jan had unconditional regard for Kellen. She didn't restrict her, but instead allowed her to be herself.

> Jan was the teacher I felt the most comfortable with. She didn't put any requirements on me. I didn't have to measure up in some way or another. She never asked me to change any of my basic principles or my basic moral judgments. I never felt restricted around her, because she allowed me to be myself. I think she was good with all the students, but it just seemed like there was something special between us.

Unlike other teachers who were distant, tense and rigid, Jan encouraged Kellen to let go and be comfortable.

> When Jan was in class with you, she might put her arm around you and say, "come on, relax a little." I know that even after she was teaching at Fort Sanders years later, she didn't mind her students calling her when they had a problem. She never lost her ability to nurture them.

Since their classroom days together, Kellen and Jan have remained close and have continued to visit each other across several states for more than thirty years. "All these years later, Jan still helps me write essays. In fact, she helped me polish my essay for my Indian fellowship."

Jan continues to assist Kellen in both academic and personal ways, supporting and sustaining her choices. At the same time, Jan challenges her. As the years have passed, Jan describes their relationship as having evolved into a kind of sisterhood.

> Jan is still the one person in the world that I could ask for anything, talk to about anything. If I hadn't met Jan when I did, I probably wouldn't be here. I would have been dead. It would have been by my own hand. I wouldn't have been alive if I hadn't had that beginning relationship with her; the pressures in my life were just too great.

4   Dr. Noy

Like Jan, another college professor named Dr. Noy made a significant contribution to Kellen's life. From the beginning he went the proverbial extra mile with her, supporting, encouraging, and having faith in her. He was gentle and warm.

> For example, the first day of classes, I was lost. Dr. Noy came up and put his arm around me and said "I'll show you where to go," and I didn't even know he was the teacher. He took me up to the laboratory and he introduced me to the lab technician. He treated me just like family. It's much easier when you feel at home in a classroom.

Laughter was an important element of Dr. Noy's classroom atmosphere.

> Sometimes he would talk too fast, he is from Taiwan. He would start laughing and then we would all start laughing. I remember one time he really set it off. He brought this paper cup in and he mixed this and that, and he looked at it and said "it isn't working," and he turned around to the blackboard and there was a big smoky explosion. Absolutely set the class crazy. He would do funny things pretty often, because he wanted that kind of atmosphere, he wanted it open. He did it deliberately.

The many ways that Dr. Noy accommodated Kellen impressed her. Those accommodations caused her to remember something she had once heard.

> I learned in psychology, that if a teacher singles out a student and says "that one is going to excel," the student will excel, because the teacher unknowingly does things to help them. On the other hand, if a teacher looks at someone and says "here's a real dummy," he'll turn out to be that way, because unconsciously the teacher considers him that way and won't go the extra mile with him. If Dr. Noy would have been that way, he would have said, "Kellen is a real dummy, she probably is senile, so why should I do anything." Instead, he just seemed like he knew I could. He was there for the students. He wanted them to learn chemistry.

Kellen feels that Dr. Noy worked with her and her limitations, and tried to work for her to overcome some of those limitations. She and her teacher developed a friendship and affection for each other. Kellen adds,

> He and his wife Susan came to my wedding. Susan said, "I'm so sorry that I'm just getting to know you now, when we were getting ready to leave. I wish we could have been here longer, because we could have all been just great friends, and helped each other."

Kellen remains in touch with Dr. Noy and Susan even though he now lives in Taiwan. Clearly, such relationships have brought great meaning to the lives of all involved.

5   Dr. Ball

A third professor, Dr. Ball, also had a major impact on Kellen. Because of him, Kellen decided to enter a second professional field, that of criminal justice. Kellen is most impressed with Dr. Ball's efforts to be honest, "dead honest" with his students, and she is fascinated with his class.

> I said, "my heavens, this man is telling us the truth." He sees things like they are. At my age, I have been through a lot and I have worked all over the country and everything. Some of the things that he comes up with nonetheless surprise me, but I can follow up on and verify that it is the truth.

Dr. Ball nurtured Kellen's natural interest in criminology. He treated Kellen warmly, and he was enthusiastic for her. He made her feel she had something to contribute to the field of criminology.

He encouraged her to conduct research, and showed genuine interest in her efforts by sharing his own research with her.

> I did a case study on serial killers and I got really involved with the research. Dr. Ball wanted to read the paper, and he said, "you know I've done research on what causes sociopathic personalities for years, and if you want to read it I'll bring you a copy of all the stuff I have come up with so you don't have to repeat it." That's one reason why I have changed fields. He asked if I really wanted to do research and find out the cause and the treatment. I said "yes I do." Then he said "you can go anyplace you want to and drive any kind of car you want to, because you will receive the Nobel Prize."
>
> Everybody in the class soon knew what I was going to do professionally. It was funny because Dr. Ball talked about the levels of crime and he would say "these are the delinquents, Kellen's bunch." Dr. Ball seems real pleased that I'm going to graduate school in Criminal Justice.

Throughout it all, Dr. Ball affirmed Kellen and her choices as Kellen began to revise her entire perspective on her life and its possibilities. This was a turning point for Kellen.

"I see Dr. Ball as somebody I want to see after I graduate from college, somebody that I might want to call once in a while, or someone I might want to write and let him know what's going on."

Despite the many contributions he makes to others, as Kellen puts it, "Dr. Ball doesn't even know what he does. He's completely oblivious to the fact that 200 people are now in criminal justice because of him."

As a nurse working in prisons, Kellen wants her clients to feel that she "is there" for them, that she will work on their behalf, and that she will be there to help them grow and rehabilitate.

> If there is some skill I can help them develop for when they get paroled, if they can get along better in society, maybe we can find out how together. Actually my position in the prison will be an RN-3 and counselor. I'm going to approach the prisoners I work with in prison as people. I'll ask "what do you think you would like to improve here, what is giving you trouble, that maybe would give you trouble if you were out, if you were getting paroled and wanted to get a job? Is it something about the way you talk; is it something about your demeanor? What would you like for us to work on?"

Kellen intends to take the risk for the prisoners as Jan once took it for her. "If they have a problem with one of the correctional officers or with someone in administration, I would hope they would tell me their point of view and let me go and mediate for them." Kellen encourages educators to show learners kindness, attention and to "draw them out, give them approval, give them encouragement starting real early in life. These kids need someone to reach out to them." She believes students need intimate and open types of relationships with their teachers. You need "someone who will accept you, warts and all. These kinds of relationships actually keep you living, keep you going, keep you human." Kellen feels that the student has a great deal to offer the teacher as well. The student gives the teacher support, and encouragement, helps the teacher feel at ease. Because of the support and influence of students, Kellen has witnessed teachers transform from lifeless, dull, classroom personas to extroverted, fun and funny teachers. Kellen believes that both the teacher and learner have abilities, experiences and gifts to share with each other. Teaching goes two ways. "You know, it's sharing back and forth, learning new things, learning about people, learning about each other."

To summarize, Kellen has known great personal and physical hardships that have caused her to regard relationships as being critically important. Those enduring special relationships are characterized by unconditional regard, faith, accommodation and nurturance. Kellen has observed, and been the beneficiary of, teachers who took risks to care, to love and to be loved.

Her relationships have enabled her to overcome her limitations, and even to avoid suicide. Kellen views the teacher learner relationship as being a matter of two-way sharing and learning about each other, and she plans to carry that on in her work with incarcerated individuals.

6   Portrait of Dr. Ball (Kellen's Professor)

> It always bothered me that some people thought they could "lord it over" other people.
> DR. BALL

One of Kellen's role models and a source of inspiration for her, Dr. Ball, wears dark framed glasses; his dark hair falls over his earthy comfortable face. He was raised during the Depression in Preston County, West Virginia. He was not afforded many of the luxuries some take for granted, such as indoor plumbing and financial stability. While he was still a small child, his family went to live in a shipbuilding community in Maryland. It astonished him that residents of the community, operating on stereotypes about West Virginians, were rude enough to walk up to the windows of his house and look in to see whether he and his family were wearing shoes. As he and I observed, one winter in West Virginia without shoes would render one without feet to put shoes on.

It further bothered Dr. Ball that "some people thought they were superior to other people and could lord it over them." That is to say, he was put off by individuals who viewed themselves as being superior to others and who acted to disparage, oppress or dominate others. When Dr. Ball was in the service, his Captain demonstrated a different approach to life.

7   The Service

It impressed then Lieutenant Ball that even though the Captain easily could have, he didn't engage in "chest thumping," did not "pull rank" or buy into what Dr. Ball called the "silliness" of the military. The Captain seemed to have it all in perspective. Dr. Ball said,

> He could have easily pulled rank because I was pretty naive about the military. I had only been there for four or five months and it's a whole different world, like I say. He treated me the way I always felt people should treat each other. Among the career officers there was more than

a tendency, I mean they actually enjoyed holding the second lieutenants in place, making clear to them they didn't know anything. It didn't take much effort and they delighted in it. The Captain could have done that very easily. This guy wasn't like that; this guy could see that there was a world outside the military.

The Captain was open with Dr. Ball, and the Captain had an outsider's view. He could laugh about adult men saluting each other, donning spangles and all. It refreshed Dr. Ball that the Captain did not take it all so seriously. As persons with graduate backgrounds in psychology, Dr. Ball and the Captain seemed to connect as they confronted the dynamics of military life. Rather than discuss rifles, football and women, for example, the two of them shared personal philosophies and perspectives on life. As Lieutenant Ball's Captain, he treated Dr. Ball as he would have asked to be treated.

> This guy probably had a lot of influence on me because I was a young man trying to learn how to deal with people and I liked the way he handled himself. I probably picked up style from him; maybe I imitated him in some of the ways he dealt with the enlisted men. He was very good with them, I thought. He was able to maintain his authority without giving them any feeling that he was stepping on them or pushing them around, or anything like that. That's the kind of officer I wanted to be, so I watched this guy.

The Captain, seven or eight years older than Lieutenant Ball, interacted with Ball, then in his early twenties, like "a big brother." Dr. Ball said he liked the Captain, who was "a kindred spirit."

8   More Background

Dr. Ball's teaching philosophy also seems to have originated from his childhood encounters, when it bothered him that people in the helping professions often hurt others rather than helped them. Those individuals seemed to contribute to what he calls the collective "burden of misery." "It bothered me that people, preachers for example, always think you need this or you need that. It didn't seem like anybody needed what they were trying to peddle at all, trying to get them so goddamn frightened, scaring them to death with hell, fire and damnation and everything."

He observed teachers as well scapegoating particular children because, perhaps, they had not brushed their teeth. For Dr. Ball, teachers, like others in position of authority or power, should not employ insensitive, intimidating or disrespectful approaches when they interact with learners.

9   Dr. Ball, the Teacher

Dr. Ball wants to treat learners more fairly than he was treated and not add to their burden of misery. He wants them to become kinder, gentler, and fairer, about crime and criminals for example, and to be smarter and more informed. He has difficulty dealing with human hierarchies. For example, Dr. Ball does not talk much differently to a child than he does to adults at the top of the hierarchy.

> Larry Nichol's daughter first came into this office when she was 5 years old. I think I talked to her in the same tone of voice I talk to the Dean. I mean it's hard for me not to. I have to strain to remember this guy is the Dean, and I'm supposed to speak with him differently than with Larry's little girl. That's why the army was so weird to me. I had to remember he's the General and you had to snap a salute to a Colonel, and all that. I don't really see that, to tell you the truth. The differences seem to me to be real superficial. I feel like we're about 99.9% the same, kids or whatever. I wouldn't say it's gotten me in trouble, but it makes time management pretty hard when you spend as much time talking to a 5 year old as you do talking to the Dean, that's for sure.

Instead, Dr. Ball believes in having conversation with, and compassion for learners.

> You go into a class and you don't know what's going on with all of these students, but you know from just talking with some of them, everybody has problems. If they don't have a health problem, they have a problem with a parent bouncing them off the wall, or they have a problem with a boyfriend or girlfriend, or they are all confused about what they want to major in, or something else. I call it compassion. A lot of it is a feeling that life is not easy and it wouldn't be so hard if people would work with each other.

10   The Teacher as Empowerer, Not as Helper

A lot of school teachers really want to help people. That's not exactly what I want to do, because I don't know how to help. In other words I don't know what they need. It's always kind of baffled me that people thought I knew what other people needed. I never really felt like I knew.

Dr. Ball said that if, as a teacher, he wanted to *help* learners, it would not be through teaching them how to diagram a sentence, for example. That doesn't seem to make any difference. He would not profess to know how to *help* in that way. As a teacher, Dr. Ball said that he

> would rather students learn *how* to learn. They would be better off. I clown around a lot because I feel like they are going to learn better that way. Not necessarily for a multiple-choice exam, but there are many ways of knowing, and the way I want them to know is in the gut. The other type of learning doesn't last very long anyway, and so I feel like I'm clowning around. They start laughing and then they open up a lot. I want them to like me, laugh, open up, and feel a sense of being free. I don't want to overwhelm them with a lot of facts, names, or things like that.
>
> On tests for example, I try to ask them about some idea rather than about some name. I would rather they leave the class with a feeling like "Hey, this isn't too bad. This guy is all right." I feel like stuff will soak in more and they will be kinder, gentler, fairer people if I do it this way. That's really how I want them to be. I want them to be kinder, gentler, and fairer about crime and criminals and other issues when they leave, and smarter too, more informed about it and so on. If I have to drop or neglect a point of information to get another laugh about something, better to see me as somebody who is some poor, rapidly aging guy who is trying to figure out things and is having a hard time himself.

Dr. Ball questions the meaning of phrases like,

> "do the right thing." I kid in the criminology class; in fact, I was kidding the students the other day. I said, I don't know what "do the right thing" means. I don't know how to "do the right thing." I just developed a rule long ago, half-joking. I said that "I'll just try to create the minimum amount of harm. I'll just try to go along." I don't know if this is right or that is right, but I take the path that seems to hurt the fewest number of people.
>
> In *Escape From Freedom* (1969) Erich Fromm makes a distinction between, I think it's freedom from, and freedom to. And he says, freedom from means, "I want the world off my back." But freedom to is the idea that if I could, I would do this, and this, and this, and this. So when you're teaching your class, you almost don't want to tell the students too much so as not to subvert their freedom.

11   Humor and Answers

Dr. Ball believes in the power of humor, when it is used discriminatingly, to open people and enable them to learn in more lasting ways, ways he has referred to as "in the gut." Humor provides an opportunity to lighten the classroom tone. He attempts to reduce the "stonefaced" sort of seriousness that many classrooms exude. Rather than diminish learners by deifying the great authorities and historical figures they study, Dr. Ball humanizes and personalizes those individuals for the learner. Rather than provide the learner with the answers he would suggest that neither he, nor the disciplines as he sees them, really have the answers.

> For example, students tell me they think that there are answers and they want the answers, and I am supposed to know because that's what I'm being paid for, then I'll try to find some way of conveying to them (not in this kind of language), that I'm not sure there are any answers. We don't know. Does time exist? Does space exist? Probably not. Emmanuel Smith said they are concepts of the mind that allow us to think. That's all they are. What the hell is real? Is a thing solid? Probably not.
>
> Why are there not any answers? That's the problem. That's why people ought to be fairer, kinder, and gentler. If there were answers, we would just do what the answers told us. We wouldn't have to rely on ourselves. In fact, we don't so much as know what the questions are. That is why people should be kinder and fairer. All we have to do is do whatever helps us make it through this stuff without hurting each other. "By their fruits shall you know them."

To summarize, as a small child and as a West Virginian, Dr. Ball remains disturbed that some individuals, either by virtue of their perceived superiority or place in the hierarchy, felt that they could dominate or oppress others. His relationship with his Captain affirmed for him that a better way was possible. The Captain did not "pull rank," but instead treated subordinates with humor and openness. The Captain was like a "big brother," a kindred spirit to Dr. Ball.

As a teacher, Dr. Ball's frustration with human hierarchies dictates how he interacts with his learners. He does not view himself as the purveyor of answers and help. Instead, he wants to explore the questions with them in an atmosphere of freedom, openness and laughter. He wants to help them out and in so doing, encourages them to be kinder, fairer and gentler persons. As an individual who struggles with authority, he questions whether an individual can have "the answers" or even the appropriate questions to ask. He does not

PORTRAITS OF TRANSCENDENT RELATORS 165

act to *help* learners because the concept of helping is too elusive or unstable for him. Instead he attempts to facilitate their abilities to be self-directed, to know *how* to learn and how to avoid hurting others, all within the context of a world without answers.

12   Questions for Thought

1. What hardships has Kellen experienced?

2. Why does she seek out family?

3. How did Kellen's teachers and professors meet her needs and become her family?

4. What do you find most appealing about Dr. Noy? Dr. Ball?

5. Would you like to have a teacher like Jan? Why or why not?

6. What qualities or characteristics of shamanism exist in Kellen's and Dr. Ball's Portraits, if any?

7. What are Dr. Ball's concerns about bigotry as it relates to one's native region or state?

8. How was the Captain different from the other officers?

9. Why and how was that significant for Dr. Ball?

10. What is the nature of Dr. Ball's conflict with the "helping" professions?

11. How is humor important to Dr. Ball?

12. What is Dr. Ball's perspective on "the truth" or having "the answer?"

CHAPTER 12

Reconciliation, Banking Education, Problem Posing Education, the I-It and I-Thou Relationships, and the Teacher as Midwife

> Finally we got to the place where [Jerry] was playing the piano .... I was pushing him, all through the whole piece.... I was pushing him that way until he was so furious with me .... It was a real chance. When we came to the biggest musical spot ... I just said "this is the spot where you let it out ...." Jerry was able to release all of his pain, a wall of pain into the music. It was amazing.
>
> LESLIE

∴

Paulo Freire was born into a Brazilian middle class family on September 19, 1921. During, and because of the Great Depression, Freire's family lost most of their assets. By the time Freire was in the fourth grade, his family was living in poverty. Freire, hungry throughout childhood and adolescence, fell four grades behind. Later Freire shared how poverty and hunger profoundly impacted his ability to learn. He realized that he was not dumb or disinterested, he was instead starving. Moreover, Freire grew to understand that his poverty and hunger limited his access to quality education. Freire's years in poverty shaped his concerns for poor people and became the foundation for much of his outlook, as well as his scholarly and other professional work. He readily discerned how social class impacts one's access to knowledge thus blocking their access to the power. Freire acted to change the very system that was deliberately designed to keep inequities in place. Throughout his life, Freire worked to improve the plight of the poor.

I heard Paulo Freire speak as part of a panel that included Maxine Greene and Nel Noddings at the 1991 Annual Meeting of the American Educational Research Association (AERA). I was certainly impressed with his narrative but I was even more impressed with his humbleness, his kindness and his gentleness. He was instantly at one with his audience. People in the audience felt that he was speaking to them privately, even when hundreds were there in person.

© HUNTER O'HARA, 2021 | DOI: 10.1163/9789004445321_012

1 Reconciliation between Teacher and Student

According to Freire, during the teaching-learning process, the teacher and learner roles may blur as each one gives to the other. As the roles blur, teacher and learner are liberated. In his book, *Pedagogy of the Oppressed* (2012), Freire describes the role freedom can play in education. Upon that backdrop of freedom, Freire places great emphasis on what he calls the drive towards *"reconciliation between teacher and student."* In other words, "education must begin with the solution of the teacher-student contradiction, by reconciling the poles of contradiction so that both are simultaneously teachers and students" (p. 72).

2 Banking Education

The teacher-student contradiction, or opposition, exists because of the practice of education systems and too many teachers: depositing information into a depository (the student). Freire calls this misguided process *banking education*. The depositor makes a deposit via narration (also called lecture) into the student (metaphorically the bank). Rather than to do something, the teacher narrates *about* something while students and the environment remain motionless, static. Students develop *narration sickness* in response to the seemingly endless, one-way flow of information with no opportunity to meaningfully respond or to react. The one way flow of voice, teacher to student, establishes a *culture of silence* in the classroom and trains students to be inclined to be silent in the face of powerful people and those who would oppress them throughout their lives. Banking education produces people who become fodder for domination.

Even though students may learn particular lessons from banking education, the nature of that learning is ultimately designed to serve the dominant, powerful class, not most learners. In Chapter 9 the teacher-student contradiction manifested for Jerry in banking educator, Ms. Gilzenskolds. That teacher acted as if she were impervious to error, fear, insecurity, and nervousness. She seemed devoid of feeling, could not empathize with learners, nor ever begin to think of them as equal to her. That teacher left Jerry with feelings of resentment and frustration. He would always remember her for the many ways in which she managed to make him and his peers feel *badly* about themselves.

A solution to what Freire calls the teacher-student contradiction, or opposition, is not found, nor can it be found, in banking education. Freire states "On the contrary, banking education maintains and even stimulates contradiction

between teacher and learner via the attitudes and practices" present in oppressive cultures that are embodied in the banking education teacher:
- The teacher teaches and the students are taught.
- The teacher knows everything and the students know nothing.
- The teacher thinks and the students are thought about.
- The teacher talks and the students listen meekly.
- The teacher disciplines and the students are disciplined.
- The teacher chooses and enforces [those choices], and the students comply.
- The teacher acts and the students have the illusion of acting through the action of the teacher.
- The teacher chooses the program content, and the students (who were not consulted) adapt to it.
- The teacher confuses the authority of knowledge with own professional authority, which sets in opposition to the freedom of the students.
- The teacher is the Subject of the learning process, while the pupils are mere objects (Freire, 2012, p. 73).

3   Problem Posing Education

Freire's brilliant alternative to banking education is *problem posing education*. With problem posing education, the revolutionary teacher, unlike Ms. Gilzenskolds, acting on the side of freedom, deliberately enters into a partnership of dialogue with the student. Through that dialogue, knowledge is formulated collaboratively as teachers engage learners in critical thought. Profound trust, hope, love and creative power emerge throughout this process. Thus, the teacher-student contradiction, or opposition, is reconciled. The co-dialoguers, teachers with students, are then enabled to move toward freedom and a *culture of voices*. A culture of voices occurs in a conversation-centered community where access to power and to voice are shared equitably between all members of the community. Those who participate in a culture of voices learn to pursue freedom for themselves, their families and their communities. Having experienced freedom fully, they are far less likely to fall subject to domination throughout their lives. Problem posing education creates a yearning for more and more freedom.

Problem posing education involves interaction that develops the student's capacity to think independently, to reach toward more and deeper learning and *again*, to stand up for oneself, one's own interests, one's family interests and the interests of the community as a whole. Evidence of this reaching toward freedom is discussed in each of the preceding portraits, including

Kellen, Dr. Ball, Jerry and Leslie, and later particularly in the example of Laura and Melinda.

Blurring of the traditional teacher learner roles and the reconciliation of the teacher-student contradiction Freire believes, occurs because all humans are in the process of becoming something more; that is, teachers and learners alike are unfinished beings. Both exist in, and with, a correspondingly unfinished reality. Both teacher and learner are evolving and both learn from each other. Likewise, as Laura explains in Chapter 13, equality and freedom, as in the example of problem posing education, are starting points in the process of becoming something more.

> I think equality between a teacher and a student is like freedom, at least from my experiences, equality is always something that can be pursued. It might be obtained in a moment, and then you work to pursue it again, just like freedom. I don't think equality and freedom refer to stages, I think they are beginnings. A kid may come in with the preconception of what their world is and what your world is like. All you can really do is start to strip those rules away, present yourself in honesty *and* invite them to question things. I really think that resistance is necessary in the effort to obtain equality between individuals. I don't think one can say "OK, now we're all equal in here," because it's not really seen as equal. But when you move beyond those roles, then you can say "we've moved into equality."
>
> Freedom should be the beginning so that there is something to struggle for and to pursue; it's not the end product, it's the beginning. Once you have had it, you have to keep working to *really* have it. I don't think you ever arrive at a conclusion or a finish. Theoretically, learners already have equality, they already have freedom, but it is always a process. It used to surprise me sometimes when they would do what I asked them just because I was a teacher. Once you shed your pretense and meet your student as another human being, that's when genuine power begins, power to become and to transform lives. I think a lot of it has to do with our interaction with learners. It depends on how we perceive their nature. We must perceive them as people first. I see my students as inherently good. In fact I used to *want* the "trouble-makers" because I knew that inside they were good people.

The act of reconceiving the teacher learner relationship requires a new or "revolutionary leadership." The practice of education must become *co-intentional*. That is, with problem posing education, both teacher and learner are co-intent in the task of unveiling a reality. Further, they come to the reality critically as they engage in the task of re-creating knowledge as in the example of Leslie and Jerry. Through common reflection and action they become permanent re-creators. In Chapter 9, for Jerry, "There is a feeling that we're in this together."

In Chapter 1, I describe how the co-intentional process works:

> My teacher Peggy explained very early on that our goal in her class would *not* be individual, independence-oriented learning pursuits. Rather, the goal would be what we could accomplish together through collaborative learning projects. I remember her talking about each of us being links in a chain, the chain itself worthless without the strength of each link. She held learners in high regard and I never felt that she took advantage of her position of authority in a negative way.

Through dialogue, the teacher-of-the-students and the students-of-the-teacher cease to exist and new terms emerge: teacher-student *with* student-teachers. The teacher is no longer merely the one-who-teaches, but one who is also taught in dialogue with the students, who in turn, while being taught, also teach. They become jointly responsible for a process in which both grow. In this process, arguments based on traditional perceptions of "authority" are no longer valid; in order to function well, authority must be distributed on the side of freedom, not against it. As teachers begin to learn from learners and relators grow together, their relationships become reciprocal and mutual in orientation. To interpret Freire in terms of the desired intent and outcomes for problem posing education as well as the process of reconciling the teacher-student contradiction, each of the following occurs with Freire's problem posing education:

– Both teacher and learner teach and are taught by each other.
– Both teacher and learner possess relevant knowledge to contribute to the act of teaching and learning.
– Both teacher and learner are actively engaged in the process of cognition, including critical thought, analysis, synthesis and evaluation of content.
– Both teacher and learner engage in bold dialogue with each other and with other learners.
– Both teacher and learner engage in the process of developing and refining self-discipline.
– Both teacher and learner develop and select learning processes, projects and activities, as well as implement those processes and procedures.
– Both teacher and learner fully engage in the process of authentic, active teaching and learning.

RECONCILIATION, BANKING EDUCATION, PROBLEM POSING EDUCATION   171

- Whenever possible, both teacher and learner choose the program content and thus, both teacher and learner are devoted to the content, as they are to each other.
- The teacher remains "in charge" and responsible for the welfare of the learner overseeing the learner's development even as the teacher acts to increase the freedom of the learner in the process of achieving authority with learners rather than over them.
- Both teacher and learner are "Subjects" of the learning process, neither teacher nor learner are "objects" of the learning process.

How specifically does banking education differ from problem posing education? I created a dichotomy table to illustrate the contrast between Freire's two education system classifications:

DICHOTOMY 1

Banking education	Problem posing education
Oppressor/oppressed dynamic	Group purpose, group-inquiry dynamics
"Culture of silence"/inertia	Culture of voices/action/involvement
"Narration sickness" purpose/involvement	Mutual dialogue/inspiration/
Automatons/robots/dehumanization	Fully human interaction, all acting on their own and collective best interests

Recall Chapter 2 and Theoni's dialectic-based motivation, "I want them to recognize, listen to, associate, understand, and commiserate with the social side of education to better prepare them to support their future students as they progress through similar experiences." Theoni describes what occurs in her problem posing classroom,

> I am there to support, encourage, promote, and challenge. ... I intuitively make these connections with students; it may be experience, it may be my desire to make meaningful connections with these young adults, it may be my compassion for their situations that allows me to interact in such a way with my students.

Dialogue between teacher and the learner, as well as between learner and learner, is the cornerstone of problem posing education as well as mutual understanding, mutual learning, mutual inquiry and questioning, mutual reflection and mutual problem solving. The traditional mode of communication, the mode used by the banking education teacher is *didactic,* whereas problem posing educators facilitate a *dialectic,* that is discourse between two or more individuals, instruction via dialogue. I created a dichotomy table below to illustrate the contrast between didactic instruction, that is prominent in banking education and dialectic instruction that is the foundation of problem posing education.

DICHOTOMY 2

Didactic instruction	Dialectic instruction
Teacher talks "at" learners	Teacher converses with learners
Learner is passive	Learner is engaged/active
One-way flow of information	Multi-directional flow of information
Efficient delivery for short-term recall	Efficient delivery for long-term recall, deep, meaningful learning
Lecture/Sometimes Q&A	Conversation/activity/imagery/graphs/film/role play/debate/group-pair-share
Reaches auditory learners	Reaches visual, kinesthetic as well as auditory learners
Unequal access/opportunity for success	Equal access and opportunity for success
"Culture of Silence"	Culture of Voices

4 The I-It Relationship

Martin Buber, a social existential philosopher, contrasts below the difference between his I-Thou relationship and the I-It relationship as well as the communion, dialogue, mutuality and reciprocity present in I-Thou relationships. That is, Buber posits two primary attitudes and relations between people. In the *I-It relationship,* one individual knows and uses other persons without allowing them to exist as unique entities (Buber, 1965b). In I-It relationships, the one individual (I) sets himself apart from the other (it), thereby increasing distance between the two relators (Buber, 1958). The It individual exists as an object for the I individual's use and exploitation (1965b). When the I individual uses the It individual as an object, the I individual's powers to relate are decreased

(Buber, 1958). Terms such as use, observation (see below), exploitation, power and destiny characterize the I-It relationship. Jerry's teacher, Ms. Gilzenskolds, deliberately constructed an I-It relationship with her learners, a relationship fraught with relational distance.

5   The I-Thou Relationship

A positive relationship however, is created when one makes oneself fully present to the other (Buber, 1965). For Buber, the purpose of relation is to "touch" the other (1958) rather than to thicken distance. One can become oneself more fully *only with* the other which suggests that an individual becomes whole through being with another individual. Moreover, one cannot develop authentically without the *I-Thou relationship*. The I-Thou relationship is one of presence, mutuality, directness and openness (Buber, 2002). The I-Thou relationship is intense and ineffable (1965). The I individual heeds, or gives consideration to the Thou individual rather than observes him or her, receives rather than uses the Thou individual (1958), and encounters rather than experiences the Thou individual. With I-Thou, the focus is tenderness, rather than power, toward the Thou individual. Leslie worked to create a tender I-Thou relationship with Jerry. Leslie was deliberately *with* Jerry, never over him. In Chapter 11, Kellen explains the phenomenon on of being with her teachers, their tenderness, openness, and success is reducing relational distance:

> ... [T]he first day of classes, I was lost. Dr. Noy came up and put his arm around me and said "I'll show you where to go," and I didn't even know he was the teacher. He took me up to the laboratory and he introduced me to the lab technician. He treated me just like family. It's much easier when you feel at home in a classroom.

Jan was present for Kellen in a similar way:

> When Jan was in class with you, she might put her arm around you and say, "come on, relax a little." I know that even after she was teaching at Fort Sanders [Regional Medical Center in Tennessee] years later, she didn't mind her students calling her when they had a problem. She never lost her ability to nurture them.

The I-Thou relation is reciprocal (Buber, 1958). It can occur only if the teacher is able to develop a real mutuality between herself and the learner. Mutuality can exist only if the learner "trusts the teacher and knows that she is really there for him" (p. 176). Mutuality makes a desirable educative relationship possible as it enables the learner to be trusting and accessible (Cohen, 1983). Peggy describes reciprocity and mutuality in teaching as "a light that shines back and forth from teacher to student, and then from student to teacher, and so on, depending on the situation. Rigidity prevents that shifting." Laura's connection with Melinda is an archetypical example of Martin Buber's I-Thou relationship particularly because of the mutual growth they shared. In Chapter 13, Laura explains the back and forth phenomenon of mutuality:

> I know that I only supported [Melinda] in her growth, but I do think we both grew because of our friendship. For a long time I thought I was the only one giving in that relationship, but looking back I realize that she was one of my only friends those first years in teaching. She was giving to me all the while. As I watched her resolve family, social, and personal image issues, I finished resolving them in my own life. I wonder sometimes where I would be if she had not entered my life. A year passed before I really knew how much Melinda meant to me.

As described above, the I-Thou relationship is similar to the transcendent teacher learner relationship in that both are mutual and reciprocal. However, while the transcendent teacher learner relationship is reliant upon mutuality (O'Hara, 2015), it also specifies three *requisite types* of mutuality: mutual trust, mutual respect and mutual care, which are the foundation of a transcendent relationship. Unlike Buber, O'Hara's transcendent relationship also requires a warm social atmosphere in which all members of the teaching learning community feel cared for, valued and valuable.

6 Becoming Mutual

Mutuality is won by "direct and ingenious participation in the life of one's pupils" (Buber, 2002, p. 127). "When the pupil's confidence has been won, his resistance against being educated gives way to a singular happening: he accepts the educator as a person. He feels he may trust this man, that this man is not making a business out of him, but is taking part in his life, accepting him before desiring to influence him" (p. 126).

> He must know [the learner] not as a mere sum of qualities, aspirations and inhibitions, he must apprehend him, and affirm him as a whole.

RECONCILIATION, BANKING EDUCATION, PROBLEM POSING EDUCATION   175

> He must practice the kind of realization I call embracing. The pupil too should intend and affirm his educator as this particular person. (Buber, 1958, p. 178)

This affirmation process is demonstrated, for example, in the relationships between Hunter and his students as they began to see him as a fellow human being rather than an exotic character.

Buber emphasizes, however, that a relationship can become mutual only "when the other comes to meet me as I him" (Buber, 2002, p. 14). Mutual relationships cannot be generated by one individual or by one's own will and action. The relationship can only come into being if the relator responds with their "whole being" (p. 14). Again, such a response must include trust because trust is "the most inward achievement" in the educative relation between teacher and learner (p. 116). When the teacher fosters genuine trust and contact with the learner and "experiences [the learner's] side of the relationship," then "through the selection of the effective world" the learner can realize meaning in life and what he or she can become (p. 120). Teacher and learner share mutuality, no small achievement as external forces act against it. Teacher learner mutuality may be regarded as one of an array of non-remunerative positive feelings one gains from engaging in teacher learner relationships that go beyond or transcend barriers of traditional relationships and of I-It relationships. In Chapter 9, Jerry describes mutuality from the learner's perspective:

> I like the equality I feel ... It's not that I'm as good ... as she is, or I know as much as she does, or that my knowledge is equivalent to hers. It's not that kind of equality. It's not so much she treats me like an adult, but that she treats me as an equal ....

From the teacher's perspective, in Chapter 15, Beth describes:

> In the classroom I never saw myself as the big boss because we all talked about things and all accomplished things. I was really aware of that. I didn't want to go in there dressed in a suit; I didn't want to make myself seem better than them, look better than them or act superior to them. I would try to talk more on [the learner's] level. I didn't want to be above Alexander, for example, I wanted to be with him. You see, that's how we could get through things.

In Chapter 9, I describe mutuality between Jerry and me as the kind of interaction that happens in some professional environments where individuals really have each other's best interests at heart. I have not found such a situation to be common in life. The possibilities for creative pursuits are endless.

In Chapter 1, I quote Helen Keller's (1988, pp. 29–30) description of the mutuality that emerged in her relationship with her teacher Anne Sullivan:

> … My teacher is so near to me that I scarcely think of myself apart from her. How much of my delight in all beautiful things is innate, and how much is due to her influence, I can never tell. I feel that her being inseparable from my own, and that the footsteps of my life are in hers. All the best of mine belongs to her – there is not a talent, or an inspiration, or a joy in me that has not [been] awakened by her loving touch.

7 Dialogue and Inclusion

At the core of Buber's mutual relationship, as with Freire's problem posing education, is *dialogue*. Buber's dialogue is facilitated through the practice of *inclusion*. Buber's use of the term inclusion is different from its contemporary use. With Buber's inclusion, one individual "experiences the other side of the relationship" (Buber, 1965, p. 70). In the inclusion process, "… I imagine to myself what another man is at this very moment wishing, feeling, perceiving, thinking and not as a detached content but in his very reality" (p. 70). The teacher's capacity to meet the learner's needs more fully, and to relate more effectively, is increased because the teacher's overall level of awareness has expanded. With this expanded awareness, the teacher is enabled to dialogue with the learner in more meaningful, more profitable ways.

Recall Chapter 2, wherein Anne practices inclusion by drawing on her inner *sharpsightedness*, her acute perception, intuition, discernment and understanding to reach Helen. Anne demonstrates a capacity to assess Helen's predicament and to draw sound conclusions, the outcomes of which were to benefit Helen day-by-day, frequently moment-by-moment for the rest of her life.

Buber's inclusion capacity could actually be the defining line that distinguishes very effective teachers from moderately effective or ineffective teachers. The presence of mutuality, trust and inclusion do not suggest that relators will always agree (Buber, 2002, p. 127). In fact, conflict has educational value and may arise in environments where learners are not required to respond in unconditional agreement with the teacher. When learners are allowed to disagree, teachers help them to arrive at answers for themselves. Again, conflict educates when it is resolved through authentic dialogue. In fact, whether the teacher and learner meet in agreement or disagreement is not what matters. What matters is the meeting itself as was demonstrated in the example of Leslie and her challenging professor. It is the healthy atmosphere of mutual confidence that sustains the relationship through conflict (Buber, 2002, p. 127), through the tension and the uncertainty of disagreement. In Chapter 15, Beth explains one dimension of the role dialogue and inclusion play in her interaction with her students, "I use trial and error, intuition. I can tell by having conversation with them, I would talk with them and determine where they were" rather than rely on tests to determine a learner's level of development.

Recall Chapter 2, Theoni describes the impact of authentic, open, even raw, dialogue:

> The entire group was riveted; the story was so personal that the adjacent group stopped reading in order to listen to Veronica. The energy in the room was dreamlike: a group of sixteen people let go of fears, misconceptions, judgments, and thoughts beyond the present moment. We all focused on this opportunity to learn from one another, to grow together and to begin to understand each other.

The teacher's role is one of "critical guide and directing spirit" (Cohen, 1983, p. 32). The teacher does not coerce the learner. The teacher's role is founded on the principle of freedom and it expresses a particular "point of view and an orientation" (p. 32). In Chapter 11, Kellen shares Jan's process of increasing freedom while avoiding coercion:

> Jan was the teacher I felt the most comfortable with. She didn't put any requirements on me. I didn't have to measure up in some way or another. She never asked me to change any of my basic principles or my basic moral judgments. I never felt restricted around her, because she allowed me to be myself. I think she was good with all the students, but it just seemed like there was something special between us.

8 The Teacher as Midwife

For Belenky, Clinchy, Goldberger, and Tarule (1997) teachers must work, metaphorically, as *midwives* in the process of recreating knowledge with the learner through collaborative dialogue. Rather than deposit knowledge, in the learner's head, midwives draw it out. They assist students in giving birth to their own ideas, in making their own tacit knowledge explicit and elaborating on it (p. 217). While teachers-as-midwives support the learner's own thought, they do not think *for* the learner nor do they "expect the students to think as they do." Rather, midwives encourage and "assist in the emergence of consciousness" (p. 218). The midwife's first priority is to be responsive to, and to preserve the child's vulnerability (p. 218). Assistance at this level often requires critical work at intense moments. The child's fragile newborn thoughts must be born with their truth intact. Teachers-as-midwives help the learner "to speak in [her] own active voice" (p. 218), to "deliver [her] words to the world" (p. 219).

Robin Williams creates an extraordinary portrayal of midwifery as John Keating in the film *Dead Poet's Society* (1989). In the film, shy, socially uncomfortable student Todd Anderson has not written the poem that he was required to write for his teacher Mr. Keating. On the pretext of expressing a "barbaric yawp," Mr. Keating in full midwifery mode, brings Todd to the front of the classroom and draws a poem out of Todd, on the spot, as it were. First he asks Todd to describe an image of Walt Whitman that sits above the blackboard. Mr. Keating covers Todd's eyes and ears thereby taking Todd's mind off of what his peers may be thinking of what he is about to create. Then Mr. Keating conducts Todd through the creation of his poem by cuing him with prompts. Before Todd has time to shrink and before his classmates or he can stop the creative process, Todd is midwifed by Keating into writing an expressive poem.

In Chapter 2, Theoni acts as midwife as she enable Veronica in the process of reading her gut wrenching biography. Theoni guided from within by understanding and awareness, "I leaned in very close to Veronica and I said, 'you *can* do this, *you need* to do this.'" Veronica describes her reaction in that moment:

> Her telling me I had to read it myself made me feel stronger somehow. Dr. Soublis' tone was even and there was a soft strength to it, if that makes sense? She seemed sure in her words, and that transferred to me, making me feel sure. Most importantly, there was no negativity in her voice, no demand, just support.

Theoni, still standing behind her, put her hands on Veronica's shoulders and her chin on Veronica's head and quietly said, "It'll be okay." Theoni stayed close behind Veronica and Veronica continued to be soothed by Theoni's nearness and confidence in her.

Belenky, Clinchy, Goldberger, and Tarule (1997) also refer to a *connected knowing* encounter, which emerges out of relationships of equality and intimacy between oneself and the other. Such connected knowing has many similarities to Buber's I-Thou relationship. In such relationships, distance and impersonality are reduced or eliminated. The goal of the relationship is understanding (p. 183) and to connect is "to enter into each student's perspective" (p. 227). The connected teacher attempts to create learning atmospheres where participants "can nurture each other's thoughts to maturity" (p. 221). Whenever a diversity of human perspectives is considered and respected, however, vagueness or uncertainty will emerge. That uncertainty needs to be recognized as a desirable quality of evolving thought. In fact, within the teaching and learning context, uncertainty leads to a sense of growing confidence in the process of learning. In Chapter 11, Kellen explains how her connnected knowing increased with Dr. Ball:

> I did a case study on serial killers and I got really involved with the research. Dr. Ball wanted to read the paper, and he said, "you know I've done research on what causes sociopathic personalities for years, and if you want to read it I'll bring you a copy of all the stuff I have come up with so you don't have to repeat it." That's one reason why I have changed fields. He asked if I really wanted to do research and find out the cause and the treatment. I said "yes I do." Then he said "you can go anyplace you want to and drive any kind of car you want to, because you will receive the Nobel Prize."
>
> Everybody in the class soon knew what I was going to do professionally. It was funny because Dr. Ball talked about the levels of crime and he would say "these are the delinquents, Kellen's bunch." Dr. Ball seems real pleased that I'm going to graduate school in Criminal Justice.

9   Communion

Communion, the act of being received or "opened up and drawn in," is best facilitated through the medium of love. Eduard Spranger, a German professor of philosophy and pedagogy, and recipient of the Pestalozzi World Prize as well as numerous other awards, expands on the importance of reciprocal *love* in education. "Genuine education can only subsist in the element of love. [Love] creates an ambiance of affection" (Spranger, 1972, p. 536). Love between the teacher and learner is not a new idea as it finds support, for example, in the work of Plato and Pestalozzi. Pestalozzi, "presupposes a medium of love" in teaching and learning that implies an atmosphere or climate in which the individuality of the one mingles with the individuality of the other. Spranger (1972) refers to love as "... a union of two personalities whose spirituality has been awakened, provided the inclination is mutual" (p. 541). The genuine educator, for Spranger, is the embodiment of the love attitude.

In Chapter 4, I describe the act of communion, of being "opened up and drawn in," the climate in which the individuality of the one mingles with the individuality of the other. The excerpt also describes Peggy's process of midwifery, wherein midwives encourage and "assist in the emergence of consciousness."

> Peggy, the conductor, embraced the mood, and controlled it. She always told us that singing was an intellectual as well as a spiritual endeavor, and so she stood, as Athena, the goddess of intellectual pursuits, with chin up, waiting for the best moment to begin. Finally, with all eyes looking into hers, all minds and hearts of one accord, the downbeat was given. The sound wafted across the warmly lit floor and began to spin. The singers' song and ambiance projected such intimacy. Listeners seemed breathless.
>
> "He's gone away for to stay a little while, but he's coming back if he goes ten thousand miles."
>
> They sang tenderly, thoughtfully. Their faces were glowy and angelic. The conductor shaped every phrase with her entire body, particularly her eyes. The singers responded to every nuance with sophistication and poise. Peggy ended the piece with a tiny bow like gesture of two fingers. The audience and the chorus were quiet, motionless. Something pure and seemingly effortless, something larger than life engulfed us. The second selection was a Shaker hymn.
>
> "Tis a gift to be simple tis a gift to be free, tis a gift to come round where we ought to be, and when we find ourselves in that place just right we will be in the valley of love and delight."
>
> That was it. We were in the place just right. I was in the valley of love and delight. I never wanted to leave. We were the music. My throat had that tight, speechless feeling. For me, Peggy was a heroine. She and her students had delivered a prize of incomparable worth to the audience. She was a star and she was also my teacher. She was mine to learn with and grow with. She had changed that gym and she had changed me. My life had a new purpose, although as yet I could not begin to understand where it would lead. She was an artist, and I wanted to be an artist, to transcend time and space as she had. Together we would become co-creators, magic makers. I did not know then that I was experiencing a transcendent shamanic teacher at work.

As part of the embodiment of Spranger's love attitude and inasmuch as love is responsive to the loved one's needs, new forms of education must be developed that are responsive to current issues that might ultimately affect the loved one. Traditionally, education forms have been developed commensurate with the perceived purposes of education as viewed in those bygone eras. That is, the purposes of education in the industrial age were different from those in the information age. A factory worker in an early twentieth century sweatshop or factory would need to possess a very different set of skills and knowledge levels than a twenty-first century computer repair technician. As new forms of education are conceived, developed, and implemented, affection or love must continue to play a pivotal role so that all involved derive maximum benefits from teaching-learning experiences.

Educators may turn to appropriate examples of care provided by parents as "their guiding pattern" (Spranger, 1972, p. 537). Moreover, "Genuine education is born in the family" (p. 537). Pestalozzi repeatedly advocates parental love as a model for love in education. Indeed, in "simpler cultures" there is no educator except for the family member" (p. 537).

In the school environment, one's official designation as educator does not guarantee or create "a genuine educational relationship" (Spranger, 1972, p. 542) between educator and learner. The learner is not transformed simply by virtue of the official position of the teacher. Rather, what is first required is that the educator must envision what is possible for the learner and must believe in the worth of the learner. If this love and belief in the learner are not forthcoming, "there can be no genuine educational relationship" (p. 542). The beloved's devotion to the educator follows the teacher's love and belief in him or her. What is both provocative and inspiring is that when the learner returns the affection of the educator, "a wonderful power is awakened" (p. 544). "The relationship is one of the most beautiful possible in human life. It is not without reason that poets have celebrated it as much as the meeting of men and women in that love which leads to a union creative both physically and spiritually" (p. 544).

The type of love called for here, Spranger (1972) admits, is difficult to develop and sustain. "Unlike other forms of love, this affection cannot simply well up and stream out. It is necessarily bound up with thought and is indeed more painful than any other type of affection" (p. 545). Nonetheless, this love is at the heart of education. In Chapter 3, Mr. Santon's love for Peggy, and the impact of that love, is described.

Mr. Santon's caring about Peggy made her feel special. "It made me feel worth something." He said that he was lucky to be her teacher. He made her feel good about herself. Peggy notes, "And, oh, my gosh, we would kill for that man. I mean, it wasn't a cult. It's just that I wanted to be around him all the time because he made me feel good about myself. Now as a teacher myself, that's the most marvelous compliment when kids want to hang around you!"

Love alone, of course, does not lead to powerful learning. One must "be something before [one] can become an ideal for the pupil, one must have something in order to give, *one must oneself have expanded energy* in order to be able to arouse energy" (Spranger, 1972, p. 546), an expanded energy demonstrated by Leslie with Jerry in the piano playing example in Chapter 9:

> I just knew Jerry was hurting a lot. I mean, he told me some of his problems and yet our biggest thing beyond that was that it was all held in. There was no emotion coming out in his playing. Finally we got to the place where he was playing the piano and I was singing in my usual off-key way and stomping, anything to get some emotion to come out. I was pushing him, all through the whole piece. He allowed me to make him really mad. I kept telling him musical things to do. I was pushing him that way until he was so furious with me, I knew he was mad and yet, I knew he wasn't really mad at me. He was mad at everybody but he was taking it out on me, so that's why I kept pushing. It was a real chance; I knew I was taking a chance. He could have put his arm up to my face in a second, but I had to take the chance. When we came to the biggest musical spot, the last page, which is just humongous, I just touched him and said "this is the spot where you let it out. You just let us know, let us know how much it hurts. I want you to say to me right now all those things you wanted to say to your parents; you release that." Jerry was able to release all of his pain, a wall of pain, into the music. It was amazing. I knew that if you can't express yourself and you're not living as a human being, and you are totally distraught, then how in the world can you make sense out of something as emotional as music? The private and the personal are ultimately the music the person makes.

The true educator possesses what Spranger calls, "an inner fullness of life which flows over and fertilizes his neighbors field. He has an aspiring energy within him which carries others along with it .... In giving, he himself receives inner riches. But he never attains that moment in which he can say, 'It is fulfilled.' He is always on the way, accompanied by enduring and silent hope" (p. 546).

Spranger's description of the educator's love for the learner is a love of unselfishness. As the educator helps and gives to the learner, the educator must make demands on the beloved learner even though the learner may not at first recognize such demands as an expression of love.

10   Questions for Thought

1. For Paulo Freire, what must be reconciled? *How* must it be reconciled?

2. What is Freire's banking education and how does it function?

3. What is Freire's problem posing education and how does it function?

4. What is Martin Buber's I-It relationship and how does it function?

5. What is Buber's I-Thou relationship and how does it function?

6. How are Buber's I-It relationship and the I-Thou relationship vastly different?

7. What does Buber say about mutuality?

8. What does Belenky et al.'s teacher-as-midwife analogy refer to and how is that analogy appropriate for understanding the relationship between teachers and learners? How does the teacher-as-midwife function?

9. What does Eduard Spranger believe about *love* between teacher and learner? How does love play a central role in the teacher learner relationship?

10. How does the teacher learner relationship suffer in the absence of love?

11. Describe a relationship in which you felt love from a teacher as Spranger describes it, and discuss the impact of that love. If you have not had such an experience, how do you imagine it would feel to have it and what do you believe the outcome of such an experience would be?

CHAPTER 13

Portrait of Transcendent Shamanic Teacher
Laura

> Once you shed your pretense and meet your student as another human being, that's when genuine power begins, power to become and transform lives.
> LAURA

∴

1 Laura

Laura is an empathetic person. She is soft, but strong as steel. She is the mother of two children.

When Laura was an undergraduate education major, her Sunday school teacher identified one of her talents. The teacher said that Laura had a unique ability to befriend people who, for one reason or another, were shy, hurting, or not likable. She said that Laura had the capacity "to look inside and see the worthy person," the capacity to nurture those individuals and bring out their very best. The teacher called this "frog kissing." The teacher's revelation had a significant impact on Laura's development. No one had ever said that there was anything special about Laura. She explains, "I still remember that like it was yesterday. You want to live up to expectations and when you can see a unique feature that you can contribute, you practice it. It was really significant to me that she saw it. She saw my compassion." And so Laura became a teacher with compassion.

Laura had always been a "good kid," insightful and mature for her age. She took care of her family, holding them together through times of upheaval, such as during her mother's struggles with mental illness. In effect, Laura bore the family burden. Although she received a lot of encouragement for her contributions from other family members, she would have appreciated more effort on their part to encourage her parents to assume more responsibility as adults and as parents.

2   First Transcendence

When Laura became a teacher, a student named Melinda, who had a reputation for rudeness and aggressiveness, came into her life. Melinda began to call on Laura to help her meet life's challenges. Though Laura was somewhat unwilling to take that risk, Laura remembers the moment when she opened the door and allowed Melinda into her life.

> I remember exactly when the relationship started. I saw it coming one evening when I was walking home from practice. I lived only two blocks from the high school. Melinda started to walk with me. She only lived a block from my house. I knew she was coming up behind me and I remember thinking "do I want to talk to this person; open myself up to this person?" Before that moment I had not crossed any boundaries in the teacher-student traditional roles, and I wasn't sure at all if I wanted to. But I knew she needed somebody.

Laura decided to make herself available to Melinda. She described,

> Over the next two years I was there for her. I took her shopping to help her pick out dresses for dances or for basketball awards night. She hated wearing dresses. She felt awkward in them. I understood that. My relationship with Melinda was tied-up in my own background. When I was young, I hated the fact that dresses called attention to my body. People noticed my body when I wore a dress. I was very self-conscious and like many young women I had a pretty unhealthy view of my own appearance. When I taught school, I wore dresses all the time, so Melinda couldn't believe it when I told her I understood how she felt about "girl clothes." When she wore a skirt to school on game days because they were supposed to, everyone pointed it out and made a "deal" about it. I never did. In fact, I never mentioned it. I knew that what she needed was time to get comfortable with herself.
>
> We also had a lot in common with our family backgrounds. My family had mental illness on my mother's side, which I think provides an environment that is similar to the alcoholism that afflicted Melinda's family. Although my family all graduated from high school, like Melinda, I was the first to graduate from college. So there were some similarities in our family life, although hers seemed much more intense, because I think there had been some physical abuse in her childhood. So I saw myself in

Melinda and I wanted to bring her "along" when in reality, at least looking back now, I was bringing myself along and resolving some unfinished business in my own growth.

3   The Confrontation

At one point Laura was going through a tough situation with Melinda. Laura cried as she told Melinda about her concerns and anger over some of Melinda's negative behavior. She told Melinda that she felt she was taking advantage of the relationship they shared, and that she did not want their relationship to enable Melinda's aggressive and rude behavior with others. Laura told her that their relationship instead needed to be an impetus for their mutual growth. She explained to Melinda that she would not remain in the relationship unless, in fact, mutual growth did occur. Laura added, "There really wasn't a tremendous breakthrough that evening.

She showed no emotion there in front of me. But after that night, something did change. Melinda became more open, the relationship became more reciprocal."

Even though for some time Laura had seen herself as a teacher who went out of her way to accommodate learners, somehow it became reciprocal during that cathartic experience with Melinda. Melinda was no longer passive, but became active in the relationship. Laura explains,

> I became the person she confided in. She would show up on my doorstep when she and her mother had a fight. I was always careful to be very professional with her and I think most of the conversations we had that year had to do, at least in my mind, with building her character. She had not had positive role models.
>
> I tried to get her to set goals academically and personally, and I tried to support her in making a commitment to make her own choices about drinking and partying. I tried to get her to consider spirituality as a source of inner strength without pushing my religion on her. I tried to get her to check how she interacted with her teammates and friends in positive and sometimes unhealthy ways. I tried to empower her concerning her family and to show her that she did not have to be just like them. At the same time I encouraged her to have deeper relationships with her family. I did all of that through our conversations, by my example, and by sharing with her my personal experiences with her. I was really investing myself in this kid.

4 The Transformation

Everything changed and Melinda started to speak her mind without violence. She stopped being an outsider in every group. She started to laugh more. She got serious about her future. She started getting along better with her parents. She applied to colleges and even tried out for and was accepted on a US soccer team that spent the summer competing in Europe. I thought that she would never get on that plane, but she did. A true transformation occurred.

Today Melinda is about to graduate from college. She is looking into physical therapy programs. No longer is she an introvert, without reflection. When we talk on the phone she shares her life with me. I am amazed at how far she has come.

5 A Mutual Relationship

> I don't take credit for her success. I know that I only supported her in her growth, but I do think we both grew because of our friendship. For a long time I thought I was the only one giving in that relationship, but looking back I realize that she was one of my only friends those first years in teaching. She was giving to me all the while. As I watched her resolve family, social, and personal image issues, I finished resolving them in my own life. I wonder sometimes where I would be if she had not entered my life. A year passed before I really knew how much Melinda meant to me.

Laura's connection with Melinda is an archetypical example of Martin Buber's I-Thou relationship particularly because of the mutual growth they shared.

6 Laura the Teacher

Laura spoke of her philosophy as a teacher. She believes that the teacher must enable learners to "understand their own values and experiences and how they treat each other." If this occurs, the teacher does not have to talk about social problems in the classroom. If teachers teach learners how to care, those issues will take care of themselves.

Like Dr. Ball, Laura says she does not see a lot of difference between herself and the learner. "The differences that are there are really artificial. They are put in place by a system – they are not really there." She speaks of Maria Montessori's conception of the learner as being divine, indeed, as being the teacher. As a teacher, Laura struggles not to squelch the wealth of creative and imaginative capacity that students have, but instead to respect and encourage that capacity. She explains that "every student could do something I couldn't do and they could teach me."

7 Equality and Freedom

Laura finds it extremely difficult as a teacher to assume the role of the great authority.

> I think equality between a teacher and a student is like freedom, at least from my experiences, equality is always something that can be pursued. It might be obtained in a moment, and then you work to pursue it again, just like freedom. I don't think equality and freedom refer to stages, I think they are beginnings. A kid may come in with the preconception of what their world is and what your world is like. All you can really do is start to strip those rules away, present yourself in honesty *and* invite them to question things. I really think that resistance is necessary in the effort to obtain equality between individuals. I don't think one can say "OK, now we're all equal in here," because it's not really seen as equal. But when you move beyond those roles, then you can say "we've moved into equality."
>
> Freedom should be the beginning so that there is something to struggle for and to pursue; it's not the end product, it's the beginning. Once you have had it, you have to keep working to *really* have it. I don't think you ever arrive at a conclusion or a finish. Theoretically, learners already have equality, they already have freedom, but it is always a process. It used to surprise me sometimes when they would do what I asked them just because I was a teacher. Once you shed your pretense and meet your student as another human being, that's when genuine power begins, power to become and to transform lives. I think a lot of it has to do with our interaction with learners. It depends on how we perceive their nature. We must perceive them as people first. I see my students as inherently good. In fact I used to *want* the "trouble-makers" because I knew that inside they were good people.

8 Humor

Laura uses a lot of kind humor.

> When you use humor or give them a chance to back down instead of having a mouthy confrontation, it gives them a chance to save face. I looked at them. I made eye contact. When I was teaching, the kids used to come into the class and they would say right out loud, "I just love coming in this class, you know I just look forward to coming in this class." When I asked why, they would say, "I just came out of calculus and I just hate the last class, but I look forward to this class," and I would say "Why?" They would say "I can just be *myself* in here." I think that came from the fact that I was always myself in there.
>
> I just never could figure out how you could be different than who you really are, whether you're with a bunch of high school kids or people in a seminar or your family. I think that sets a certain tone in the class and maybe kids feel comfortable to be themselves.

9 The Mutual Exchange

Laura spoke of the ways the learner gives to the teacher.

> Any teacher can remember the first class of the semester and how vulnerable you felt when you saw those twenty faces looking at you. You are so conscious that day about how the students will perceive you. "Will they make fun of my appearance? Will they reject me?" We can be so insecure. You can either face it with honesty or with distance and intimidation. One of my teachers told me that she just tells her students that she is scared that she will fail them, and that because of this they embrace her.

For Laura, once a classroom community is established, the teacher does not have to worry about students taking advantage of their trust. Likewise, she uses grade contracts so that learners do not feel their trust of the teacher has been violated by subjective grading. She believes in providing every effort for the learner to acquire an understanding of the material being taught.

Laura told of her efforts to accommodate another student in a relational context. In that example, the experience was also positive, both accepting and affirming for the student, but the student was not enabled at that time to move beyond her personal situation. "She seemed content just to be with me, to read her romance novel, play Bingo with her family every Friday night. I had to learn to be comfortable with that and with my limits."

The teacher learner relationship can also *go beyond* in the direction of the negative. As a young learner, Laura had an experience with a math teacher in which he humiliated her in front of the class. It was a powerfully negative, but transformative experience for her as a person destined to become a teacher, even though as a mathematician it permanently scarred her.

> Some teachers probably would say that what Mr. Brown did was right because it made me "rise to the occasion and overcome my fear," but actually it only instilled fear deep within my core being. To this day if someone asks me to add numbers in my head I am instantly filled with so much anxiety that any response is either blocked or just delayed until I can work through the emotion.

Laura is able to avoid situations, such as the one described, by not abandoning the learner as Mr. Brown did to Laura. Instead, the appropriate pedagogical response is to feel as if "you're the one struggling when a student loses it. Yes, it is much more than empathy or simply putting yourself in 'someone else's shoes.' You really have to *feel* for them with compassion."

10   Reciprocal Relationships

Laura believes that her responsibility is to love her students, but she feels that it is the learner who *allows* her to teach them. They must accept the teacher before a meaningful learning exchange can occur. Along with that acceptance comes a wonderful benevolence from the learner which is all forgiving when things do not go just as the teacher planned them. Laura adds, "They gave me forgiveness, and they give you lots of things. They gave me friendship. Teachers are not used to articulating what we learn from, and are given by learners. It's an important realm of thought that is still unexplored."

To summarize, a turning point occurred for Laura when her Sunday school teacher identified her ability to bring out the best in other individuals. No one had ever pointed out her own unique qualities, or her compassion before. She felt a responsibility to live up to her teacher's observations. As a teacher, Laura was sought out by Melinda, a learner. Even though Melinda needed a

PORTRAIT OF TRANSCENDENT SHAMANIC TEACHER   191

friend, she was not able to really "open up" to Laura until a very honest, cathartic moment occurred for the two of them. After that, they began to share more deeply in conversation and Laura realized her biographical connection with Melinda seeing herself in Melinda. Their friendship became a mutually giving one that continues today.

Laura feels that it is her responsibility to love her learners, to support and empower them, and to teach them understanding, trust and care. She believes that she must actually struggle through with the learner, as she strips away artificial roles. Humor and eye contact also play important roles. Laura finds that learners return her love, and they give her acceptance, forgiveness, benevolence and friendship.

11   Questions for Thought

1. How did Laura's Sunday school teacher play a significant role in Laura's development?

2. What were three key transcendent events that occurred in Laura's relationship with Melinda?

3. What biographical connections did Laura and Melinda share?

4. How is the relationship between Melinda and Laura a mutual one as described by Martin Buber?

5. How do equality and freedom emerge and maintain in Laura's relationships with learners?

6. How do Laura's learners "allow" Laura to teach them?

7. How would you feel if you were one of Laura's learners?

8. How was Laura transformed by her relationship with Melinda?

9. What qualities and characteristics of transcendent shamanism exist in Laura's portrait? How is Laura a shamanic teacher? Use concepts and terms from Sections 2–10 to answer these questions.

CHAPTER 14

Power, Rhythm, the Turning Point, Limits, Limitations and Labeling

> I knew she was coming up behind me and I remember thinking "do I want to talk to this person; open myself up to this person?" But I knew she needed somebody…. So I saw myself in Melinda and I wanted to bring her "along" when in reality, I was bringing myself along and resolving some unfinished business in my own growth.
>
> LAURA

∴

1   Compelling Powers and Rhythm

Clark Moustakas' *Heuristic Research: Design, Methodology, and Applications* (1990) provides a model that I chose to guide and structure my original and subsequent research on the transcendent teacher learner relationship (see Appendix A for details). Heuristic research is a phenomenological investigation approach in which the researcher becomes personally involved in the process. Wanting to confirm that I was in the right track with my research, in my inimitable way, I called Clark Moustakas on the phone. I explained my work to him and asked if he could spare a few minutes to discuss my project. Immediately I sensed he was interested in my topic and plans. He was gracious and generous with me and highly supportive. We had several phone conversations wherein he gave me careful guidance and support throughout the process of completing my research. I remember his lovely gentle personality and tenor voice, pleasant and understanding, soft and airy. When I completed my research and before my dissertation defense, I sent my dissertation to him for his approval, which he gave overwhelmingly in a typed two page letter. I am indebted to him for his commitment to me, his advice and his writings.

American psychologist Moustakas is one of the leading experts on humanistic and clinical psychology, an educator and author of numerous publications on teaching, learning and creativity. Moustakas (1966) sensed at an early age that a radical wrong was being perpetrated on him as a learner. "Authoritarian demands were violating [his] right to choose, to maintain [his] personal uniqueness and distinctiveness"(Moustakas, 1977, p. 86). Therefore, Moustakas challenges teachers to overcome the ordinariness of reality, present in a "production oriented society" (p. 51). The process of overcoming, Moustakas recognizes, is no easy task and to accomplish this "it is often essential to create *compelling powers* in the classroom, forces that are strong enough to overcome past conditioning" (p. 51). An example of this is Laura's transcendent shamanism and her ability to create a power that led to Melinda's transformation.

The teacher may apply compelling powers to accomplish a variety of goals. To operationalize such powers, it is critical that the teacher approach the learner as a person of unique value. Such valuing leads a teacher to avoid comparing an individual learner with her or his peers. Further, teachers must believe that all individuals possess a "core of goodness" (Moustakas, 1981, p. 29), "a wisdom" that enables them to make choices that satisfy, and to seek experiences that affirm him or her. Laura's Sunday school teacher helped Laura recognize her ability to see the "worthy person" beneath the façade. Laura's ability played a pivotal role in Melinda's transformation. Teachers must be passionate but patient and willing to wait as that process is allowed to evolve. Moustakas believes that everyone maintains an inner "source of life," regardless of the disastrous events that many experience in childhood. That source is a kind of "magic energy" that is impervious to the blows of disaster. A magic energy such as this remains naive, fresh and childlike, and it is that energy that makes it possible for teachers to facilitate positive change in learners and themselves (Moustakas, 1977). The teacher uses compelling powers to appeal to that energy in the learner. Mr. Santon appealed to Peggy, Peggy to Hunter, Leslie to Jerry and Laura to Melinda. As described in Chapter 2, Theoni's compelling powers enabled Veronica to overcome her past conditioning that included extended periods of bullying and neglect. Thus, Veronica was paralyzed and had an overwhelming sense that it was impossible to rise to the supreme challenge of reading her most intimate narrative aloud before her peers. Monitoring Veronica closely, Theoni moved in and deployed her compelling powers that enabled Veronica to rise above her past conditioning:

> I saw Veronica hand her paper off to another student to read. I immediately made my way over to that group and stood behind Veronica. I wanted to take the paper out of the hand of her peer and give it back to Veronica, but I knew it needed to be Veronica's choice to continue.

Veronica's "ugly cry" came from the deepest regions of her being. When she handed the paper to a friend to read, Theoni guided from within by understanding, awareness and power, "... leaned in very close to Veronica and I said, 'you *can* do this, *you need* to do this.'" Veronica describes her reaction in that moment:

> When Dr. Soublis said that, it felt like more of a reassurance than a demand. I felt like Dr. Soublis was telling me it's alright to be this upset, it's valid, and that it's alright if I'm crying and upset while I read. That was a part of the healing. That put *power* into it. Her telling me I had to read it myself made me feel stronger somehow. Dr. Soublis' tone was even and there was a soft strength to it, if that makes sense? She seemed sure in her words, and that transferred to me, *making me feel sure*. Most importantly, there was no negativity in her voice, no demand, just support. (emphasis added)

The teacher "must often depart from external demands and meet the learner as an individual" (Moustakas, 1966, p. 20). In the effort to meet the learner as an individual, the teacher must establish a *rhythm* between the teacher and individual learner (Moustakas, 1981, p. 9). Rhythm is defined as a regular pattern of ebb and flow, tension and release at regular intervals in human interaction. Such an interactional rhythm enables the relators to cope with tension, to renew attitudes and to resolve issues. One must make an effort, must seek to locate that rhythm (p. 15) as was evident in Laura's relationship with Melinda. Laura used the rhythm established in her relationship with Melinda to discern when to intervene in Melinda's struggles and when to wait and as a result, Melinda began a path toward transformation. Laura was also transformed. Polarities, which exist within any relationship, must be recognized, expressed and accepted (p. 47). "We can only know the full measure of what is by also knowing its opposite," Moustakas writes (p. 44).

As a prelude to the life teachers and learners are to share with each other, a trust and openness must be built, creating a secure base for the relationship. The establishment of trust and openness creates the first layer of meaning in a relationship (Moustakas, 1981, p. 15).

2 Establishing a Bond with the Learner

According to Moustakas (1966), two ways in which teachers may establish significant bonds in their relations with learners are the *confrontation* and the *encounter*. The confrontation is a meeting between persons who are involved in a conflict or controversy and who remain together, face-to-face, until feelings of divisiveness and alienation between them are resolved. Such feelings are replaced by genuine acceptance and respect, even though differences in belief and attitude may continue to exist (Moustakas, 1966, p. 22). The reader will recall Chapter 13, in which Laura and Melinda shared a confrontation that Laura said led to a tremendous breakthrough, and the relationship became deeper and more reciprocal as a result.

At one point Laura was going through a tough situation with Melinda. Laura cried as she told Melinda about her concerns and anger over some of Melinda's negative behavior. She told Melinda that she felt she was taking advantage of the relationship they shared, and that she did not want their relationship to enable Melinda's aggressive and rude behavior with others. Laura told her that their relationship instead needed to be an impetus for their mutual growth. She explained to Melinda that she would not remain in the relationship unless, in fact, mutual growth did occur. Laura added, "There really wasn't a tremendous breakthrough that evening. She showed no emotion there in front of me. But after that night, something did change. Melinda became more open, the relationship became more reciprocal.

Moreover, the learner and facilitator must be free to disagree openly. To reinforce the importance of this point, Moustakas clarifies that "the child must have the right to be in disagreement with his teacher" (pp. 22, 23).

Confrontations, such as those Moustakas describes, occurred in my relationships with my learners at St. Albans High School during my first year there as a teacher. They were not reserved in their criticism of me and tact was not the strong suit of several of them. I was ultimately able to *hear* them because of their directness, even if that hearing was painful for me.

Although it may seem paradoxical, people can establish genuine bonds only when they can openly disagree (Moustakas, 1966). In this process, both must be aware of the other's full legitimacy, and must value the other as a person whose views are worthwhile and contain unique insight. Then relaters expect that in the end such views, if carefully considered, help pave the way for positive change. Otherwise, one must be prepared for the consequences of broken relation_that include "evasiveness, distortion, and alienation" in the teacher learner relationship (p. 22). As Rogers (1967), Klein (1989), Shaffer (1977) and others have indicated, such broken interactional consequences distort the process of meaningful learning.

The second dimension of the process of risk and challenges is the *encounter*. "The encounter, in contrast to the confrontation, is a meeting of harmony, mutuality and oneness" (Moustakas, 1981, p. 89). It "is a sudden, spontaneous, intuitive meeting between teacher and child in which there is an immediate sense of relatedness and a feeling of harmony and communion" (Moustakas,

1966, p. 22). Relaters move outside secure boundaries "onto deeper and richer layers of meaning" in relationships and toward more meaningful learning (Moustakas, 1981, p. 53). The relationship growth hinges more often on inner connection, such as intuition, than on spoken messages or outwards signs. "I depend on internal states to guide me. I am willing to risk and experiment with new resources and possibilities in behalf of these values, and to accept the ultimate mystery of growth" (p. 38). The encounter is an imminent reality between the two relaters in which an absolute relatedness exists, a relation replete with mutuality (Moustakas, 1966). During the encounter, "there is a dropping off of conventions, systems, and rubrics, and a letting go ..." (p. 119). Again, Laura's interaction with Melinda in Chapter 13 provides an exemplary model of Moustakas' encounter. Laura explains:

> I tried to empower her concerning her family and to show her that she did not have to be just like them. At the same time I encouraged her to have deeper relationships with her family. I did all of that through our conversations, by my example, and by sharing with her my personal experiences with her. I was really investing myself in this kid.
>
> I became the person she confided in. She would show up on my doorstep when she and her mother had a fight. I was always careful to be very professional with her and I think most of the conversations we had that year had to do, at least in my mind, with building her character. She had not had positive role models.

Receptiveness, relatedness and openness each are pivotal qualities of the encounter. Regardless of pressures and responsibilities, the opportunity for relaters to meet is *ever present*, and encounters become reality if the teacher is willing to make the required commitment. The encounter is a shift that establishes a rhythm that unites, a rhythm that connects (Moustakas, 1981, p. 89).

3   The Turning Point

The encounter represents a shift in growth. Moustakas' (1977) *turning point* "significantly alter[s] the world in which the person lives" (p. 3) and occurs as the result of some sort of catalyst, such as challenge, crisis or a time of upheaval. As example, Moustakas cites the story of an individual whose relationship with her authoritarian father improved as the result of a turning point experience. The experience involved her refusal to accept her father's directive to join in playing a board game. That refusal led not only to her asserting herself for the first time, but also to a more loving and mutually respectful friendship with her father. For the father this was *the* turning point in that relationship. Other dialogues with her father and mother during personal crisis situations also awakened "new attitudes" (p. 14) that altered her sense of self in a way that strengthened her, a strength that served her well throughout her life. The confrontation, described above between Laura and Melinda, led to a turning point experience in their relationship and in their mutual healing. Laura explains:

> Everything changed and Melinda started to speak her mind without violence. She stopped being an outsider in every group. She started to laugh more. She got serious about her future. She started getting along better with her parents. She applied to colleges and even tried out for and was accepted on a US soccer team that spent the summer competing in Europe. I thought that she would never get on that plane, but she did. A true transformation occurred.

Throughout such relational encounters, new strengths, new resources, new ways of being with others are realized and expanded. New potentials are opened and made more accessible. Individuals are affirmed throughout such processes.

When teachers express and give affirmation to the learner, they contribute to the establishment of an encouraging climate wherein children are free to "test out their feelings and pursue their interest" (Moustakas, 1977, p. 103). The learner must be free to maintain their own identity, and to trust their own senses (Moustakas, 1966). Freedom of choice is central in the quality learning process (Moustakas, 1977). Whenever authoritarian or external values are imposed (Moustakas, 1966), whenever standards and concepts are forced on the child, the child's uniqueness and creativity are compromised. Moreover, "when the will is blocked, a counter will, or negative will, is created, one that operates in negative directions, a force against someone or something – sheer stubbornness, opposition and negativism" (Moustakas, 1981, p. 76). If freedom within structure is withheld, the learner either begins the construction of defenses in preparation to fight, or conforms at the expense of uniqueness and creativity (Moustakas, 1977). When the learner's will is left intact, however, risk, experimentation, inner-directed leaps can occur (Moustakas, 1966). The learner is inspired to "transcend restraints" (p. 30). The inner-directed leaping that transcends restraint is the essence of invention, leadership and creativity. Clearly, such characteristics are highly prized in professional and business environments and the learner's attainment of such characteristics are valid learning objectives. For Veronica, the encouraging and liberating climate Theoni created led to a turning point for Veronica.

I felt stronger and stronger as I read it. I could hear the quiet feedback of my group as I read and whenever I occasionally looked up I could see there was sympathy, patience and interest. I think I was still tearful, but by the end of it, I felt empowered and I felt braver for having read it. I felt more composed once I was done reading. I was also relieved when my group had questions about my experience and I could answer them. There is nothing worse than crying in front of people and they just look at you in awkward silence. Again, part of it was the support I felt coming from not just Dr. Soublis, but also my peers listening. Nobody seemed ambivalent towards me or my story. I gathered strength from that, knowing that my pain was not in vain. I felt like a great weight was lifted off me; it was *very* cathartic.

Prior to her turning point experience in Theoni's class, Veronica was alone with her pain, fully disconnected from those around her because of her past that was rife with abuse and neglect. Through the turning point experience with Theoni and all of her colleagues surrounding her in the most attentive way possible, Veronica was empowered, liberated, healed and authentically united with her colleagues in a profound and delightful way.

4 Limits and Limitations

Moustakas, like Greene, does not suggest that learners be released to act at will, in whatever manner they choose. All freedom requires responsibility, self-discipline, and limits including "the realization of other's right to be, respect for materials and property, sharing of resources and opportunities, etc." (Moustakas, 1981, p. 78). The learner's will, the right to be, to feel, to protest or be in opposition are valued by the teacher. The teacher nonetheless firmly establishes and maintains limits, rather than limitations. Limitations are "external to the situation, blocks and deterrents to growth" (p. 82). Limits instead, "define the uniqueness of the relationship, the characteristics that differentiate the two persons in the relationship" (p. 82) and the boundaries of the relationship. However, these limits must "not throttle the will of the child" or in any way reduce the self-esteem of the child (Moustakas, 1966, p. 76).

If the limits that establish the parameters of the relationship are broken, the structure of the relationship may be damaged. Laura was very clear about the limits that existed in her relationship with Melinda. Without those limits Laura and Melinda could not have shared the mutuality that led to Melinda's and Laura's transformation. The limits, that is the structure, facilitated transformation. Such situations present an opportunity for the relationship to gain more depth. If both relators share in the effort to resolve a conflict by staying fully engaged, no matter how turbulent it may be, deeper roots, stronger relational structures may be formed (Moustakas, 1981).

Learners are more likely to stay with the conflict through resolution if the teacher shows that he deeply cares for, respects the uniqueness of, and accepts the learner without qualification (Moustakas, 1966). The learner must be received by the teacher. Receiving is not a matter of rewarding, approving or agreeing with the learner. Instead, when receiving the learner, the teacher affirms and embraces the learner saying, "yes I see. I hear" (Moustakas, 1981). Moustakas' receiving has to do with being present to and for the learner. To receive or be present, the teacher must respond to the "immediate moment in all its fullness, not holding back, being fully there" (p. 37). To take this a step further, Moustakas concurs with Buber (1958a). The teacher must, with "unbiased attitude, see what an experience means to a child" (Moustakas, 1966, p. 30), and must attempt to know and understand the learner's attitudes, beliefs, concepts and values as they are perceived by the learner.

5   The Damaging Impact of Labels

The authentic relationship then, includes freedom, responsibility, trust, care, encouraging climates, acceptance, confirmation and respect for uniqueness. Particularly destructive of each of these qualities is the use of punishment, labeling and competition, each of which contributes to the learner's sense of alienation. Labeling, in particular, stigmatizes and deprives learners of choices. For Moustakas (1977), labels act as missiles, which encourage the ingraining of negative behavior patterns. Labeling occurs, for example, whenever a teacher refers to one learner as lazy, "slow" or "behind" and to another learner as "gifted." Unfortunately teachers apply all sorts of labels, "labels to motivate and push learners, labels to fix individuals, forms of prophesying and forecasting" (p. 92). Labeling is destructive because it deprives learners of a sense of possibility, of potentiality and of opportunity.

Consider this example of a lost sense of possibility, potentiality and opportunity. A high school learner has a passion and aptitude for architecture. But because of poor performance on standardized tests, this learner might be denied the chance to rise above their previous academic performance and be denied the opportunity to take architecture-relevant high school courses necessary for undergraduate studies in architecture. Learners are regularly labeled "average," "gifted," "disabled" and so on, labels most learners accept as a "fact" that looms not only throughout elementary and secondary school, but indeed, their entire lives. The life-persistent label dictates what so many people expect of themselves, or deny themselves, throughout their lives.

Human uniqueness, of course, includes the human intellect. Using standardized test scores, schools purport to measure and thus label intellectual ability, when in fact, standardized test scores measure only a fraction of the spectrum of human intellect. Specifically, standardized tests measure what Howard Gardner (2011) has classified as *verbal-linguistic* and *logical-mathematical* intelligence. Gardner, an American developmental psychologist and professor at the Harvard Graduate School of Education at Harvard University, has identified other intelligences that include: *intra-personal, inter-personal, visual-spatial, bodily-kinesthetic, naturalistic* and *musical intelligences*. None of these intelligences are measured by standardized tests and thus a vast measurement deficiency exists. For example, consider Claude Monet, an artist with an extraordinary visual-spatial intellect, Ludwig van Beethoven, a composer with extraordinary musical intellect or Martha Graham, a dancer and choreographer with an extraordinary visual-spatial intellect would *not* be labeled "gifted" if they were learners today in United States schools, *unless* of course, they happened to also have high verbal-linguistic or mathematical intelligence. Profound intellects, the *"giftedness"* of those such as Monet, Beethoven and Graham do not register on standardized test radar. Thus, a faulty intellectual caste system is firmly entrenched in the United States, wherein only verbal-linguistic and mathematical intelligences, the only ones assessed by standardized tests, are valued and labeled as "gifts." Based on standardized test scores, schools label a few learners "gifted" and passively label all other learners *non-gifted* because standardized testing measures only a fraction of the human intelligence spectrum.

6   Precocious Learners and Labeling

Precocious learners, those who learn quickly at first, energize the teacher's inclination to label them positively for their precocity while passively labeling others negatively for their lack of it. Precocity becomes the justification for making artificial ability distinctions between learners, for providing exciting instruction for some and dull instruction for others. All of this fuels the competitively-oriented classroom arena because the precocious child, who is not necessarily more capable, or even as capable as less precocious learners, is given more access, more opportunity to learn and to proceed developmentally in an unrestrained manner. Because of the perceived level of advancement of some learners, others who are not labeled precocious are often pulled into uninspired, substandard, drill-laden instruction that constricts the learning process and their potential even more. A lost sense of possibility emerges.

On the other end of the labeling spectrum, the person who is afforded the label-promise "gifted" on the basis of standardized mathematical and verbal-linguistic intelligence test scores may feel frustrated later in life because their life accomplishments are only average, even as they watch the learner who was labeled "average" in K-12 school become extraordinarily successful after graduation. A label-promise is not fulfilled for the one and a label-barrier is fortunately transcended by the other. Thus all labels, whether they are misleading promises or barriers, positive or negative, are destructive.

The competitive classroom of unequals emerges wherein such disparities exist and so some are put at risk of failure while others are given additional encouragement. Some must become losers for others to succeed or win. Thus, the learner who is inspired via their "gifted" label to greater academic achievement and additional opportunity, does so at the expense of those who are denied the label. Moustakas suggests that an authentic relational environment (one of trust, care, confirmation, etc.) cannot exist where learners are set up to lose or fail. The teacher is thus called upon to create a culture wherein all persons involved are perceived to be equal even as individual strengths and weaknesses are respected, valued and built upon.

7   Questions for Thought

1. What concerns does Clark Moustakas have regarding "authoritarian demands?"

2. What are Moustakas' "compelling powers" and how do they function? What teacher in your life do you believe demonstrated "compelling powers?" *How* did that teacher demonstrate compelling powers?

3. What is meant by Moustakas' *confrontation* in teacher learner relationships? How does Moustakas' confrontation function?

4. How does Moustakas define a turning point encounter? Applying Moustakas' definition, have you ever had a turning point encounter with a teacher? If so, describe. If not, how could a turning point encounter with a teacher change your life for the better? How so?

5. How and why are labels debilitating? How do standardized tests facilitate destructive labeling?

6. In terms of the measurement of intellect, how are standardized tests immensely limited?

CHAPTER 15

Portrait of Transcendent Shamanic Teacher
Beth

> I didn't want to be above Alexander, I wanted to be with him. You see, that's how we could get through things.
> BETH

∴

1   Beth

Beth is a fresh faced, animated and enthusiastic teacher and mother of two young daughters. One immediately senses her commitment to those who are in her charge. That commitment germinated before the death of her father when she was five. Until that time, Beth received unconditional regard from her family. They encouraged, accepted and affirmed her, and allowed her to feel free. Themes such as encouragement, acceptance and affirmation emerge prominently in Beth's style as a teacher.

> I received a lot of positive reinforcement and freedom from both parents as well as my grandparents. I felt free to try anything. I didn't know about failure, nor did I experience it, but I remember that I learned quickly, enthusiastically and *well* without an awareness of failure. In retrospect, because of this, I do not view feelings of failure as being a necessary dimension of meaningful learning.

2   Beth's Classroom

Beth delves deep into her childhood to remember what it was like to not know failure. She sees no positive result from allowing a child to feel like a failure. Consistent with that belief and thanks to the progressive school environment in which she works, Beth does not give grades. Instead, she tries to make her class "the most supportive and open place possible. My class may be the only positive atmosphere and interaction they receive that day."

Beth tries to nurture learners in ways that she was not nurtured herself after her father's death.

> My attitude is that my class is a restful kind of place. My students are all from foster homes and those homes are not all ideal. And so I meet them at the door in the morning or in the hallway, or on the porch of the school, and say "all right, let's get ready to roll" and try to help them share about themselves with me.

Beth tries to make a personal connection with each learner every day, even if it is eye contact and a smile. Via empathy, she discerns whether learners are having a bad or good day, and gauges her interaction with them accordingly. "You just know, you get a sense that something's just not right. I give them just a little 'Hey how's it going? I'm glad to have you here today.' or whatever."

Beth also employs the use of humor in her teaching. She believes humor removes barriers and creates a relaxed atmosphere. Humor, when sensitively applied, does not bruise fragile egos, and it helps people avoid aggressive behavior and increases their understanding of each other.

Beth believes her own learning experiences and her learning background contribute greatly to her development and style as a teacher. Her experiences with familial mental illness, economic hardship and other problems provide a unique insight into the problems her learners experience. She uses those insights to inform her teaching.

> I knew because there were times in my life that we didn't have enough to eat, so I certainly knew what it felt like to be hungry. It helped me a lot as a teacher. One thing I want to say is that I have had about every experience a child could have; a parent that died, mental illness in my family, I was sexually abused by a stepfather, I had lots of siblings, natural and adopted ones and I moved a lot. So it was real easy for me to practically know where all of my students are coming from. I never lived on the street, but that was the only thing.

When Beth was very young, she had concerns her peers never gave thought to. For example, as a first grader, she worried whether soldiers in Vietnam had enough to eat. At the same time, Beth remembers feeling lost as a child, trudging through the days, one after another. She felt lost in a second grade classroom of thirty students, but she developed an extraordinary relationship with her third grade teacher.

PORTRAIT OF TRANSCENDENT SHAMANIC TEACHER   205

> She knew who I was and what I was about. She liked the things I did. She made me feel like I was worth something. It certainly was an affirmation for me and it definitely made me more free to do things, to explore things.

That teacher had a profound effect on Beth, because their relationship went beyond traditional teacher-learner interaction. "I remember having these same kinds of exchanges with her that I had with my student, Alexander (see Section 4 below) as far as eye contact and a lot of non-verbal messages."

Beth's middle school teacher valued her unique qualities. Before this teacher came into her life, Beth was mystified by the frivolity of her peers and some teachers.

> Those people seemed so happy, you know, with their little frivolous ways, always giggling. I told my Mom "you know, it would really be nice to not know about other people's struggles because the people I know seem so happy." I couldn't have been oblivious of other's struggles if I had wanted to be. I just didn't think along those lines.

As she observed others, Beth was seeking out a teacher who could be genuine, who could be concerned "with what really matters."

At the middle school age, Beth was depressed and felt there was no purpose for her existence, because she felt that no one, not even her mother, would miss her if she were gone. If her teacher had not intervened, Beth believes she would be dead, probably of suicide brought on by depression. That teacher, Beth observes,

> recognized me as an individual. When I think about her I can remember the feeling of being close with her even clear across the room, the feeling she truly believed in me and who I was. She knew exactly what I was about and she still believed in me. I was valuable to her. Because of her, I made the conscious decision that I would be a teacher also. I want to make that kind of difference to someone. I mean, what more valuable thing can you do with your life. I still see her from time to time, and it's still the same.

Beth added that she could feel her teacher's "inner self." "I related to her and didn't feel as if there was an age difference between us. Rather, it felt like two souls, relating."

3   Beth the Teacher

Beth gauges her success as a teacher by the affirmation she receives from her learners, who have been labeled *behaviorally disabled*. Her first concern is to "open up their minds and enable them to think in new ways, and to think creatively." Rather than the subjects she teaches, Beth's first concern for her students is to facilitate their *individual* development as learners. In her classroom, for example, as far as reading is concerned, whatever provokes and challenges reading, and the development of reading capacity, is fair game, whether it is *People* magazine or *The Enquirer*. Using such publications as reading material, Beth is able to cultivate and establish a sense of personal competence in learners.

> To tell you the truth, more than even their ability to read, I am most concerned with their emotional growth. I never felt the subjects I taught were the most important outcomes. Most of my students were very creative and that's why they ended up in trouble a lot in school.

Applying an individualized approach, Beth does not rely on tests to gauge a learner's academic development. She believes test results are inaccurate indicators for skill development because of the emotional stress they inflict on the learner. That stress interferes with cognitive, affective, and psychomotor processes and performance. Instead of having faith in tests, Beth explains, "I use trial and error, intuition. I can tell by having conversation with them, I would talk with them and determine where they were."

She also attempts to undo the negative self-images that teachers have established in the minds of so many of her students. Beth believes that the teachers who created those images caused her learners to disbelieve in themselves.

> I think a lot of learning mistakes occur because people are afraid to just let go. In the past, teachers have told my students that they are stupid bums who can't do anything. Then they come to me and say "I'm too stupid, I can't do this." I say, "I don't believe that for a minute and neither do you. I can see in your eyes that you have the intelligence of a genius." If they feel that you truly believe in them, they can do it, but the fear and the emotional rape that has been put on them by those teachers, or whomever, has kept them from letting out their true selves and thereby their capacity to learn well.

> Teachers in the past had been so overbearing to my students, real disciplinarians. And of course they were coming through the justice system, you know. I don't think anybody had ever treated them as equals, not even their own peers. They felt like dirt, because they didn't have money. One can see why kids from the streets would be into selling drugs to get money. I tried to get them to realize that they weren't any worse than anyone else and they weren't any better than anyone else and also that we need to accept other people.

When personal issues and disputes emerged with learners, Beth had class meetings in which students openly verbalized their frustrations. The effort was intended so that students could grow to understand each other. "A lot of times, we talk about what a particular kid has been through. We have a group session so that people understand the underlying problems."

Beth deliberately creates projects that require cooperation and collaboration amongst peers. She uses herself and her personal life as example for discussion.

> You see, often they can't succeed right away because they have never seen it done and they don't know how to do it. I bring my past or home life into the discussion. I become very open with them. There are no secrets about my home life. They know everything.

In general, Beth avoided behavioral problems and confrontations through her intuitive assessment of classroom interaction and her responding personal dialogue with individuals. Students learned to moderate their own behavior in Beth's classroom, choosing when and how often to remove themselves from their classmates. "We have "time out" rooms. I have one right off my classroom. But rather than me putting them in there, I allow them to choose to go in there and have some time alone."

Beth finds that conversation with her learners facilitates increased understanding. She attempts to create an environment of open and honest dialogue. She wants her learners to feel free to discuss whatever they will as long as it does not denigrate others. "There was no embarrassment on my part with them, or them with me. I think that through discussion about intimacy you can really open up on a lot of levels. Everyone feels perfectly free to ask questions." She believes such an approach provides a way for learners to become informed and expand their awareness.

> I accept what they say and use it or go beyond it. The other students identify with each other [and] work together. We have a mutual respect for each other. What I try to do with my students is to make things open enough that they can come forward, and empathize with my concerns.

For Beth, the pursuit of mutual respect between herself and her learners is a constant concern. She can tell whether her learners are developing a sense of real equality with her and others by whether or not they feel free enough to question things.

> I want them to question. For example, I said, "Now how many people feel that your history book is the truth?" Everybody felt it was so, and they were surprised when I said, "No, this is one person's perspective." That was real important to me because nobody told me that until I was in college. Then I told them that even though all these teachers have been teaching it, it may not be absolutely true. They said, "Then, a lot of stuff that you learn is just somebody's opinion," and I told them, "yes and your opinion is valuable as well."

Beth's students demonstrate a remarkable capacity for critical thought and creativity. Emerging, as they are, from traumatic backgrounds, Beth's learners often respond in dramatic ways when they are asked to pursue less than genuine, or what they perceive to be, irrelevant projects. She believes her students are "free thinkers" overall, and that's why they have often been "in trouble."

When she is teaching, Beth highlights the learner's own personal, unique needs and tries to assess how to best help the individual learner. She feels she understands the plight of those who must "fit in" but finds it is extremely difficult. She shares her faith and confidence in her students. Beth wants to offer an atmosphere in which learners are free to behave in unorthodox ways as long as they understand that such behavior may be inappropriate or unacceptable elsewhere.

4 Alexander

Beth still thinks about a student with whom she had an extraordinary relationship several years ago. Much like her own biography, this student felt responsible for his siblings at a very early age. Alexander, her twelve-year-old student, stole to provide for his family, so that they would not go hungry. Alexander was subsequently arrested for theft, and his family was split up. While Beth had not stolen, she understood *why* this had occurred. Beth believes her class was the last stop for Alexander before a juvenile prison facility. "This kid had been kicked out of school six times. I was afraid that would put negative ideas in the teachers' heads about who Alexander was." Beth knew what it meant to have to intercede for siblings on behalf of reticent parents and so she sought to help other teachers understand Alexander's situation.

Beth and Alexander shared nonverbal exchanges, and they had a particular connection with puns.

> He was really good with them, and that's one of my areas I really used. I would say a pun, and of course he'd be the only one in the room to get it and we exchanged glances. We didn't have to talk to communicate well. All I had to do, if he wasn't doing something, was just look at him in a particular way and he knew exactly what I was thinking.

While Alexander could "con" other teachers, he could not con or manipulate Beth. That gave him a sense of security. "He realized that he couldn't manipulate me, so he relaxed in my room. I saw a lessening of the tension in his body and his face. He was more relaxed in my class." Beth knew he desperately needed the security that limits provide. For Alexander and his peers, a lack of boundaries shows that no one cares about them.

Beth talked of the extraordinary support she felt from all of her students during her pregnancy. Alexander also came to her aid.

> This kid, in this special time of my life, wasn't verbalizing it, but he was letting me know that "this is a special time of your life" and "yes, you should be nurtured" and "you might need some extra care with your emotional ups and downs." He would help me out and make me feel really good.

The caring verbal and nonverbal conversations Beth shared with Alexander were very special. Beth still worries about Alexander and what has become of him, even though she has no way to reach him. She feels certain he is now in prison. She adds, I'm not a person to cry, but I do lay awake at night thinking about him, worrying about him. And what I hope is that maybe at some point when he gets to thinking and sorting things out, he can think about people who showed him a different way.

5   Removing Barriers

Beth talked about the importance of going beyond the barriers imposed by roles and the removal of artificial hierarchy.

> In the classroom I never saw myself as the big boss because we all talked about things and all accomplished things. I was really aware of that. I didn't want to go in there dressed in a suit; I didn't want to make myself seem better than them, look better than them or act superior to them. I would try to talk more on [the learner's] level. I didn't want to be above Alexander, for example, I wanted to be with him. You see, that's how we could get through things.

To summarize, Beth's encounters as a learner contributed a great deal to her style as a teacher. Two teachers valued and respected her as an individual with unique qualities and capacities. There was a great amount of nonverbal communication, empathy and "feeling for" each other in their relationships. The teachers helped her avert her depression that may have resulted in suicide.

As a teacher, Beth creates an open, supportive positive atmosphere of mutual respect in which learners do not encounter failure. She facilitates the learner's self-esteem, emotional growth and awareness through giving them understanding, acceptance and affirmation. Her faith and confidence in learners is communicated through conversation and nonverbal forms of communication.

6   Questions for Thought

1. How could Beth understand her learners so well?
2. How does Beth's classroom differ from a traditional classroom?
3. Describe Beth's interactional style with learners.
4. Describe the atmosphere in Beth's classroom.
5. How is Alexander of particular importance to Beth?
6. How does Beth remove barriers?

7. If Beth were your teacher, could she have a life changing effect on you as a learner? How so or how not so?

8. How is Beth's approach to the learner similar to Dr. Ball's approach?

9. What qualities and characteristics of *transcendent* shamanism exist in Beth's portrait? Use concepts and terms from Sections 2–5 to answer this question.

CHAPTER 16

The Transcendent Teacher-Learner Relationship
A Class Investigation

Hunter O'Hara

As children's challenges and needs climb at an alarming rate, teachers are called to a new pedagogy, called to move beyond the barriers of the past. Moreover, to meet the needs of all learners effectively, teachers must relate to children in new ways that transcend the obstacles that have long stood in the way of meaningful learning. All children, particularly special needs children, homeless children, and neglected and abused children, need a special brand of caring, trust, compassion, and high expectations. Such children need transcendence in their relationships with teachers. In a transcendent relationship, teacher and learner go beyond their traditional interactive roles and both may undergo a "turning point" in which their life goals are altered. Caring, trust, mutual respect and love are characteristics of transcendent relationships. How transcendent relationships are mutually beneficial for both relaters and how frequently the impact of such relationships is profoundly positive are analyzed. The life-long relationship between Helen Keller and Anne Sullivan is viewed as a paradigmatic example of the transcendent teacher-learner relationship.

The implications of such relationships and their significance for learning scenarios that otherwise may be handicapped by teacher-learner alienation and estrangement, learner non-engagement and non-ownership of the learning process are also included. Through the exploration and analysis of the stories of those who have enjoyed such relationships, this discussion identifies: the qualities and characteristics that have been indicative of transcendent atmospheres and interactions, how transcendence in teaching-learning relationships has been invited and facilitated, how learning has been broadened and enhanced by the presence of transcendence, how transcendent relationships have facilitated the development of learning communities, and how transcendent phenomena affects relators.

1 Introduction/Perspectives of the Research

The conceptual and theoretical framework for transcendence in teacher learner relationships derives from an integrated body of education literature including educational philosophy, educational psychology, and learning theory. The transcendent teacher learner relationship (O'Hara, 1992) may occur when relators move beyond secure boundaries of endeavor. Both teacher and learner must drop off conventions, rubrics, and systems (Moustakas, 1966). To move beyond secure boundaries, both relators must trust and risk in the process of establishing limits, exercising self-discipline and responsibility. The learner's world is "received" and understood by the teacher. As roles are transcended in these ways, a turning point may occur. Author of Pedagogy of the Oppressed (1989), Paulo Freire, writes of the importance of reconciliation in the pedagogical relationship, i.e., reconciling the poles of the teacher learner contradiction so that both are simultaneously teachers and learners (p. 59). Together, teacher and learner may encounter a process involving expanded awareness, the emergence of new identity, and steps toward new life.

In transcendent relationships, the teacher's traditional governance stance over children is replaced by a new pedagogy of thoughtfulness and openness (Van Manen, 1991). The teacher believes in and has confidence in each learner and provides challenging expectations for learners. With such a pedagogy, the teacher tactfully mediates love and care, hope and trust, and responsibility. This application of tact is not obtrusive but is subtle, hardly noticeable. The teacher's use of tact reads the inner life of the learner, intuits when to intervene and when to remain silent. Such tact creates a warm social atmosphere, a sensitive and flexible tone that is also firm, direct, decisive, and open. Tact requires humor and commitment to one's core values. For Carl Rogers and others, "the facilitation of significant learning depends upon certain attitudinal qualities which exist in the personal relationship of the facilitator and the learner" (Rogers, 1967, p. 3). Buber (1958, 1965a, 1965b), Greene (1985, 1988), Palmer (1983), Rogers (1967), Maslow (1968), Macdonald (1974), Noddings (1984) and others call for pedagogical relationships characterized by trust, care, and mutuality between teacher and learner. Teachers and learners enter "a covenant with another, a pledge to engage in a mutually accountable and transforming relationship, a relationship forged of trust and faith in the face of unknowable risks" (Palmer, 1983, p. 1). Martin Buber emphasizes the importance of mutuality and intimacy in teacher-learner relationships (Buber, 1965a, pp. 98–100). For relationships to transcend, the teacher must "view the world through the learners' eyes" (Rogers, 1967, pp. 8–9), and must "experience from the other side" (Buber, 1965, pp. 8–9).

Transcendent teacher-learner interaction is reciprocal, liberating, and growth oriented. Such interaction is authentic or genuine by virtue of the interweaving of the active and passive (receptive) pedagogical roles. In the transcendent relationship, for example, teachers as well as learners are in the learning mode and learners are in the teaching mode on an intermittent basis.

Manipulated or deliberately assigned interaction between teacher and learner is inconsistent with the subject of this study. One cannot be assigned a transcendent relator the way, for example, one may be assigned a mentor. Again, the transcendent connection occurs spontaneously. Transcendent relationships frequently endure for a lifetime.

2   Methods/Data Source

The heuristic methodology applied in this study was developed by Clark Moustakas (1990). Heuristics provides a format for research that begins with researcher self-inquiry and then moves outward to the encounters of others. The heuristic researcher does not presuppose cause-effect relationships.

Data for this study were collected through journal writings, other written accounts, and class inquiry and discussions facilitated by the researcher. Data were organized into three categories:

1. Data generated by co-researchers prior to the course relevant to their personal relationships with teachers and learners;
2. Data generated during the course relevant to participant perceptions of the role of teacher-learner relationships in pedagogy and meaningful learning; and
3. Data collected months after the course relevant to effects of the course on co-researchers' pedagogical practice.

The data presented in this discussion retain the co-researchers' language and are organized according to qualities and themes that emerged during class investigation. The population for this study is comprised of students enrolled in the early childhood master's degree program at Towson University.

(a) Procedures for Collection and Analysis of Data in Category

Several weeks prior to the course, enrolled students received a letter that included the following assignment to be completed prior to any other assignment or reading for the course:

> Reflect and write about your relationship with a teacher or learner. Recall a teacher or learner with whom you had a very good relationship or with

whom you had a very bad relationship. What characteristics and qualities in both of you contributed to it being a good or bad relationship? How did the relationship affect how you felt about teachers, learners, school and learning? Assignment needs to be two typed, double-spaced pages.

Over the duration of the course each co-researcher shared their story with the class. Using the definition of transcendent teacher-learner relationships in O'Hara (1992), written stories were analyzed for transcendence themes. Verbatim transcendence thematic data were grouped according to their relevance to the research questions. Verbatim data were then compiled in the form of composite narratives. In the interest of coherence, pronouns were changed as needed to reflect a single gender.

(b) Procedures for Collection and Analysis of Data in Category

During the course, participants kept daily reflective journals. The selected journal paragraphs included in the findings segment convey some of the overarching core meanings and themes individual co-researchers recorded during the course.

(c) Procedures for Collection and Analysis of Data in Category

Five months after completing a teacher-learner relationships course, 13 of 15 student co-researchers who were available were contacted by phone and asked whether or not the class investigation of teacher learner relationships had affected their teaching, their reflection about teaching, or their relationships with learners. Data were recorded and categorized by theme. Co-researchers reported overarching changes related to classroom practice and their relationships with learners.

3   Composite Narratives

Co-researchers discussed the following qualities and characteristics of transcendent atmospheres and interactions in their written narratives:

Learner perspective

> The classroom was exciting but also a safe learning environment for us. We were treated with genuine care. I felt like I thrived in the atmosphere

of encouragement and respect that she created. She greatly respected her students and was very interested in their personal well-being, not merely their academic welfare. She had a very vivacious and energetic personality. (Participant 1)

Her passion was contagious and her awe genuine. She valued effort more than accomplishment. She also demonstrated a love of teaching and affection for her students. I realized I was as important to her as she was to me. She was gregarious, active, and always seemed sure of herself. Yet, she made a point of trying to involve me in activities. She was always eager and happy to teach and grow in her profession. I began to understand that your teacher can be both your friend and instructor. She accepted nothing but success from her students. She was available whenever a student had a problem. Her style of teaching was one of patience, understanding, and sincere encouragement. (Participant 2)

This narrative suggests a number of provocative concepts:
– learners may recognize and value safety;
– learners may appreciate and thrive when the teacher applies an holistic approach to relationships with learners;
– learners may recognize and value a teacher's vivacity and energy;
– learners may effectively interact with, and learn effectively from, a teacher who is simultaneously friend and instructor;
– when high expectations are balanced with patience and encouragement, learners may rise to the challenge.

The paragraph that follows is particularly significant because it illustrates the integration of several transcendence themes into one particular example. Those themes include reciprocity, mutuality, and intimacy.

Learner perspective

While we all adored her, she didn't seek to be put on a pedestal. She wanted to know us. She played basketball at recess with us, her rosary beads and veil flying. She listened to our hearts' concerns about dating and parents and dances we weren't invited to. She asked about and listened to our music. She wasn't trying to be one of us, but trying to know each of us.

The reader will note that this learner was aware and responded with adoration when the teacher transcended traditional barriers.

Teacher perspective

As a teacher, I make an extra effort to know and understand my students' wants, needs, and concerns. Caring, encouragement, and perseverance provide the inspiration learners need to continue enhancing the skills that help to develop self-confidence. Because of this I have learned exactly what true education is. It is the reciprocity of teaching and learning which makes it come alive as a profession and gives it that intangible quality of having value not only as a career, but as a way of life.

This teacher appears to view teaching as a joint pilgrimage, a comprehensive effort that emerges from one's very being. Teaching seems not, therefore, an extension of oneself, but it is the expression of one's very essence. Co-researchers believe that transcendence in teaching-learning relationships can be invited and facilitated in the following ways:

Learner perspective

From the moment I walked into his classroom, I felt welcome. He had a warm smile and a very pleasant disposition. His sincerity and trust were evident to me. The interaction and atmosphere that he created caused me to respond differently to this class. We worked together as a team and no student was ever left out. He was available to talk to me whenever we both had free time. I was able to talk to him about anything such as my loneliness, my troubled family relationships, and my fears. He listened without judging, offered advice and encouragement, and repeatedly told me I was a valuable person.

In the example above, the reader will note the teacher's facilitation of transcendence through acting as counselor and friend as well as the subsequent positive impact on this learner.

The following paragraph is another illustration of the integration of several transcendence themes that include humor and moving beyond secure boundaries of endeavor.

Learner perspective

One day, she started to laugh so hard that her face turned red. The class, at first shocked to see a teacher laugh so hard, soon caught the fire and began laughing themselves.

This example demonstrates the power of laughter to raise the atmospheric tone and to remove obstacles. The following teacher views teaching as an expression of love and as an opportunity to transcend.

Teacher perspective

> I want all of my students to be confident and successful. I express my faith and support in them. I shower them with as much love and attention as I possibly can without making other students jealous. I know with love and consistency, they will one day prevail.

Co-researchers reported that their own teaching and learning are broadened and enhanced within the context of transcendence.

Learner perspective

> She set high standards for our behavior and our learning; because she believed in us, we believed in ourselves and our comprehension and achievement reflected that. Because she instilled a passion, I learned, learned well, and remembered. The encouragement and support she gave increased the self-esteem of her students, both emotionally and academically. We were encouraged, for example, to enter a county science fair – not to "win" but to investigate something we wondered about. Every level of research, if it grew out of the student's genuinely wanting to know the answer, was lauded by her. (Participant 1)

> She was my greatest inspiration and my greatest challenge. I realized that my teacher never expected me to please her, but rather to please myself. (Participant 2)

> After I graduated, I returned to my high school to visit her several times. Instead of meeting at the school, we went out to lunch. I will never forget the lessons I learned from her about teaching. Effective teaching requires sharing knowledge as well as compassion, understanding, and respect for individual students. I see the relationship between the teacher and the learner as the nucleus of education. (Participant 3)

For the learners above, real standards for life-lasting learning and achievement are facilitated by encouragement, collaboration, challenge, compassion, and understanding.

Transcendent relationships facilitate the development of learning communities in the following ways:

Learner perspective

> She ran her classroom in a way I had never experienced before. She provided an environment where the whole class became a community of learners. Working together as we did was a regular occurrence in her class and that feeling of being important within the group stayed with me all through my life. Family is the word I think of. We were encouraged to express ourselves and our personalities. She allowed us to be open with our emotions, thoughts, and lives. In return, she shared her life with us.

The implication above is that teachers may generate a marvelous learning community and facilitate the development of life long transcendence-oriented skills and abilities when they move beyond traditional boundaries and facilitate the development of a genuine network of friendships.

Teacher perspective

> My classroom becomes a family, a network of loved ones and friends. I have tried to make it an open learning experience, a cooperative environment where children are both learner and instructor.

One wonders how such an approach as this could have anything but positive results.

Transcendent phenomena affect relators in a variety of ways.

Learner perspective

> The caring, motivation and teaching drive he had will always be my goals. It was the experience in class that changed me. Reflecting back I realize how it helped me to develop my teaching methodologies and beliefs. As a teacher, I make it my goal to create an atmosphere where each student will feel comfortable and successful. I recognize that it is essential to develop an atmosphere that is friendly and positive before meaningful learning can occur. I suddenly understood that my frustration was self-imposed, as was my fear of failure. If it had not been for him and his belief in me academically and personally, I would not have decided to

enter the teaching profession. Because of him, I became more open and even to a degree more extroverted. He taught me to trust myself as well as trust others. (Participant 1)

He helped me to see the beauty in all things, to appreciate everyone and everything around me; he also taught me to appreciate myself. He awakened my sense of humor and encouraged me to use my sense of humor at all times. I embrace teaching and learning with equal passion and to strive for inspiration as a teacher and a learner. A strong relationship between teacher and students builds a strong foundation for increased learning. However corny it may sound, I want to touch a child's life the way he touched mine. (Participant 2)

The discussion above demonstrates the power of transcendence to enable the learner to take risks, to transform the learner in a myriad of ways that later are passed on to the learner-become-teacher's learners.

The following selected paragraphs convey some of the core meanings and themes individual co-researchers recorded during the course (b).

Somehow it seems ironic that this should be my last graduate class; such fundamental stuff-trust, honesty, mutuality, confidence, and intimacy. Why do these characteristics feel too personal for a classroom relationship? Perhaps it is the rigidity of our present educational system or perhaps it is the rigidity of ourselves. As teachers it becomes our responsibility to make the system work for children. (Participant 1)

Teachers can effectively defuse the traditional power structure. Setting up transcendent environments can change education dramatically from the inside out-the way it should be changed. The change will eventually purge the rigid and disinterested from the system in essence purifying it. (Participant 2)

We watched a film, *The Miracle Worker,* the story of a teacher who transcended the traditional teacher's role-moving both herself and her student to the next relational level. Anne was relentless in her concern for Helen. She moved outside of herself – assuming Helen's position and demanded of her what she was capable of. It was only through the transcendent relationship with Anne that Helen was able to reach a turning point in her life. Anne demanded a reciprocal relationship with Helen, unlike the relationship Helen had with the rest of her family. The story captures so many of the concepts we had been exploring together; it somehow won another Academy Award today! Somehow Anne managed to combine a healthy amount of bluntness with grace and tact in such a way that the relationships with not only Helen, but the whole family became transcendent in nature. Anne and Helen's expectations of one another went well beyond what either could have imagined. (Participant 3)

As advocates for children we must transcend the traditional teacher's role. We must take the risk that leads to understanding and trust. If teachers are the trigger to such transcendence, then risk taking is no longer optional for us. As children's challenges and disabilities climb by an alarming rate, transcendent teacher learner relationships become more critical to children's survival. Much like Helen, many of today's children have become victims of those around them. They are the victims not of their own blindness, but of the blindness of others. (Participant 4)

This class has been a transcendent experience for me. It has moved me closer to where I need to be. Often in my life I have been a passive participant. I have allowed life to happen around me without my involvement and response. This class has redirected my journey to that place I have to go. I am committed to pursue transcendence, to grow with others in a life of grace sustained by faith and trust. (Participant 5)

Several months after completing the teacher-learner relationships course, 13 of 15 co-researchers reported the following overarching changes related to classroom practice and their relationships with learners. They reported an increase in (c):
- awareness of how comfortable atmospheres, characterized by mutual trust, help learners to become "ready to learn";
- awareness of the significant impact teachers have on learners;
- in-depth examination of teacher relationships;
- awareness of how ostensibly miniscule comments, words or actions affect learner's growth and development;
- sensitivity to learner's feelings and needs;
- compassion for and patience with learners;
- use of teaching methodologies and strategies that are learner-centered;
- reflection about class discussions has helped co researchers to effectively deal with difficult circumstances; and
- deepened understanding and awareness of self as a learner as well as a teacher.

4 Summary and Implications

Co-researchers determined that learning is broadened and enhanced when teacher and learner enter a mutual learning quest or joint pilgrimage. The learning process is made more meaningful when teaching-learning roles are reciprocal so that relators are more intimately engaged in the pedagogical process. Classroom community is generated and becomes "infectious" when atmosphere and interaction are characterized by respect, trust, love, and humor. In such contexts, teachers and learners are able to risk, to transcend realities and become different in positive ways.

The powerful, often profound, positive impact transcendent relationships have on relators has implications for both theory and practice. In light of the positive feedback recorded here from individuals who practice a transcendence-oriented approach to relating, teaching, and learning, what would the outcome be, for example, if an entire school pursued transcendence? A school district pursued transcendence? A state or nation pursued transcendence? How would interaction between teachers change? Between teachers and administrators? Between learners and other learners? Between teachers and parents? Between administrators and parents? Between the school and community? Certainly, such questions provide inspiration for future research.

Teachers and learners in transcendence are enabled to overcome common educational dilemmas such as learner non-engagement, non-ownership of the learning process, and teacher-learner alienation and estrangement. Are these not some of the most critical ills that face contemporary learning environments? Moreover, the transcendent learning relationships and interactions studied expanded participant awareness and sense of possibility. Because transcendent atmospheres can be created and transcendent interaction invited, educators wishing to effect meaningful reform may consider the qualities, characteristics and power of the transcendent relationship as they redesign learning scenarios.

To create transcendence-oriented interaction with children, the following guidelines are recommended[1]:

– Create a welcoming, supportive, warm, social and nurturing environment. Model a positive outlook on life;
– Establish a classroom community, a network of friends, in which a sense of shelter can be provided by peers as well as the classroom teacher. Engender teamwork, not competition, between children and make it safe for all learners to take risks;
– Model respectful attitudes and do not tolerate dialogue or behavior that does not convey respect for each and every individual in the classroom community. Model respect for diversity;

- Encourage humor and laugh out loudly with children;
- Demonstrate to each child that they are valued and valuable;
- Demonstrate passion for learning and for what you teach. The teacher needs to inspire learners by demonstrating inspiring behavior and ideas;
- Get to know each child personally and speak with each one individually each day as you circulate, before and after school, at recess time, at lunch, etc. Sincere and encouraging remarks and conversations are desirable. Non-curriculum related dialogue is effective in conveying that your interest in, and concern for, each child extends beyond school;
- Convey to children that you trust them, and be willing to take measured risks to demonstrate that trust;
- Look for unique interests, qualities and characteristics in each child and facilitate the child's unique development. Use your awareness to expand your repertoire of strategies to teach each child;
- Adopt an "all children will succeed in this classroom" policy and make it your business for that policy to be successfully implemented. Encourage children and expect each and every child to succeed;
- As you plan and implement exciting learning experiences, reach deep within.

Remember and feel what it is like to be in the learner's place.

5 Implications for Early Childhood Teacher Educators

When I was a young child I faced heavy issues at home including the violence and alcoholism of my father. School might have been a place of stability, support, nurturance, nonviolence and love. Such was not the case. (Instead, at school I found an impersonal, uncertain, competitive, rigid and sometimes violent atmosphere in the primary grades and beyond.)

How powerful a transcendent school environment with a loving teacher might have been at that time. How warm I would have felt and how secure I would have been. I am certain, however, that all children stand to gain from transcendent atmospheres such as those described above where children and adults come together to transcend barriers and to fulfill their dreams.

This chapter is a study of transcendent teacher learner relationships that is reprinted in this book because of the rich descriptions of transcendent relator experiences that it provides. Having read the preceding chapters, the reader may wish to skip to Section 3 of this chapter.

6   Questions for Thought

1. What must happen before a transcendent relationship can occur?

2. What is "tact" and how is it applied?

3. Can a transcendent relationship be assigned to a pair of relators? Why or why not?

4. Identify three or more qualities of transcendent atmosphere and three or more qualities of transcendent interaction.

5. How did learners feel about their transcendent teachers? Include three or more feelings.

6. How are transcendent atmospheres created?

7. How did learners feel in transcendent atmospheres?

8. Describe the impact transcendent teachers have on their learners.

9. What do you admire in the transcendent teachers discussed in this study?

Acknowledgements

This chapter is reprinted from *Journal of Early Childhood Teacher Education*, 25(4), 331–337, 2005. Reprinted here by permission of Taylor Francis llc (http://tandfonline.com).

Note

1   Author's note: See also O'Hara, H. (2000). Children and their invisible needs. *Journal of Early Childhood Teacher Education*, 20(3), 253–257.

CHAPTER 17

Miracles Can Happen

The School of Transcendence

A theoretical *school of transcendence,* as conceived by participants in a graduate course taught by me on the topic of transcendence in teacher learner relationships is analyzed herein. *Transcendent teacher learner relationships* are spontaneously occurring ones in which teacher and learner transcend, or go beyond, their traditional interactive roles. During the transcendent encounter a "turning point" occurs for one or both participants, and life goals are altered or changed. Just as transcendent relationships are characterized by particular qualities that include caring, trust, mutual respect and love, the school of transcendence is designed to support transcendent pedagogy and transcendent interpersonal relationships. Powerful transcendent relationships and correspondingly powerful learning encounters are invited by transcendent school atmosphere and interaction.

The school of transcendence is contrasted with the traditional school in terms of philosophy and approach to creating learning encounters, curricula, planning and scheduling, assessment and evaluation, physical space and school community interpersonal relationships. The conception of the traditional school as a place of violence is contrasted with the safe environment of the school of transcendence. Governance in the school of transcendence is explained. Finally, transcendence-oriented approaches currently implemented in the extraordinary Reggio Emilia, Italy public schools that I visited are identified. A series of metaphors for the school of transcendence are presented to help the reader synthesize and envision the school of transcendence.

1 Perspectives on Education

The theoretical underpinnings for the school of transcendence emerge from the study of transcendence in teacher learner relationships (O'Hara, 1992, 1997, 2005, 2011). The conceptual and theoretical framework for transcendence in teacher learner relationships derives from an integrated body of education literature. That body of literature includes educational philosophy, educational psychology and learning theory. The transcendent teacher learner relationship (O'Hara, 1992) may occur when relaters move *beyond secure boundaries of endeavor.* Both teacher and learner must drop off conventions, rubrics and systems (Moustakas, 1966). To move beyond secure boundaries, both teacher and learner must trust each other and risk the unknown in the process of establishing limits, exercising self-discipline and responsibility. The learner's world must be received and understood by the teacher. As teacher learner roles, obstacles and barriers are transcended, a turning point may occur. Author of *Pedagogy of the Oppressed* (1989), Paulo Freire, as example writes of the importance of *reconciliation* in the pedagogical relationship, i.e., reconciling the poles of the teacher-learner contradiction so that both are simultaneously teachers and learners (p. 59). Together, teacher and learner may encounter a process involving the expanding of awareness, the emergence of new identity, and the taking of steps toward a more positive new life.

The teacher's traditional governing stance over children must be replaced by a new pedagogy of thoughtfulness and openness (Van Manen, 1991). It must include belief and confidence in the learner as well as the determination of challenging expectations. Such pedagogy involves the tactful mediation of love and care, hope and trust, and responsibility. The mediation each of these requires is *tact*. Tact is not obtrusive but is subtle, hardly noticeable. It reads the inner life of the learner, intuiting when to intervene, when to remain silent. Tact creates a warm social atmosphere, a sensitive and flexible tone, but it is also firm, direct, decisive and open. Tact employs humor and the tactful individual is deeply committed to her principles.

"The facilitation of significant learning depends upon certain attitudinal qualities which exist in the personal relationship between the facilitator and the learner" (Rogers, 1967, p. 3). Buber (1958, 1965a, 1965b), Greene (1985, 1988), Palmer (1983), Rogers (1967), Maslow (1968), Macdonald (1974), Noddings (1984) and others have called for pedagogical relationships characterized by trust, care, and mutuality between teacher and learner. "One person enters a covenant with another, a pledge to engage in a mutually accountable and transforming relationship, a relationship forged of trust and faith in the face of unknowable risks" (Palmer, 1983, p. 31). Martin Buber emphasizes the importance of mutuality and intimacy in teacher learner relationships (Buber, 1965a, pp. 98–100). For relationships such as these to occur, the teacher must "view the world through their eyes" (Rogers, 1967, pp. 8–9), and must "experience from the other side" (Buber, 1965, pp. 8–9).

Transcendent teacher learner interaction is mutually reciprocal, liberating, and growth oriented. Such interaction is authentic or genuine by virtue of the interweaving of the active and passive (receptive) pedagogical roles. Transcendent interaction is facilitated when there is a spontaneous, personal and biographically oriented attraction between two people. Any teacher learner relational interaction created by virtue of planning, manipulation or deliberately assigned mentorships is inconsistent with the subject of this study. Again, the connection occurs spontaneously, but the transcendent relationship frequently endures for a lifetime (O'Hara 1992, 2005, 2011).

2 Methods/Data Source

The methodology applied in this study derives in part from Clark Moustakas' *heuristics* (1990). Heuristics provides a format for research that begins with researcher self-inquiry and then moves outward to the encounters of others. The heuristic researcher does not presuppose cause-effect relationships.

The population for this study is comprised of students enrolled in the early childhood master's degree program at Towson University. Data for this study were generated by students following their self-studies, group research and collaborative exploration of transcendent teacher learner relationships. Late in the course, having considered how transcendence emerges in teacher learner relationships, in their own and in the lives of others, the students were asked to theorize how a school characterized by transcendence might look and feel. At first students experienced what Katherine Patrick (1955) has identified as the *preparation stage* of creativity.

During this stage, the creator experiences doubt, disorganization, trial and error. I refer to this as the "cranky" stage of creativity. The crankiness emerged as students grappled with the theoretical restructuring of learning environments they had been schooled in as well as the ones where they were currently teaching. They were being asked to imagine an entirely new kind of school. Students were baffled at, and frustrated by, the poor "fit," the incongruity between, on the one hand, traditional structures, and on the other hand, transcendence, or the action of going beyond traditional structures. Ultimately, students considered their own perceptions of the characteristics of the traditional school. Having identified those perceptions, they postulated about how the school of transcendence might go beyond traditional structures. Students characterized the traditional and the transcendent schools on chart paper following extended discussion.

Using data collected from students during the course, I began to shape and develop what follows. Simultaneously, I was studying the Reggio Emilia schools and was struck by how those schools mirror the school of transcendence conceived by my graduate students.

Related Reggio Emilia practices and philosophy are discussed below. Drawing upon transcendent teacher learner relationship research and the theoretical school of transcendence data collected during the course, I developed a series of metaphors for the school of transcendence. These metaphors are also included.

3 Findings

The data collected draw sharp distinction between the traditional school and the school of transcendence. The traditional school refers to many schools that have existed in the past and continue to exist today. Perceptions of traditional school characteristics were gleaned from learning encounters that graduate course participants had during their education career as students. Those characteristics are listed as bullets, organized into six categories: philosophical orientation and approach to creating learning encounters, curricula and program implementation, planning and scheduling, assessment and evaluation, physical space, and school/community interpersonal relationships.

4 Philosophical Orientation and Approach to Creating Learning Encounters

4.1 *The Traditional School*
- It is assumed that many learners will not be successful and that only some have an exceptional intellect, "gifts" and "talents." It is presumed that gifts and talents can be identified through formal testing.
- Teaching strategies, assessment and evaluation predispose some learners for success and many others for mediocrity or failure.
- As learners attempt to be successful, learning and evaluation strategies pit them against each other.
- Learning is an independent, passive, inactive and abstract experience. Learning strategies and discourse are didactic (one way) rather than dialectic (two ways). Teachers view themselves as intellectually complete and learners as blank slates, receptacles for data.
- Teachers place themselves center stage and place learners in the audience for which the teacher performs. A one-way transmission of information occurs following the teacher's performance.
- Learner movement, choice and empowerment are regarded as permissiveness.
- Convergent thought is valued and developed to the exclusion of divergent or creative thought (as example, field trips are regarded as entertainment).

– Learner diversity is compensated for rather than valued and incorporated into teaching and learning events and experiences.

4.2   The School of Transcendence

– All learners are assumed to be intellectually capable and competent in divergent ways. It is the facilitator's responsibility to identify those divergent competencies and to teach to accommodate and develop all of them.
– Learning is active, hands-on, tactile, multisensory and interdisciplinary. Abstract lecture is minimized and drill is rarely used.
– Learning encounters are made relevant to all learners so that deep meaning is facilitated.
– Open, two-way dialogue, or a dialectic, between all members of the learning community is regularly facilitated.
– Learners are grouped heterogeneously by developmental level rather than age.
– Facilitators regard themselves as co-learners, or partners in learning.
– Learner-centered, rather than teacher-centered, cooperative and collaborative learning scenarios are implemented.
– Freedom, movement, choice and empowerment are facilitated and nurtured for all community members.
– Self-expression is sought, facilitated and developed by teachers who facilitate learning encounters designed to develop self-expression.
– The development of skills and abilities in the fine arts are valued and are developed in all learners because of the critical role they play in the facilitation of self-expression and positive self-perception.
– Learners are invited and encouraged to develop and broaden personal horizons, their unique interests and creativity.
– Divergent as well as convergent thought is developed.

5   Curricula

5.1   The Traditional School

– Curricula do not identify and build on learners' prior experience and interests.
– Discrete subjects are studied independent of other subjects.
– A subject hierarchy exists in which math and science are regarded as important, the language arts are important as support systems, social studies is not so important (frequently defined only in terms of climate, geography and economics), and art, music, dance, drama and physical education are not important at all (if they are present in curricula).

5.2 The School of Transcendence

- Curricula build on learner's prior experience and interests. Learning is reinforced by projects that are selected by learners rather than dictated by the teacher.
- Curricula are integrated and interdisciplinary, not disparate and subject hierarchy does not exist.
- The fine arts, as example, are regarded to be of equal importance to mathematics.
  There is therefore, no "core curriculum" in a school of transcendence.
- The fine arts are regarded to play critical roles in the process of facilitating self-expression and a healthy self-perception. One's individual diversity is perceived as being an intrinsic component of their self-expression and positive self-perception.

6 Planning and Scheduling

6.1 The Traditional School
- Inflexible, rigid and frequently arbitrary schedules are imposed on the teacher.
- Learners are grouped homogeneously by perceived ability levels and by age.

6.2 The School of Transcendence
- Large blocks of time for teacher-learner collaboration, planning and learning are provided. Teacher and learner are involved in a partnership wherein reciprocity, mutual respect and learning occur simultaneously involving both teacher and learner.
- Learners develop ownership of learning encounters as they assist in the conception and planning of their developmental opportunities.
- Learners are grouped heterogeneously by a wide array of developmental levels, not by age.

7 Assessment and Evaluation

7.1 The Traditional School
- Didactic teaching strategies, assessment and evaluation predispose some learners for success and many for mediocrity or failure.
- Formalized, standardized testing instruments used that are culturally biased and are not responsive to learners' economic status or culture, to divergent

thought, to their developmental level, divergent learning styles or a learner's personal existential sphere are imposed.

7.2   The School of Transcendence
- Collaborative evaluation is performance criteria based, and is never subjectively implemented. Failure is not within the lexicon of transcendent evaluatory discourse. All children are assisted in the pursuit and achievement of success.
- Authentic, formative, non-biased assessment and evaluation are implemented. Standardized tests are not given.
- Learner progress is documented qualitatively in the form of dialogue, journals, portfolios and multimedia. Cumulative progress is never reduced to a letter grade. Letter grades are viewed as yielding an inaccurate, inadequate characterization of an individual's developmental progress.
- Learners are taken seriously in terms of their ability to make responsible and creative decisions, and are taught to assess their own learning and developmental progress.

8   Physical Space

8.1   The Traditional School
- Physical school structures are dark or unnaturally bright, dull, hard, rigid, aesthetically negative, ominous, restrictive maze-like spaces.
- Inside school structure is regarded as the place for learning and outside as the place for the release of physical energy.
- The school is regarded as the structure that "houses" learning.

8.2   The School of Transcendence
- Physical learning spaces are open, cheerful, beautiful, airy, positive relationship enhancing structures where the inside flows into the outside. Both sides of school walls as well as beyond the campus, are regarded as equally valid learning spaces. Field trips, for example, are viewed as supreme learning encounters.
- The physical environment is not regarded as the structure that "houses" learning, but as the home base where powerful learning encounters are planned and initiated. The outside is perceived to offer varied and profound opportunities for observation, experimentation, group investigation and inquiry.

9 School Community Interpersonal Relationships

9.1 *The Traditional School*
- A rigid social hierarchy and interpersonal relational artificiality exists between principal, teacher, parent, and particularly between teacher and learner. Teacher and learners are not equal partners in the relationship. Relationships are not reciprocal. The teacher is perceived to be an authority figure that learned but no longer learns content in her or his classroom.
- Relationships between teacher and learner are not mutual and they are never viewed as interchangeable. Teachers may behave in a manner that is inconsistent with the manner in which they interact with all others. An artificial persona manifests.

9.2 *The School of Transcendence*
- Warm, social interpersonal relationships between all community members are developed to facilitate deep interpersonal understanding as well as intense and creative collaboration.
- Regular meetings occur between administrators and teacher, parents and learners with family involvement nights, days, lunches and picnics. Deep interpersonal relationships are sought, established and facilitated between all personnel, learners and community individuals.
- Open, two-way dialogue between all members of the learning community is ongoing.

10 Traditional Schools as Places of Violence

The atmosphere of the school of transcendence is one that facilitates physical, intellectual, emotional and social safety. By contrast, the traditional school, as described above, suggests a violent, therefore unsafe environment. Violence is defined here as an external force that inflicts social, economic, emotional, cognitive as well as physical pain and suffering. The traditional school also denies opportunity to those deemed to be less capable than others. Such a traditional school cannot be regarded as safe or as learner-centered. Teachers who uphold such traditional environments cannot be regarded as learner advocates. Elements of violence identified in the traditional school include:
- Physical violence that may occur frequently in traditional schools, as it is legal to strike children in schools in many states and even to inflict bruises on them. Corporal punishment is perceived to teach respect for authority figures.

- Social violence when, at particular junctures, learners are ostracized and denied opportunity if they are unsuccessful with testing in particular content areas. Learners may also be ostracized if they come from social, economic and ethnic minority groups (e.g., African-Americans, Buddhists, Gay, Lesbian or Bisexual, Homeless learners, etc.).
- Emotional and social violence can occur when teachers disregard and/or disrespect learners who are not having a successful learning experience.
- Cognitive and social violence that are present when learners are pitted against each other and opportunity is denied because learners are not successful in prescribed, non-responsive, often uni-dimensional learning scenarios.
- Economic violence that occurs when opportunity is denied on the basis of one's economic status or on the basis of standardized tests. Even though standardized tests are culturally biased and non-responsive to individual learning styles and needs, low standardized test scores ultimately result in the denial of economic opportunity.
- Social, cognitive, emotional and economic violence that occurs when learners are "tracked" against their will, and cognitive and economic opportunity is subsequently denied on the basis of that tracking.

11 Governance of the School of Transcendence

Unlike the authoritarian governance present in the traditional school that is based on hierarchy, power, submission and punishment, the transcendent school is non-hierarchized and governed through egalitarian sharing of authority and responsibilities by all personnel.

Punishment is regarded as a destructive and ultimately ineffective approach to modifying human behavior and output. Personnel endeavor to understand the causes of negative behavior and to respond positively to learner needs. All policies, rules and regulations are developed collaboratively by all personnel. All school responsibilities are pooled in the form of a list. Responsibilities on the list are distributed equitably among all personnel.

A team of coordinators, who assume coordinator positions voluntarily for a specified term, perform most of what have been traditionally regarded as administrative duties.

Coordinators act to facilitate the implementation of policy through maintaining the lines of communication between various other teams and through supporting personnel in the performance of their various team and individual responsibilities. There are no titles among personnel in the school of transcendence. An individual's responsibilities on a given day could include, for example, answering the phone, hosting a tea with an international focus for learners and faculty, facilitating a learner team to clean windows or floors, facilitating a team of learners to design a courtyard garden, or facilitating learners to write a book about that garden.

Assignments are not ranked according to personnel hierarchy because such a hierarchy does not exist. All personnel are regarded as equal players. The sharing of responsibilities is such that it would not occur to faculty to say, "I'm sorry, that's not my job." Pay for all personnel is equal.

12 Transcendence-Oriented Approaches Implemented in Reggio Emilia Schools

The early childhood programs in the town of Reggio Emilia, Italy have been visited by over 10,000 international educators because of their extraordinary approach to facilitating young children's development. These schools were conceived and built by the hands of parents in Reggio Emilia immediately following World War II. Reggio Emilia educators welcome visitors to the schools to stimulate reflection about teaching.

Characteristics of the Reggio Emilia schools that approximate, or mirror, those of the school of transcendence are listed below.

- The environment is beautiful and many elements of that environment are created and/or assembled by individual members of the school community. Attention is given to every environmental detail including color, furniture shape, arrangement of objects including sculpture, the presence of beautiful, healthy green plants, etc. (Hendrick, 1997).
- Children are recognized as active constructors of their own learning through social processes that include teamwork in aesthetically-oriented projects (Hendrick, 1997). Teachers are deeply aware that children have preparedness, curiosity and interest in constructing their own learning. They are viewed by teachers as capable of engaging in social interaction and of negotiating everything in the environment (Gandini, 1993).
- Relationships between teachers, parents, children and the community are reciprocal and interconnected (Gandini, 1993). When parents, children and teachers plan a task, it is mutual choice and is carried out with strong motivation and engagement (Hendrick, 1997).
- Teachers view themselves as partners with children in the learning process. Teachers enjoy and celebrate the process of discovery with children. Teachers

talk with children to explore their theories and ideas. Subsequently, teachers and learners develop learning encounters together (Gandini, 1993). An overarching spirit of cooperation is present at all times (Hendrick, 1997). "Children's own sense of time and their personal rhythm are considered in planning and implementing activities and projects" (Gandini, 1993, p. 6). The schedule provides sufficient time to complete projects and activities with satisfaction (Gandini, 1993).

- Relationships between teachers are strong. Teacher learner relationships in Reggio Emilia are based on mutual respect and trust. Teachers work in pairs as equals.
- "Schools do not have a director on the premise. Schools are run by the team of teachers and staff members to help teachers with the interpretation of philosophy, to mediate the connections with parents and administrators, to organize training sessions, to follow the development of projects and activities, and much more. Teachers are assisted toward autonomy, not dependence" (Hendrick, 1997, p. ii).
- Curriculum is not pre-established. Instead, teachers have general goals and hypothesize about what direction projects and activities might take (Gandini, 1993).
- "Transcriptions of children's remarks and discussions, photographs of their activity, and representations of their thinking and learning using many media are carefully arranged to document the work (and the process of learning) done in the schools" (Gandini, 1993 p. 8). The data provided are used to assess and evaluate children's developmental progress, but also help teachers understand children more, maintain parental involvement, facilitate communication and the sharing of ideas, and to help children see that their efforts are valued (Gandini, 1993).
- Taking John Dewey's lead, Reggio Emilia schools strive to make all learning relevant to the lives of all children (Hendrick, 1997). Reggio Emilia schools are non-selective and non-discriminatory.

Again, the Reggio Emilia schools approximate many of the characteristics of the school of transcendence. An investigation to determine the extent of such approximations is beyond the scope of this book.

13   Metaphors for the School of Transcendence

Having studied the theory for the school of transcendence developed by graduate students at Towson University, I created a series of metaphors for that school. The metaphors are designed to synthesize the myriad qualities and implications presented by the school of transcendence theory.

The school of transcendence as the *meeting house* where:
– governance is shared;
– all voices are heard and respected;
– decisions are arrived at through group consensus, and;
– conflict is addressed with care and respect.

The school of transcendence as the *kitchen* where:
– all participants "cook the education meal";
– learning experiences are delectable and tantalizing;
– only fresh, authentic ingredients are used;
– recipes are intercultural and international spices are used;
– chefs are committed to pleasing, and;
– creativity and daring abound.

The school of transcendence as the *artist's studio* where:
– the goal is to express oneself creatively;
– the artist and one's work is supported, protected and nurtured;
– the artist has adequate time to reflect and to create;
– there is room to display one's work;
– one feels a sense of ownership of space;
– marvelous projects are created, and;
– diversity is expected, respected and valued.

The school of transcendence as a *rehearsal hall* where:
– harmony and dissonance are desired and created;
– people share vision and common goals;
– the atmosphere is full of anticipation;
– efforts lead to performance before an audience, and;
– people are free and feel safe to make mistakes as they develop skills and creativity.

The school of transcendence as the *architect's drawing board* where:
– projects are conceived;
– new ideas are developed and recorded;
– a broad spectrum of concerns, regulations, needs and desires are integrated into the design;

- sharing of ideas and collaboration occurs;
- vision is given form and dimension;
- details and glitches are worked out on paper, and;
- plans and drawings are created with full intention for their implementation.

The school of transcendence as the *dinner table* where:
- nourishment is served and enjoyed;
- protocol and good manners are observed;
- the atmosphere is stimulating and is multisensory;
- people are drawn close intellectually, physically and spiritually, and;
- dialogue is engaging.

The school of transcendence as the *market* where:
- many products are examined and evaluated;
- choice is of the utmost importance;
- quality and value are sought;
- products are organized appropriately;
- judgment is applied;
- relevance and attraction are critical, and;
- people learn through experience.

The school of transcendence as the *counseling center* where:
- people feel safe to express themselves;
- individual experience is valued and regarded as relevant;
- personal growth is fundamental;
- solutions to problems are mediated;
- sharing is the primary learning medium;
- transformation is desired and facilitated, and;
- violence is not present, and when it is, it is purged.

The school of transcendence as the *stage* where:
- human experience is created, conveyed and felt;
- great meaning is expressed;
- human experience is integrated and valued;
- humor, art, music, drama and dance are central;
- people experience other's hope, pain, joy, love, laughter, etc. vicariously;
- one can learn what it means to walk in another's shoes;
- creativity is of paramount importance, and;
- both performer and audience play an integrated, active role.

The school of transcendence as the *courtroom* where:
- component parts are examined and analyzed;
- valid determinations and judgments are made;
- protocol is observed;
- many points of view are critically examined from two or more frames of reference, and;
- expert opinion is sought.

The school of transcendence as the *cafe* where:
- people meet to share, to enjoy, to be stimulated and to be authentic;
- atmosphere helps create powerful and beautiful moments;
- manners matter;
- people feel warm, comforted and nurtured;
- conversation is encouraged as an opportunity to expand, and;
- interaction is appropriate and spontaneous.

The school of transcendence as the *sacred space* where:
- people feel whole and in touch with an extraordinary power;
- people can return home;
- something beyond the ordinary can occur;
- something larger than the component parts is present;
- one is loved for being oneself, and;
- magic sparkles.

The school of transcendence as the *beach* where:
- all individuals play together;
- there are no badges of office and no bosses;
- the environment is enjoyed, admired and respected;
- there is time for reflection, and;
- beauty and aesthetics are abundant.

14 Conclusion

The school of transcendence theorized by graduate students at Towson University is unique in concept and design. Nonetheless, it is significant that many of the qualities and characteristics of the extant Reggio Emilia schools mirror those of the school of transcendence. Educators seeking to restructure learning environments can look to the Reggio Emilia schools and note several transcendence-oriented approaches practiced successfully.

The school of transcendence goes beyond the theory and practice of the traditional school as defined in this discussion. The school of transcendence is a place of genuine human equality, mutual respect, trust, flexibility and abundant opportunity. Learning encounters are conceived as safe, lively, vital and intensely collaborative. Dialogue between all transcendent school community members is intended to be continuous and mutually beneficial. Creativity and diversity are valued and nurtured. Physical environments are cheery and beautiful in the school of transcendence. The interpersonal transcendent environment as conceived is bathed in the power and grace of human dignity.

15   Questions for Thought

1. How would you define a school of transcendence?

2. How is a school of transcendence different from a traditional school? Identify three levels of difference that you regard to be the most significant in terms of the difference between the two types of school.

3. How would you feel as a learner in a school of transcendence? How would that feeling differ from how you felt in a traditional school?

4. If you attended a school of transcendence, what made the school transcendent?

5. How would your learning experiences have been different in a school of transcendence?

6. Which three metaphors for a school of transcendence do you find the most appealing and why is that the case?

CHAPTER 18

Putting It All Together

> Treat people as if they were what they ought to be and you help them become what they are capable of becoming.
> GOETHE

∴

In Chapter 1, I encouraged the reader to read and think about what it would mean if transcendent teacher learner relationships were commonplace, or even if transcendence was the standard to which all teacher learner relationships aspired. My intent was for the reader to consider where such relationships could lead if they were to become commonplace and to ponder the implications of thoroughly transformative encounters for both teacher and learner.

Findings derived from the study of transcendent teacher learner relationships and shamanic teachers have philosophical and pedagogical significance evidenced herein. Teachers and learners report that mutual trust, mutual care, mutual respect, as well as freedom, love, realness and openness allow relationships to go beyond, or transcend traditional teaching-learning relationship structures. The process of going beyond not only makes learning profoundly meaningful, but the relationships positively alter the lif paths for relators. The various interactional and atmospheric dimensions of transcendence do not act singularly, but in concert, to facilitate the development of transformative life-long relationships. Transcendent relationships involve what Van Manen (1991) has called the tactful mediation of these dimensions.

Shamanic transcendent teacher participants, following deep contemplation, deploy glamour to attract the learner. They deliberately act to merge with, uplift, heal and mobilize the learner to dream. Shamanic teachers, applying profound powers of empathy and compassion, work with the learner to accomplish that which would otherwise seem unattainable or unreachable. Below I have attempted to unify the critical components of the transcendent teacher learner relationship and shamanistic teaching as seen from multiple perspectives.

1 A Synthesis of the Research on Transcendent Teacher Learner Relationships

1.1 *Freedom and Discipline*

Freedom is not possible for relators without the balance that discipline provides. The discipline that appears to develop in transcendent teacher learner relationships, however, is self-discipline. Self-discipline can occur only when limits have been clearly established by relators. Participants find that self-discipline tends to negate the need for extrinsic or externally imposed discipline or rewards. Instead, in transcendence-oriented scenarios, learners respond to teachers and learning situations with what Phenix (1974) has called *glad obedience*. Kathy and Laura report that this obedience arises voluntarily as a self discipline develops. Participants explain that freedom is not taken advantage of when trust is established and a caring sense of community exists. For Palmer (1983), it is love that "reconciles the demand of freedom and discipline." Moustakas (1981) has pointed out that love allows for the harmonious establishment of limits (not to be construed as limitations) and the acceptance of each relator's responsibility in the interactional process. Humor also enables participants to mediate the tension that arises in the process of balancing freedom and discipline.

1.2 *Love*

Spranger (1972) and Van Manen (1990, 1991) argue the importance of love in the teacher learner relationship. Klein (1989) and Shaffer (1977) call for a love that preserves and protects, but also challenges. Love is not harsh and in Spranger's (1972) words, never rejects the learner. Teachers and learners, in fact, report that rejection of either relator does not arise in their transcendent interaction.

Love emerges as foundational for study participants. As Palmer (1983) suggests, love provides a sense of the other's value. Love provides willingness to risk for the other and enables the other to mediate the demands of freedom and discipline. Unconditional love fills in the gaps that present themselves for relators thereby opening the possibility of ever deepening rapport and the continuance of transcendent relationships. Love inspires teacher and learner participants to strive for, and to accept, something more than what would exist otherwise.

Noddings (1984) has carefully explained an ethic of care. Rogers (1967) has emphasized realness and openness in the teacher learner relationship. Participant teachers have voiced their inability to divorce these qualities from their teaching, which for them, are acts of caring and compassion. Images of home, closeness, warmth, relaxation and laughter, or what Van Manen (1990,

1991) has called a "warm social atmosphere" predominate transcendent atmospheres. Lauren, as example, describes the atmosphere and relational tone as being like family. Kathy and Kellen also spoke specifically of the familial tone of their transcendent relationships.

1.3   Trust, Risk and Tact

Rogers (1967), Noddings (1984), Van Manen (1990, 1991), Bollnow (1972, 1989) and Moustakas (1966, 1977, 1981) have all emphasized the importance of trust in learning relationships. For Moustakas (1981), trust provides a secure basis for a relationship. The security of having the teacher's trust, faith and confidence is enjoyed by the learner. The *tactful* (Van Manen, 1991) teacher affords the learner the freedom to fail without risk of the withdrawal of acceptance. Transcendent relator participants find that when they are challenged in tactful ways, they feel safe to take risks. The teacher, to use Peggy's and Phenix's (1974) term, acts as a *catalyst* that accelerates the learner's desire to imagine things, thereby "breaking through the structures of the world and creating something new" (Greene, 1988, pp. 17, 34).

Van Manen's (1991) tact, is a non-obtrusive, subtle quality of intuition that reads the *inner life* of the learner, or the learner's internal state (a quality that is also referred with differing terminology by Spranger (1972), Shaffer (1977), and Belenky, Clinchy, Goldberger, and Tarule (1997). Learners refer to teacher tact as a kind of omniscience, or universal awareness. Tactful teachers appear to learners to read, or connect with, the learner's *inner life* which is a critical component of shamanic teaching as well transcendence in relationships.

A teacher's tact or grace in teaching and relating is supported by an awareness and sensitivity to the learner's biography, as well as their own biography. The teacher draws on his or her own biography to inform teaching approaches and practices with particular learners as was demonstrated in the example of Melinda and Laura. Such processes involve what Shaffer (1977) describes as *interpersonal synchrony* and Moustakas (1981) calls *rhythm*. When the teacher's graceful approach is supported by a biographical link with the learner, learners are empowered to break through existing structures and to create something new. Such an imagining, melded with risk taking, enables relators to break free of limitations and obstacles.

1.4   Seeing from the Other's Point of View

Buber's *inclusion* refers to putting oneself in the place of another individual is similar in connotation to *connecting* by Belenky, Clinchy, Goldberger and Tarule (1997), as *attentiveness* by Klein (1989), *as engrossment* by Noddings (1984) and as *seeing from the child's point of view* by Shaffer (1977). Inclusion and humor are core qualities of the transcendent teacher learner relationships studied. Moreover, inclusion and humor are primary tools for reaching transcendence in the relationship. Inclusion, an intuitive process requiring compassion, allows one to receive and understand the other individual. Humor is used powerfully in transcendent interaction to reduce distance between relators. Humor and inclusion are practiced concurrently, for example, when teachers, and sometimes learners act to overcome uncomfortable or potentially discordant relational circumstances. Beth, as example, emphasizes the role of humor in her interaction with her learners.

1.5   Dialogue and the Reduction of Distance

Freire (1989), Greene (1984a, 1984b) and Phenix (1974) highlight the importance of ongoing and unfinished dialogue in human interaction. Indeed, dialogue is a hallmark of the transcendent teacher learner relationships chronicled in this book. Dialogue establishes and sustains caring, trust, and faith in the other. Dialogue is a primary tool for the establishment of relational reciprocity, equality, and mutuality. Through dialogue, participants consciously act to reduce the distance that has historically separated and even estranged teachers and learners. Beth and Laura concur with Buber (1958) that dialogue can occur when both participants have a consciousness of inclusion, or of seeing from the other's point of view.

To further facilitate the reduction of distance between relators, teachers have modified or removed grading. The use of grading, as Noddings (1984) has suggested, intrudes on the teacher learner relationship. Instead, in transcendent atmospheres, grading is handled in ways that avoid teacher subjectivity, increase access to new or increased learning opportunity, and facilitate the most development possible for learners by shifting the locus of control of grades into the learner's hands and away from those of transcendent teacher participants. Encouraging and empowering learners to redraft assignments until appropriate levels of mastery are reached helps to facilitate learner control of grades.

Transcendent relationships are mutually giving/receiving ones – partnerships as Shaffer (1977) has called them, that contribute to healthy development and the growth of positive self-esteem in both teacher and learner. Both parties tend to feel ennobled and enabled by transcendent relational encounters. Respect between transcendent relators is strong.

1.6   Mutuality and Reciprocity

Roger's (1967) equality and personalness, Buber's (1965a) and Moustakas' (1966, 1981) mutuality, Shaffer's (1991) and Buber's (1965a) reciprocity are inherent in the transcendent teacher learner relationships encountered by the participants. Also evident is that the teacher perceives the learner to be fundamentally and inherently good. Such a perception is consistent with Noddings' (1984) notion of always expecting "the best possible motive" from learners. Autocratic, dominance/submission style approaches are rejected by participant transcendent teachers. Learners are safe to risk, as Moustakas (1981) and Noddings (1984) point out, when autocratically-oriented barriers are removed. Belenky, Clinchy, Goldberger, and Tarule (1997) instead refer to the interchangeability and the merger of the teacher and learner, and Freire (1989) to the reconciliation of teacher and learner roles. Jerry spoke of the importance of feeling "that we're in this together." Such sentiments are mirrored in Shaffer's (1977) work as he speaks of mutual involvement and mutual adjustment, Freire (1989) of cointentionality, and Macdonald (1974) of joint pilgrimage. Palmer (1983) concurs that the teacher and the learner are challenged by one another in the pursuit of growth and expansion. For Laura, reciprocity, equality, mutuality, as well as freedom, are not acquired on a permanent basis. They are dynamic or of the moment and they must be continually nurtured, renewed and sustained.

Again, transcendent teacher learner relationships are reciprocal relationships. Teachers in transcendent relationships give in innumerable ways to their learners, ways that result in new awareness and changes in life direction for their learners. The relationship is not one of dependence, however, but one in which teachers nudge their learners beyond dependence.

What is clear is that for participants, teacher-giving is reciprocated by learner-giving in transcendent relationships. Teachers indicate that learners give to them in many ways that include reliability and dependability. But learners also respond to teachers with thoughtfulness, concern, emotional support, cheerfulness, love and laughter. Laura indicated that her work with Melinda had allowed her to work through and resolve many of the issues in her own past. Learners also bring a beguiling quality to the transcendent relationship that Bollnow (1989) has called *the morningness of youth*. In fact, teacher participants find that it is the learner who bestows the very distinction of teacher on them.

2 Transcendent Impact

Relator participants have suggested that the teacher, or the learner, involved in a transcendent relationship may not know the impact their behavior and responsiveness is having on the other relator. Instead the giving relator simply attempts to do her job in the most response-able way possible. But, what Moustakas (1977) has called a *turning point* may occur for an individual relator because of the slightest, briefest, personalized effort one makes on behalf of the other. Efforts such as these give relators hope Phenix (1974) as is evidenced in the examples of Kellen, Beth and Peggy. Each relator was enabled to forgo thoughts of suicide because of the impact of their relationships with their teachers, even though it is unlikely that those teachers were aware of the impact they were having on their learners at the time or even since that time.

3   Community

Transcendent teacher learner relationships, for relators such as Jerry, may ultimately evolve into a network of relationships, or what Greene (1992) and Palmer (1983) have called *community*. In the community Jerry depicts, individuality is not only upheld, but valued and championed. Once the teacher provides the lead of valuing individuality, as Moustakas (1966), Noddings (1984) and Phenix (1974) have suggested, participants find that learners respond in like manner. Community comes, for Kathy and others, when individuals respect and value each other in a way that is not possible if they compete against each other. A mutually respectful network of relationships is facilitated by an absence of competition. In such a collaborative, genial community, respect and dignity are attended to reciprocally between teacher and learner, and other learners. Teachers operating in a community not only foster unconditional regard, love, respect and dignity, but in doing so they also contribute to the development of healthy self-esteem for each of the community members. Transcendent teachers and learners repeatedly remarked that their relationships made them feel that they "mattered," that they were "worth something." Their teachers gave them a sense of what Phenix (1974) has called "unrealized possibilities." Jean and Peggy concur with Van Manen (1990, 1991), that when the teachers trust learners, learners are enabled to trust themselves and each other.

4   The Transformative Impact of the Transcendent Teacher Learner Relationship

Transcendent relator participants found that whether they encounter a positive, or even a negative transcendent teacher learner relationship, the relationship tends to alter the individual's perspective in ways that influence future relationships. Participant perspectives strongly suggest that negatively transcendent teachers, those who are distrustful, uncaring and "distant" do not have a positive transcendent impact on learners. Also, teachers who are not willing to risk for their learners, do not transcend barriers with learners because the act of going beyond traditional roles is in itself a risk for both relators. Risks emerge when relators drop off what Moustakas (1966) has called the conventions, rubrics and systems that secure teacher learner boundaries provide. For Bollnow (1972, 1989), trust itself is a kind of risk. In the same way, if a teacher does not expect to learn from learners, it is not likely that mutuality, reciprocity, or collegiality can develop between relators.

Transcendent teacher learner relationships occur for participants because of a cluster of atmospheric qualities and interactive features that converge in such a way as to enable teacher and learner to transcend barriers and create new realities. It is clear that participant biographies predisposed them to relate in transcendent ways with the other.

Teacher and learner participants report that they have gone beyond the lackadaisical, dull, and meaningless interaction that exists in so many teaching-learning environments. Those who are well familiar with bland classroom atmospheres and dull pedagogical relationships have found another way of being via transcendent relationships, in which learning takes on a profoundly positive meaning. Difficult, often dire personal circumstances seem less severe as the learning relationship expands relator awareness and their sense of possibility increases. The barriers presented by loneliness, wheelchairs, repression, hopelessness, shock treatments, and even suicide contemplation are transcended. Visions of better realities take their place even as better realities emerge.

5   Questions for Thought

1. What does O'Hara say regarding balance between freedom and discipline?

2. What does Palmer say regarding balance between freedom and discipline?

3. What does Buber say regarding balance between freedom and discipline?

4. What does Greene say regarding balance between freedom and discipline?

5. What does it mean to reach beyond oneself in the pursuit of personal freedom?

6. What are the characteristics of a transcendent space?

7. What makes a learning community supportive?

8. Explain wonder, awe and reverence as they relate to transcendent relationships.

APPENDIX A

Heuristic Research Methodology and Procedures

Because of the lived connection and experience I have had with the phenomenon of transcendent teacher learner relationships, I chose the heuristic research paradigm. Clark Moustakas, author of *Heuristic Research: Design, Methodology and Applications* states, "In heuristic research, the investigator must have had a direct, personal encounter with the phenomenon being investigated" (Moustakas, 1990, p. 14). The researcher's encounter must be vital and intense because it is that vitality and intensity that creates in the researcher a passionate drive to know.

Heuristic research "involves self-search, self-dialogue, and self-discovery" (p. 11). Such an inner experiential process leads to the development of "methods and procedures for further investigation and analysis …" (p. 9). "Whatever presents itself in the consciousness of the investigator as perception, sense, intuition, or knowledge represents an invitation for further elucidation" (p. 10). "In heuristics, an unshakeable connection exists between what is out there, in its appearance and reality, and what is within me in reflective thought, feeling and awareness" (p. 12). "One brings one's own knowledge and experience into poetical depictions" (p. 14). Heuristic research is appropriate for this study because heuristics allows one to take one's own autobiographically derived question and pursue it from the internal frame of reference outward, always keeping the internal referential foremost.

The heuristic researcher does not presuppose cause-effect relationships, as is the case with traditional empirical investigations. Instead, the intent of the heuristic researcher is to "discover the nature and meaning of the phenomena itself" (Moustakas, 1990, p. 38). Because the research question focuses on how individuals encounter transcendent teacher learner relationships, this study is *emic* or particularizing in nature, rather than etic, or generalizing in nature (Denzin, 1989, pp. 20–21). Emic studies seek to study experiences from within, through the use of personal accounts that capture what a particular moment or phenomenon means to the experiencer. Each case is viewed as unique, shaped by the individuals who create it. The individual voice and encounter is not to be lost in the texts that are reported (Moustakas, 1990, p. 39). The research effort is designed to recreate the lived encounters of the participants through complete depictions. Sources for depictions include:

Analogies   Journals Artwork

Autobiographical logs   Metaphor
Case histories   Narrative descriptions
Conversations   Poems
Correspondence   Records
Creative renderings   Stories
Dialogues   Other personal documents
Diaries Documents
(Moustakas, 1990, pp. 9, 24, 42, 44, 52)

Although co-researchers, or participants, provide the data mentioned above, the bulk of reporting is provided by the primary research. Heuristic research methods are open ended and each research process opens in its own way. "As long as the method is congruent with responsible ethical concerns, any course that a researcher's ingenuity is capable of suggesting is an appropriate method for scientific investigation" (Moustakas, 1990, p. 43). The researcher feels completely free to choose any method or device which seems likely to illuminate the phenomenon.

1   The Population

The population for this study is divided into three tiers. Consistent with the heuristic approach, the first tier includes an investigation of the primary researcher's encounters with transcendent teacher learner relationships, both as teacher and as learner. The second tier, or significant others, includes interviews with two teachers and three students with whom I have experienced and shared transcendent relationships. The third tier, the community of teachers and learners, involve individuals who responded to an advertisement for participants, and who were chosen on the basis of the selection criteria.

2   Data Collection

The majority of data collected were derived from interviews. In heuristic research, the primary researcher is called upon to create an atmosphere that will encourage the natural expression or disclosure of thoughts, feelings, images and ideas. The intent is to allow the co-researcher "to respond comfortably, accurately, comprehensively and honestly" (Moustakas, 1990, p. 47). To accomplish this, Moustakas recommends a conversational or dialogue approach as being most "consistent with the rhythm and flow of heuristic exploration and search for meaning" (Moustakas, 1990, p. 47). "This approach relies on a spontaneous generation of questions and conversations in which the co-researcher participates in a natural, unfolding dialogue with the primary investigator" (Moustakas, 1990, p. 48). In heuristics, however, the primary researcher must respond flexibly (Moustakas, 1990, p. 47) to the co-researcher's lead, and may elect a second option, the "general interview guide." In the general interview guide, a set of issues or topics are outlined "to be explored that might be shared with co-researchers as the interview unfolds, thus focusing on common information to be sought from all the co-researchers" (Moustakas, 1990, p. 47). After each co-researcher had been interviewed independently, a seminar was held in the 1992 study. The seminar provided an opportunity for sharing experiences using primarily the conversational method.

3 Description of the Research

- A set of instructions was prepared to apprise potential co-researchers of the nature of the research, its purpose and process, and what was expected of them.
- The criteria for the selection of participants included ability to articulate the experience, cooperativeness, interest, willingness to make that commitment and enthusiasm.
- A contract was developed which included a statement of confidentiality, permission to tape record, informed consent, opportunities for feedback, permission to use material in a dissertation and other publications, and verification of findings.
- Every effort was made to facilitate a climate "of comfort, relaxation and at homeness" (Moustakas, 1990, p. 46).

Data were gathered in three tiers of concentration, as discussed in Section 1.

> In heuristic research, the primary researcher must respond flexibly and openly, and listen with empathy to the co-researcher. The accurate generation of data depends on this (Moustakas, 1990, p. 48). "The researcher is free to vary procedures to respond to what is required in the flow of dialogue" (Moustakas, 1990, p. 48). For example, the primary researcher may elect to share a personal "experience that will inspire and evoke richer, fuller, and more comprehensive depictions from the co-researcher" (Moustakas, 1990, p. 47). Interview lengths are not timed by the clocks, but conclude only when the co-researcher has had an "opportunity to tell his or her story to a point of natural closing." (Moustakas, 1990, p. 47)

4 Procedures for the Analysis and Reporting of Data in Heuristic Research

1. In the first step in organization, handling, and synthesizing, the researcher gathers all of the data from one participant.
   The data include primarily interview transcripts, but also include narrative descriptions, stories, metaphors, analogies, correspondence and personal documents. All interviews were tape recorded and later transcribed except for the example of Veronica and Theoni. Notes were taken by the primary researcher immediately following the interview. Depictions include verbatim examples, used to form an individual experiential portrait for each co-researcher … (Moustakas, 1990, p. 54).
2. The primary researcher enters into the material in timeless immersion until it is understood. Knowledge of the individual participant's whole experience and in its detail and is comprehensively apprehended by the researcher.
3. The data are set aside for a while, encouraging an interval of rest and return to the data, procedures which facilitate the awakening of fresh energy and perspective. Then, after reviewing again all of the material derived from the individual, the researcher takes notes, identifying the qualities and themes manifested in the data. Further study and review of the data and notes enables the heuristic researcher to construct an individual depiction of the experience. The individual depiction retains the language and includes examples drawn from the individual co-researcher's experience of the phenomenon. It includes qualities and themes that encompass the research participant's experience.
4. The next step requires a return to original data of the individual co-researcher. Does the individual depiction of the experience fit the data from which it was developed? Does it contain the qualities and themes essential to the experience? If it does, the researcher is ready to move on to the next co-researcher. If not, the individual depiction must be revised to include what has been omitted or deleted and what are or are not essential dimensions of the experience. The individual depiction may also be shared with the research participant for affirmation of its comprehensiveness and accuracy and for suggested deletions and additions.
5. When the above steps have been completed for one research participant, the investigator undertakes the same course of organization and analysis of the data for each of the other research participants until an individual depiction of each co-researcher's experience of the phenomenon has been constructed.

6. The individual depictions as a group, representing each co-researcher's experience, are gathered together. The researcher again enters into an immersion process with intervals of rest until the universal qualities and themes of the experience are thoroughly internalized and understood. At a timely point in knowledge and readiness, the researcher develops a composite depiction that represents the common qualities and themes that embrace the experience of the co-researchers. The composite depiction, referred to a portrait herein (a group depiction reflecting the experience of individual participants) includes exemplary narratives, descriptive accounts, conversations, illustrations, and verbatim excerpts that accentuate the flow, spirit, and life inherent in the experience. The depictions are intended to be vivid, accurate, alive, and clear, and encompass the core qualities and themes inherent in the experience. The composite depiction includes all of the core meanings of the phenomenon as experienced by the individual participants and by the group as a whole.
7. The heuristic researcher returns again to the raw material derived from each co-researcher's experience, and the individual depictions derived from the raw material. [Because of the diversity of themes that emerged from participants, a portrait is included for each of them.] Raw data include individual depictions and autobiographical material that were gathered during preliminary contacts and meetings, contained in personal documents, or shared during the interview. The individual portraits should be presented in such a way that both the phenomenon investigated and the individual persons emerge in a vital and unified manner (Moustakas, 1990, pp. 51, 52).

APPENDIX B

Transcendent Teacher Inventory

1 Transcendent Teacher Dispositions

The teacher searches for their own freedom and intellectual passion, following a path that inspires them.

Not evident *Sometimes evident* *Frequently evident*

The teacher's intellectual passion and effort toward self-liberation inspire hope and wonder in the learner.

Not evident *Sometimes evident* *Frequently evident*

The teacher's manner of expressing their intellect, particularly with their physical bearing, attracts and broadens the learner's scope of awareness, builds the learner's interest, and later intellectual passion, for content.

Not evident *Sometimes evident* *Frequently evident*

The teacher desires and creates attractive, magnetic learning encounters for all members of the learning community.

Not evident *Sometimes evident* *Frequently evident*

The teacher creates conditions that facilitate the learner's capacity to imagine, to dream, to see things as they could be otherwise.

Not evident *Sometimes evident* *Frequently evident*

The teacher coaxes and persuades learners in terms of the value of what is taught, inviting contemplation, conversation and careful consideration, even disagreement, regarding content and content-related matters.

Not evident *Sometimes evident* *Frequently evident*

The teacher facilitates intense conversation and critical analysis of content and relevant matters.

Not evident   *Sometimes evident*   *Frequently evident*

The teacher avoids the need to demand or require creativity by modeling her own creativity thereby inspiring learner creativity.

Not evident   *Sometimes evident*   *Frequently evident*

The teacher acts as a catalyst for the learner's development and transformation on multivariate levels, including intellectual, social, emotional and spiritual levels.

Not evident   *Sometimes evident*   *Frequently evident*

The teacher's goal is to teach learners how to learn, as well as passion for learning, far more than what to learn.

Not evident   *Sometimes evident*   *Frequently evident*

The teacher collaborates with learners to develop, negotiate and maintain learning encounters.

Not evident   *Sometimes evident*   *Frequently evident*

2   **Transcendent Atmosphere**

The teacher deliberately creates, facilitates and maintains a warm, social atmosphere in the learning community.

Not evident   *Sometimes evident*   *Frequently evident*

The teacher creates an emotionally, socially, physically and intellectually safe learning environment for all members of the learning community.

Not evident   *Sometimes evident*   *Frequently evident*

The teacher creates an atmosphere that demonstrates valuing and regard for all dimensions of human diversity.

Not evident   *Sometimes evident*   *Frequently evident*

3   Transcendent Interaction: Trust

The teacher is fully present to the learner, relating to learners with their whole being.

Not evident   *Sometimes evident*   *Frequently evident*

The teacher deliberately establishes and maintains relationships of mutual trust with all members of the learning community.

Not evident   *Sometimes evident*   *Frequently evident*

The teacher fully trusts learners and in every circumstance, ascribing the best imaginable intention to the learner's behavior.

Not evident   *Sometimes evident*   *Frequently evident*

The teacher facilitates the development of the learner's capacity for trustworthiness.

Not evident   *Sometimes evident*   *Frequently evident*

The teacher takes measured risks on behalf of learners to demonstrate trust in them.

Not evident   *Sometimes evident*   *Frequently evident*

The teacher inspires the learner to have faith and confidence in them.

Not evident   *Sometimes evident*   *Frequently evident*

The teacher inspires the learner to have faith and confidence in themselves.

Not evident   *Sometimes evident*   *Frequently evident*

4   Transcendent Interaction: Care

The teacher deliberately establishes and maintains relationships of mutual care with all members of the learning community.

Not evident   *Sometimes evident*   *Frequently evident*

The teacher empathizes with the learner to increase awareness of how to best to meet the learner's needs.

Not evident   *Sometimes evident*   *Frequently evident*

The teacher empathizes with the learner to contemplate the learner's struggles and intellectual passions in order to derive premium levels of development in the learner.

Not evident   *Sometimes evident*   *Frequently evident*

The teacher makes the learner's struggles their own, intuiting the learner's needs so they may determine the best and most effective way to meet the learner's needs.

Not evident   *Sometimes evident*   *Frequently evident*

The teacher demonstrates empathy and compassion for all members of the learning community as well as for each member's academic and personal struggles.

Not evident   *Sometimes evident*   *Frequently evident*

The teacher deliberately creates relationships with learners that are characterized by tenderness and challenge.

Not evident   *Sometimes evident*   *Frequently evident*

The teacher demonstrates devotion to learners along with firmness and strength.

Not evident   *Sometimes evident*   *Frequently evident*

The teacher demonstrates inspiration and ingenuity via the creation of and facilitation of compelling learning encounters.

Not evident *Sometimes evident* *Frequently evident*

The teacher protects and nurtures each learner's vulnerability and emerging, yet delicate, confidence.

Not evident *Sometimes evident* *Frequently evident*

The teacher cares more about the learner's development as a human being (socially, emotionally, physically, cognitively, spiritually) than curricula.

Not evident *Sometimes evident* *Frequently evident*

The teacher demonstrates appropriate judgement in terms of when to intervene and when not to intervene, to maximize learner development.

Not evident *Sometimes evident* *Frequently evident*

5 Transcendent Interaction: Respect

The teacher deliberately establishes and maintains relationships of mutual respect with all members of the learning community.

Not evident *Sometimes evident* *Frequently evident*

The teacher's authority is most frequently characterized by mutual collaboration with learners rather than traditional power over learners.

Not evident *Sometimes evident* *Frequently evident*

The teacher avoids coercing learners. Instead, the teacher works with them to negotiate learning encounters, facilitating the learner's power to choose and, when appropriate, to yield voluntarily to the teacher's guidance and direction.

Not evident *Sometimes evident* *Frequently evident*

The teacher does not discipline or punish learners in pursuit of learner compliance. Instead, the teacher creates circumstances and learning structures that allow natural consequences for behavior to unfold thereby developing the learner's capacity for self-discipline.

Not evident		*Sometimes evident*		*Frequently evident*

The teacher creates and maintains learning structures and interpersonal interaction that develop learner self-discipline and move the learner toward more and more freedom and stimulation within those structures.

Not evident		*Sometimes evident*		*Frequently evident*

The teacher does not compel learner interest or compliance through an artificial reliance on the threat of grades or demerit systems.

Not evident		*Sometimes evident*		*Frequently evident*

The teacher reveals their authentic self without façade to learners.

Not evident		*Sometimes evident*		*Frequently evident*

The teacher shares appropriate self details that relate to what is being learned and experienced in the learning environment.

Not evident		*Sometimes evident*		*Frequently evident*

The teacher models democratic principles in interactions with all learners and creates learning structures that teach and apply democratic principles.

Not evident		*Sometimes evident*		*Frequently evident*

The teacher creates and facilitates learning structures that teach deep understanding, and regular application of democratic principles.

Not evident		*Sometimes evident*		*Frequently evident*

APPENDIX C

Role Play Scenarios

Directions: For the following five scenarios, please read and discuss with your group members how a traditional teacher would approach the problem verses the transcendent teacher. Then prepare a role play for each teacher that fully conveys the approach of each teacher.

1. Sarah comes to Ms. Jewell and says that her friend told her the gym teacher touched her inappropriately. What do you do? Remember to first answer as a traditional teacher and then as a transcendent teacher.
2. Christy tells Ms. Wells that she just found out that she is pregnant. How do you respond? Please answer as a traditional teacher and then as a transcendent teacher.
3. James has been falling asleep in class, has dark circles under his eyes, and has lost weight in the past few weeks. You notice that he has been coming to school in the same clothes and hasn't bathed. How do you approach him? Please answer as a traditional teacher and then as a transcendent teacher.
4. It's story time and Mr. Nico decides to read *The Berenstein Bears Visit the Dentist*.
   Mr. Nico points to the pictures of mom, dad, brother and sister. Annie raises her hand and says that she has two mommies. What do you say to Annie and the rest of the class in response? Please answer as a traditional teacher and then as a transcendent teacher.
5. Madison walks into class, sits down, and begins to cry. As class continues, her crying becomes a distraction to other students. How do you respond to this situation? Please answer as a traditional teacher and then as a transcendent teacher.
6. Nick comes from a prosperous family and does well in class. His parents are very active in the school. However, Nick frequently makes remarks to his colleagues that can be interpreted as sexist, homophobic and racist. How do you respond to this situation? Please answer as a traditional teacher and then as a transcendent teacher.

References

Ayers, W., & Millner, J. (Eds.). (1998). *A light in dark times: Maxine Greene and the unfinished conversation.* New York, NY: Teachers College Press.

Belenky, M. F., Clinchy, B. M., Goldberger, N. R., & Tarule, J. M. (1997). *Women's ways of knowing: The development of self, voice, and mind* (10th anniversary ed.). New York, NY: Basic Books, Inc. Publishers.

Berry, D. L. (1985). *Mutuality: The vision of Martin Buber.* Albany, NY: State University of New York Press.

Bloom, B. S. (1982a). *All our children learning: A primer for parents, teachers, and other educators.* New York, NY: McGraw Hill Book Company.

Bloom, B. S. (1982b). The master teachers. *Phi Delta Kappan, 63*(10), 664–668, 715.

Bollnow, O. (1972). Risk and failure in education. *Education, a Biannual Collection, 6,* 37–52 [Reprinted]. In J. P. Strain (Ed.), *Philosophy of education* (1971) (pp. 520–535). New York, NY: Random House.

Bollnow, O. (1989). The pedagogical atmosphere: The perspective of the child. *Phenomenology and Pedagogy, 7,* 12–36.

Bourgeault, C. (2010). *The meaning of Mary Magdalene: Discovering the woman at the heart of Christianity.* Boston, MA: Shambala.

Bronte, C. (1847). *Jane Eyre.* Retrieved from https://www.planetebook.com/free-ebooks/jane-eyre.pdf

Buber, M. (1958). *I and thou* (R. G. Smith, Trans.). New York, NY: Collier Books, MacMillan Publishing Company. (Original work published 1923)

Buber, M. (1965a). *Between man and man.* New York, NY: Macmillan.

Buber, M. (1965b). Chapter 2. In M. Friedman (Ed.), *The knowledge of man: A philosophy of the interhuman* (M. Friedman & R. G. Smith, Trans.). New York, NY: Harper Torchbooks, Harper and Row.

Buber, M. (2002). *Between man and man.* New York, NY: Routledge Classics.

Canning, I., Sherman, E., Unwin, G. (Producers), & Hooper, T. (Director). (2010). *The king's speech* [Motion picture]. Troy, MI: Anchor Bay Entertainment.

Clawson, J. G. (1980). Mentoring in managerial careers. In C. B. Derr (Ed.), *Work, family and the career: New frontiers in theory and research* (pp. 144–165). New York, NY: Praeger.

Coe, F. (Producer), & Penn, A. (Director). (1962). *The miracle worker* [Motion picture]. Culver City, CA: MGM/UA Home Video.

Cohen, A. (1983). *The educational philosophy of Martin Buber* (pp. 25–54). Rutherford, NJ: Associated University Presses.

Conrad, C. (1985). *Strategic organizational communication: Cultures, situations, and adaptations.* New York, NY: Holt, Reinehart and Winston.

Corbett, L. (2002). *The religious function of the psyche*. New York, NY: Brunner-Routledge.

Craffert, P. (2008). *The life of a Galilean: Jesus of Nazareth in anthropologica-historical perspective*. Eugene, OR: Wipf and Stock.

Craig, P. (1978). The heart of the teacher: A heuristic study of the inner world of teaching. *University Microfilms International, 78*, 80–57.

Crucher, C. (2003). *Staying fat for Sarah Byrnes*. San Francisco, CA: Greenwillow Books.

Denzin, N. K. (1989). *Interpretive interactionism*. Newbury Park, CA: Sage Publications.

DeVito, D., Shamberg, M., Stacy, S. (Producers), & LaGravenese, R. (Director). (2007). *Freedom writers* [Motion picture]. Paramount Home Video.

Emerson, R. (1983). *Essays and lectures*. New York, NY: Library of America.

Fab, J., Hiltzik, M., Johnson, R., Pinchot, A. (Producers), & Berlin, E. (Director). (2004). *Paper clips* [Motion picture]. Miramax/Arts Alliance America.

Foshay, A. (1984). The peak/spiritual experience as an object of curriculum analysis (Report No. SO-015-787). *Joint Meeting of the Social Science Education Consortium and the Bundeszentrale fur politische Bildung*, Irsee, Bavaria, West Germany. (Eric Document Reproduction Service No. ED 247 169)

Freire, P. (1989). *Pedagogy of the oppressed* (M. Ramos, Trans.). New York, NY: Continuum.

Freire, P. (1994). *Pedagogy of hope*. New York, NY: Continuum.

Freire, P. (2012). *Pedagogy of the oppressed* (M. Ramos, Trans.). New York, NY: Bloomsbury.

Frey, B., & Noller, R. (1983). Mentoring: A legacy of success. *Journal of Creative Behavior, 17*(1), 60–64.

Friedman M.S. (1976). Martin Buber: *The life of dialogue*. Chicago, IL: University of Chicago Press.

Fromm, E. (1994). *Escape from freedom*. New York, NY: Holt Paperbacks.

Gandini, L. (1993). Fundamentals of the Reggio Emilia approach to early childhood education. *Young Children, 49*(1), 4–8.

Gardner, H. (2011). *Frames of mind: The theory of multiple intelligences* (3rd ed.). New York, NY: Basic Books.

Greene, M. (1969). The arts in a global village. *Educational Leadership, 26*(5), 439–446.

Greene, M. (1982). *Equality of opportunity: Perspectives and possibilities*. Boston, MA: National Council for the Social Studies. (Eric Document Reproduction Service No. ED 224 447)

Greene, M. (1984a). *The master teacher concept: Five perspectives* (Report No. SP 027 725). Austin, TX: Research and Development Center for Teacher Education. (Eric Document Reproduction Service No. ED 270 447)

Greene, M. (1984b). *Perspectives and visions: A rationale for "foundations" in teacher education*. (Report No. SP 025 655). College Station, TX: Texas A&M University, College of Education. (Eric Document Reproduction Service No. ED 253 503)

Greene, M. (1985). A philosophic look at merit and mastery in teaching. *The Elementary School Journal, 86*(1), 25.

Greene, M. (1986). *Toward possibility: Expanding the range of literacy* (Report No. CS 008 504). San Francisco, CA: American Educational Research Association. (Eric Document Reproduction Service No. ED 272 B46)

Greene, M. (1988). *The dialectic of freedom.* New York, NY: Teachers College Press, Columbia University.

Greene, M. (1989). The teacher in John Dewey's works, Socrates to software: The teacher as text and the text as teacher. In *Eighty-ninth yearbook of the NSSE* (pp. 24–36). Chicago, IL: University of Chicago.

Greene, M. (2011). Maxine Greene. In T. Johnson & R. Reed (Eds.), *Philosophical documents in education.* per Hunter: New York, NY: Pearson.

Haft, S., Witt, P., Thomas, T. (Producers), & Weir, P. (Director). (1989). *Dead poet's society.* Buena Vista Home Video.

Hamilton, N. (Producer). (2012). *Helen Keller in her story* [Motion picture]. Phoenix Learning Group, Inc.

Hendrick, J. (Ed.). (1997). *First steps toward teaching the Reggio way.* Upper Saddle River, NJ: Merrill.

Jones-Hunt, J. (2011). *Moses and Jesus: The shamans.* Blue Ridge Summit: Moon Books.

Katz, M., Noddings, N., & Strike, K. (Eds.). (1999). *Justice and caring: The search for common ground in education.* New York, NY: Teachers College Press.

Keen, E. (1975). *A primer on phenomenological psychology.* New York, NY: Holt, Rinehart & Winston.

Keeney, B. (2006). *Shamanic Christianity: The direct experience of mystical communion.* Merrimac, MA: Destiny Books.

Keller, H. (1998). *The story of my life.* New York, NY: Signet Classic.

Keller, H. (2015). *The story of my life.* Create Space Independent Publishing Platform.

Klein, T. (1989). Teaching and mother love. *Educational Theory, 39*(4), 373–383.

Lee, H. (1988). *To kill a mockingbird.* New York, NY: Grand Central Publishing.

Levine, J. (2014, May 29). *Maxine Greene, TC's great philosopher, dies at 96.* New York, NY: TC Media Center from the Office of External Affairs.

Macdonald, J. B. (1974). A transcendental developmental ideology of education. In W. Pinar (Ed.), *In heightened consciousness, cultural revolution, and curriculum theory: The proceedings of the Rochester Conference* (pp. 85–116). Berkeley, CA: McCutchan Publishing Company.

Maslow, A. (1968). *Toward a psychology of being* (2nd ed.). New York, NY: Van Nostrand Reinhold Company.

Merriam Webster. (2020). *Pleroma.* Merriam-Webster.com. Retrieved May 21, 2020, from https://www.merriam-webster.com/dictionary/pleroma

Moustakas, C. (1966). *The authentic teacher: Sensitivity and awareness in the classroom.* Cambridge, MA: Howard A. Doyle Publishing Company.

Moustakas, C. (1977). *Turning points*. Englewood Cliffs, NJ: Prentice-Hall, Inc.

Moustakas, C. (1981). *Rhythms, rituals and relationships*. Detroit: Center for Humanistic Studies.

Moustakas, C. (1990). *Heuristic research: Design, methodology, and applications*. Newbury Park, CA: Sage Publications.

Noddings, N. (1984). *Caring: A feminine approach to ethics and moral education*. Los Angeles, CA: University of California Press.

Noddings, N. (1992). *The challenge to care in schools: An alternative approach to education*. New York, NY: Teachers College Press.

Noddings, N. (2011). Nel Noddings. In T. Johnson & R. Reed (Eds.), *Philosophical documents in education*. New York, NY: Pearson.

Noddings, N., & Shore, P. (1984). *Awakening the inner eye: Intuition in education*. New York, NY: Teachers College Press.

Noe, R. A. (1988). Women and mentoring: A review and research agenda. *Academy of Management Review*, *13*, 65–78.

O'Hara, H. (1992). *Transcendent teacher-learner relationships: A vision for pursuit*. Dissertation, West Virginia University (University Microfilms No. 9322936).

O'Hara, H. (1994a). *The transcendent teacher-learner relationship in Denmark: Building the community* (Unpublished manuscript). Morgantown, WV: West Virginia University.

O'Hara, H. (1994b, March). *Liberation in Lithuania: Teacher-learner transcendence in the face of oppression*. Paper presented at the annual meeting of the Comparative and International Education Society, San Diego, CA.

O'Hara, H. (1995, February). Great music teaching: Commitment, passion, persuasion. *Choral Journal*, *35*(7), 27–29.

O'Hara, H. (2000). Children and their invisible needs. *Journal of Early Childhood Teacher Education*, *20*(3), 253–257.

O'Hara, H. (2005). Transcendent teacher learner relationships: A class investigation. *Journal of Early Childhood Education*, *25*(4), 331–337.

O'Hara, H. (2011). *The transcendent teacher learner relationship: Toward a philosophy of transcendence*. Virginia Beach, VA: Academx Publishing Services.

O'Hara, H. (2014, November). *On bullying: A gay teacher remembers*. Retrieved from http://www.OutHistory.org

O'Hara, H. (2015). *Transcendent teacher learner relationships: The way of the shamanic teacher*. Rotterdam, The Netherlands: Sense Publishers.

Palmer, P. (1983). *To know as we are known: A spirituality of education*. San Francisco, CA: Harper.

Palmer, P. (1993). *To know as we are known: A spirituality of education*. San Francisco, CA: Harper One.

Patrick, K. (1955). *What is creative thinking?* New York, NY: Philosophical Library.

Phenix, P. H. (1974). Transcendence and the curriculum. In E. W. Eisner & E. Vallance (Eds.), *Conflicting conceptions of curriculum*. Berkeley, CA: McCutchan Publishing Company.

Pinar, W. (Ed.). (1998). *Curriculum: Toward new identities*. New York, NY: Garland Publishing, Inc.

Polanyi, M. (1958). *The study of man*. Chicago, IL: The University of Chicago Press.

Polanyi, M. (1969). *Knowing and being* (M. Greene, Ed.). Chicago, IL: The University of Chicago.

Rogers, C. (1967a). *Freedom to learn*. Columbus, OH: Merrill.

Rogers, C. (1967b). The interpersonal relationship in the facilitation of learning.In R. R. Leeper (Ed.), *Humanizing education: The person in the process* (pp. 1–18). Washington, DC: Association for Supervision and Curriculum Development, NEA.

Rogers, C., & Freiberg, J. (1994). *Freedom to learn* (3rd ed.). New York, NY: Merrill.

Rosenblatt, L. (1938). *Literature as exploration*. New York, NY: D. Appleton-Century.

Ryan, R. E. (2002). *Shamanism and the psychology of C.G. Jung: The great circle*. London, UK: Vega.

Schaffer, R. (1977). *Mothering*. Cambridge, MA: Harvard University Press.

Schlipp, P. (Ed.). (1991). *Albert Einstein: Philosopher-scientist*. LaSalle, IL: Open Court.

Spranger, E. (1972). The role of love in education [Reprinted]. In J. P. Strain (Ed.), *Philosophy of education (1971)* (pp. 536–546). New York, NY: Random House.

Tapert, A. (1998). *The power of glamour*. New York, NY: Random House.

Tewksbury Almshouse (n.d.). *American Federation for the Blind: Expanding possibilities for people with vision loss*. Retrieved April 8, 2020, from https://www.afb.org/about-afb/history/online-museums/anne-sullivan-miracle-worker/formative-years/tewksbury-almshouse

Tewksbury Almshouse investigation. (1883, April 24). *The Lowell Weekly Sun*. Retrieved May 15, 2020, from https://socialwelfare.library.vcu.edu/issues/tewksbury-almshouse-investigation/

Tzu, L. (1999). *Tao Te Ching* (S. Mitchell, Trans.). London, UK: Francis Lincoln Limited.

Van Manen, M. (1990). *Researching lived experience: Human science for an action sensitive pedagogy*. New York, NY: State University of New York Press.

Van Manen, M. (1991). *The tact of teaching: The meaning of pedagogical thoughtfulness*. New York, NY: State University of New York Press.

Viereck, G. (1929, October 26). What life means to Einstein: An interview. *The Saturday Evening Post*, p. 117.

Willis, D. (2013), *Hollywood in Kodachrome*. New York, NY: !T-imprint of HarperCollins Publishers.

Witherell, C., & Noddings, N. (Eds.). (1991). *Stories lives tell: Narrative and dialogue in education*. New York, NY: Teachers College Press.

Yamamoto, K. (1988). To see a life grow: The meaning of mentorship. *Theory into Practice, 27*(3), 183–189.

www.ingramcontent.com/pod-product-compliance
Lightning Source LLC
Chambersburg PA
CBHW061436300426
44114CB00014B/1709